Independence, Propertylessness, and Basic Income

A Theory of Freedom as the Power to Say No

Basic income is one of the most innovative, powerful, straightforward, and controversial proposals for addressing poverty and growing inequalities. A Basic Income Guarantee (BIG) is designed to be an unconditional, government-ensured guarantee that all citizens will have enough income to meet their basic needs. The concept of basic, or guaranteed, income is a form of social provision and this series examines the arguments for and against it from an interdisciplinary perspective with special focus on the economic and social factors. By systematically connecting abstract philosophical debates over competing principles of BIG to the empirical analysis of concrete policy proposals, this series contributes to the fields of economics, politics, social policy, and philosophy and establishes a theoretical framework for interdisciplinary research. It will bring together international and national scholars and activists to provide a comparative look at the main efforts to date to pass unconditional BIG legislation across regions of the globe and will identify commonalities and differences across countries drawing lessons for advancing social policies in general and BIG policies in particular.

Series Editors:

Karl Widerquist is a visiting associate professor of Philosophy at Georgetown University-Qatar.

James Bryan is an associate professor of Economics at Manhattanville College.

Michael A. Lewis is an associate professor at Hunter College School of Social Work.

Basic Income Reconsidered
Simon Birnbaum

Alaska's Permanent Fund Dividend
Edited by Karl Widerquist and Michael W. Howard

Basic Income Guarantee
Allan Sheahen

Basic Income Guarantee and Politics
Edited by Richard K. Caputo

Exporting the Alaska Model
Edited by Karl Widerquist and Michael W. Howard

Citizen's Income and Welfare Regimes in Latin America
Edited by Rubén Lo Vuolo

Independence, Propertylessness, and Basic Income: A Theory of Freedom as the Power to Say No
Karl Widerquist

Independence, Propertylessness, and Basic Income

A Theory of Freedom as the Power to Say No

Karl Widerquist

palgrave
macmillan

INDEPENDENCE, PROPERTYLESSNESS, AND BASIC INCOME

First published in 2013 by
PALGRAVE MACMILLAN®
in the United States—a division of St. Martin's Press LLC,
175 Fifth Avenue, New York, NY 10010.

Where this book is distributed in the UK, Europe and the rest of the world, this is by Palgrave Macmillan, a division of Macmillan Publishers Limited, registered in England, company number 785998, of Houndmills, Basingstoke, Hampshire RG21 6XS.

Palgrave Macmillan is the global academic imprint of the above companies and has companies and representatives throughout the world.

ISBN: 978–1–137–27472–4

Library of Congress Cataloging-in-Publication Data

Widerquist, Karl.
Independence, propertylessness, and basic income : a theory of freedom as the power to say no / Karl Widerquist.
p. cm.—(Exploring the basic income guarantee)
ISBN 978–1–137–27472–4 (alk. paper)
1. Property. 2. Liberty. 3. Distributive justice. 4. Guaranteed annual income. I. Title.

HB701.W52 2013
330—dc23 2012035150

A catalogue record of the book is available from the British Library.

Design by Newgen Imaging Systems (P) Ltd., Chennai, India.

First edition: February 2013

10 9 8 7 6 5 4 3 2 1

Other Books

Karl Widerquist

Economics for Social Workers: The Application of Economic Theory to Social Policy and the Human Services. With Michael Anthony Lewis (2002)

The Ethics and Economics of the Basic Income Guarantee. With Michael Anthony Lewis and Steven Pressman (eds.) (2005)

Alaska's Permanent Fund Dividend: Examining Its Suitability as a Model. With Michael W. Howard (eds.) (Palgrave Macmillan 2012)

Exporting the Alaska Model: Adapting the Permanent Fund Dividend for Reform around the World. With Michael W. Howard (eds.) (Palgrave Macmillan 2012)

Basic Income: An Anthology of Contemporary Research. With Jose Noguera, Yannick Vanderborght, and Jurgen De Wispelaere (eds.) (forthcoming)

Prehistoric Myths in Modern Political Philosophy: Challenging Stone Age Stories. With Grant McCall (forthcoming)

Contents

Preface and Acknowledgments

I don't know exactly when I began thinking about the ideas that made their way into this book. The general philosophical outlook is something that has been bouncing around in my head for a long time. The outlook didn't appear as a whole at any one point; it gradually developed. My interest in social justice began when I was a kid. My parents were politically interested, liberal Christians (a rarity these days). They, my brother, my sister, and I regularly discussed politics around the dinner table. Growing up in that context in the 1970s, I was optimistic about the progress the United States had made against racism, and I began to believe that the biggest problem remaining in most democratic countries is the horrible way we treat the poor.

The television series *Free to Choose,* by Milton Friedman, first introduced me to the idea of a guaranteed income, which is now more commonly known as a basic income guarantee. He presented it mostly as a way to simplify the welfare system, but having thought about it over the years, I began to see it as the centerpiece of a just society and a serious challenge to the Left: If we really care about other people in society, we should care about them *unconditionally*. The effort that has so far resulted in this book is a self-exploration of why I think this perspective is so important.

As I see it, from the hanging gardens of Babylon to the modern sweatshop, one social problem occurs over and over again in different ways: advantaged people force disadvantaged people to serve them. Can this be justified? I find the social contract answer extremely dissatisfying: it's okay to force people to do things as long as you can imagine conditions under which they would have signed a contract subjecting themselves to force. For some time I thought I was a libertarian, but I eventually came to see the right-libertarians, who call themselves "libertarians" in the United States, in a similar light as social contract theorists. I find their answer even more dissatisfying: it's okay for owners to force the propertyless to do things, because someone did something before we were all born to give owners special rights over the Earth and its resources, so that the propertyless have no right to refuse the duty to serve owners. Right-libertarians talk about freedom from force, but they invite everyone to ignore the tremendous amount of freedom-threatening force involved in the establishment and maintenance of property rights to the earth and all its products. Without rectifying this issue, "libertarianism" becomes the defense of privilege at the expense of liberty.

Although these issues were important to me, I didn't do much direct work on social justice until the mid-1990s, when I taught several semesters of the History of Economic Thought at New York University while working on a PhD. in economics at the City University of New York. Some ideas from in-class discussions with students (from all the institutions at which I have taught) have probably made their way into this book. Also in the mid-1990s, Michael Lewis, Pam Donovan, and I decided to have weekly breakfasts to talk about the progress we were making on our theses. These discussions usually turned to politics, and one day we found the one thing we could all agree on was an unconditional basic income guarantee. So, Michael Lewis and I wrote a paper on it that was eventually published (about ten years later and in heavily revised form) as "An Efficiency Argument for the Basic Income Guarantee," in *International Journal of Environment, Workplace and Employment.*

One paper on the basic income guarantee led to another as well as to involvement with the Basic Income Earth Network and to writing the Newsletter for the U.S. Basic Income Guarantee Network. I read a lot of impressive literature on basic income, but none of it quite seemed to articulate the reasons I thought it was so important. So, I had to explore my ideas further.

In 2001, I held a half-year fellowship at the Chaire Hoover at the Catholic University of Lovain in Belgium where Philippe Van Parijs was an influential mentor. By this time I had realized that my interest in economics was secondary to my interest in social justice, and I decided that the best way to work full-time on social justice was to go back to graduate school and get a doctorate in political theory. Getting a second doctorate still feels like a crazy idea, but in hindsight, it was the right thing for me. I started at Oxford in October 2002, and by April 2006 I completed a doctoral dissertation entitled "Property and the Power to Say No: A Freedom-Based Argument for Basic Income," which is my initial statement of the theory of justice as the pursuit of accord. Many of the ideas in this book appeared first in that thesis—often in a slightly different form.

My supervisor, Stuart White, gave me extremely helpful feedback on several versions of each chapter. Other faculty also gave me useful help and encouragement, including Dan McDermott (my substitute supervisor), Adam Swift and David Miller (my "transfer-of-status" examiners), Gerald A. Cohen (my internal thesis examiner), and Michael Otsuka (my external thesis examiner).

Some of the most valuable help I received was from discussing writings and ideas with my fellow graduate students at Oxford, both while we were students and since we left. These include Ayelet Banai, Ben Saunders, Christian Schemmel, Clare Heyward, John Filling, Katherine Eddy, Kieran Oberman, Miriam Ronzoni, Olly Dowlen, Omar Khan, Peter Balint, Rob Jubb, Sara Ababneh, Sarah Fine, Shlomi Segal, Steve Winter, Teun Dekker, Tiziana Torresi, and others.

Other friends and colleagues have been helpful including Almaz Zelleke, Angela Cummine, Carole Pateman, Chris Brooke, Daniel Butt, David Casassas, Drew Chastain, Eri Noguchi, Gijs van Donselaar, Jason Berntsen, Jason Burke Murphy, Jeremy Koons, José Noguera, Julia Maskivker, Jurgen De Wispelaere, Marc-Andre Pigeon, Michael Howard, Michael Lewis, Nir Eyal, Pascal Couillard (who coined the term "passive contribution"), Paul Schumacher, Richard Caputo, Stephen Nathanson, Yannick Vanderborght, and many others. I have discussed these ideas with so many friends, colleagues, students, and mentors that I can't possibly name everyone who has influenced this book, and so I know when this comes out I'm going to owe apologies to several people for leaving them out. If I've discussed politics or philosophy with you in my lifetime, you might have influenced this book in some way. So, thanks.

I received useful comments from participants at more conferences and seminars than I can name in Europe, North America, the Middle East, South Africa, South America, and New Zealand. For the most part, I don't remember the name with the comment. But I do remember Peter Vallentyne asked a question that made me revise my definition of status freedom; Erik Olin Wright asked a question that made me reformulate a criticism of Nozick; and John Baker asked a question that made me realize I had to clarify all kinds of things about the relationship between this theory, liberal-egalitarianism, and the argument for a social responsibility to work.

I published four chapters of my thesis in the following journals: *Public Reason*, *Human Rights Review*, *Political Studies*, and *Politics, Philosophy, and Economics.* Although text from only one of these articles (the one in *Human Rights Review*) has made it into this book, anonymous referee comments from these (and other) journals made me think further about what this project ought to be.

Since leaving Oxford, I have continued to rework and extend the ideas from my thesis on and off while working on other projects. Not long after Laurie Harting of Palgrave Macmillan approached me about becoming series editor for their new book series Exploring the Basic Income Guarantee, I thought about turning my thesis into a book. In the spring of 2012, I set out to do that, but as I revised it, I found that the chapters in the first half were growing and splitting into more chapters. I finally realized that the book would be an extension of the first half of my thesis—concentrating on an exploration of the theory of freedom as Effective Control Self-Ownership and leaving the development of most of the rest of justice as the pursuit of accord for later works.

Elizabeth Smith Widerquist (known professionally as Elizabeth Smith Rousselle) and I met after I completed my thesis, and got married before I started trying to turn it into a book. She has been extremely kind and encouraging as I worked on my laptop while traveling between Qatar, the UAE, Oman, Jordan, Israel, Cypress, Northern Ireland, England, California, Louisiana, North Carolina, New York, Indiana, and Michigan.

I worked on my thesis and then on this book in more cafés than I can remember, but one toward the end stands out. In late June and during the whole month of July 2012, I spent up to seven days a week and up to 14 hours a day at the Cru Wine Bar/Coffee Shop in Beaufort, North Carolina. I appreciate the tolerance of the staff (especially Kerry Guist and Kayla Lewis) and the other customers for my monopolization of the spot by the window.

Now that the book is almost done I still feel that it is tentative in many ways. I could spend years revising it, but it is best to get it out. Although tentative, it is a sincere expression of my beliefs on the issues discussed at this point. I hope to explore these ideas much more in the future.

KARL WIDERQUIST,
Mojo's Coffee House,
New Orleans,
Louisiana,
August 2012

Prologue: The Big Casino

All descriptions of artwork, architecture, documents, and secret rituals in this novel are accurate.

—*Dan Brown*[1]

Suppose you're driving down a desolate highway through the semi-arid plateau of eastern Oregon on the way home to your birthplace in Winnemucca, Nevada, at the end of your first year studying political philosophy at the University of Northern British Columbia. You day-dream about the time when you will finish your studies, homestead some land near your hometown, raise sheep, eat mutton, and write papers that no one will ever read.

Just over the Nevada Stateline, you see a sign on the side of the road reading "Welcome to the Small Casino." The casino stands alone in the middle of an otherwise empty landscape. While you were gone, your home state legalized gambling, and someone built the Small Casino here to serve gamblers who drive down from population centers such as Bend, Oregon and Walla Walla, Washington. You stop in for a free shrimp cocktail. You observe the people at the casino.

Except for the fact that everyone chose to be here, nearly every principle of distributive justice you learned in your studies is violated inside the Small Casino. At every table the odds are stacked in favor of the house, and otherwise, the games do a poor job of rewarding desert, merit, productivity, hard work, diligence, skill, welfare, or need. Some of the games, to some extent, reward some desirable characteristics, but all of the games incorporate a large element of luck and reward for undesirable characteristics, and on average, at every table, the house always wins. Although people choose to be here, not everything can be dismissed as "option luck," because they make their decisions against a background of brute luck inequalities. Gamblers with advantaged backgrounds tend to do better than others, and deep pockets have a perpetual advantage. Disadvantaged people don't have the option to gamble in places that compensate for their disadvantages—but that is not the responsibility of the house. People choose to come to this place that accentuates their disadvantages, when they could easily have stayed home.

You meet a poker player who seems to have no spirit of cooperative enterprise. He tells you, "I play vicious, and I play to win. I didn't twist people's arms to make them come here. The game isn't always fair, and I make use of any advantage I can to get ahead. The only thing that's fair about it is that everybody knew the nature of the game before they chose to play. There's nothing but available open land for hundreds of miles in every direction that people can use any way they want. If they don't want to play our way, they don't have to step into the Small Casino."

Although you may be able to think of reasons to change background conditions, you can't think of any legitimate justification to force people like him to stop doing what they want. Somehow, you happen to know that there are no compulsive gamblers here; everyone is a rational, fully informed adult who chose to come here to do what they are doing, knowing the risks and the inequities. They were free to stay away, but they chose to come to the Small Casino. You finish your free shrimp cocktail and leave without placing any bets—consuming something for nothing in violation of the norm of reciprocity. Like everyone else who doesn't like the Small Casino, you are free to ignore it.

Every year as you return home from your studies, you see that the Small Casino has grown larger; more and more of the land and resources of Nevada are taken up and used for a purpose you do not want to be a part of.

Twenty years later, you complete your study of political philosophy, come of age, and head home to Winnemucca. When you reach the Nevada Stateline, you pass under an arch over the road with a sign across it reading "Welcome to the Big Casino." It straddles the highway, and covers the hills in all directions. From border to border, everything is owned by the Big Casino. You have nowhere to sleep and nothing to eat without the permission of the Big Casino. You were mistaken about the Homestead Act; you should have known it was repealed decades before you were born. Long before you came of age, all the land and resources of your homeland were made someone else's property. You can't just take natural resources and use them for your own purposes. If you want resources you have to buy them from someone who owns them. That is, from the house—one of the many small houses that make up the Big Casino.

The Big Casino is willing to let you buy in, to buy your own piece of whatever you want. All you have to do is to work for the Big Casino.

If you provide some service to one of the owners, you can make it in their interest to part with some of their property, and you can get your own property to use as you will. Service to the people who control property is the only legal means of survival.

So, you walk into one of the small houses that make up the Big Casino and ask for a job. They say, "If you want to work here, play baccarat with the other applicants to help us determine whether we should hire you and in what capacity. After that you'll play poker with the other employees to see how soon you will advance." Another Small Casino asks you to try your hand at craps, blackjack, or the slot machines. Wherever you go, you're in the Big Casino. A casino element is involved in whatever you do. To some extent the Big Casino rewards merit, skill, desert, talent, hard work, and diligence in ways that are relevant to the performance of beneficial actions. To another extent, it rewards luck or the skills that are not directly relevant to productivity but that are relevant only to the casino games associated with attaining a position. It serves the needy only in proportion to how much the needy succeed in serving it. The Big Casino creates risk and unfairness, and it creates inequality in terms of who is subject to the risks created by the casino system. And always, the odds are stacked in favor of the house. You see that people born with disadvantages tend to remain disadvantaged throughout their lives, sometimes performing dull, degrading, low-status, or low-reward jobs for their entire working lives.

Depending on the combination of your luck, your relevant abilities (such as your skills at doing your job), and your irrelevant abilities (such as your skill at the casino games involved with your job), you might strike it rich and attain your independence in one day; or as it does for the least advantaged people, it could take a lifetime. If you succeed, you have succeeded in the Big Casino. You have become one of the shareholders of the Big Casino. You have become part of the house. But you don't want to play that game.

You complain to the owner of a Small Casino that you don't want to play his games or serve his interests. He responds, "I'm not forcing you to be here. If you don't want to play, you can go somewhere else." The owner of every Small Casino denies responsibility for the whole, because they are only responsible for one part. But there is no more open land; wherever you go, you're still inside the Big Casino. You can avoid any one Small Casino, but you can't avoid all of them; you can't avoid the Big Casino as a whole.

You go to the main office of the Big Casino Association, but it takes no responsibility for the way individual casinos behave. The

Big Casino is merely a loose association of Small Casinos; it simply enforces rules of ownership and exchange, and leaves the owners of property to do with it as they will. "The Big Casino's rules benefit everyone. Many goods and services are produced that would not otherwise be produced. Many opportunities are created that would not otherwise exist." You see that the Big Casino benefits you in some ways, but you also see that it burdens you and reduces your freedom in other ways. You did not choose to trade the burdens for the benefits. That trade was imposed on you. By demanding you trade your labor even for access to natural resources, every Small Casino owner takes credit for the benefits the Big Casino provides, but no one takes responsibility for the burdens and the unfreedom created by system as a whole.

The available work is varied and there is a choice of employers. You can work for any one of them, but no matter which employer you work for, you work in the Big Casino, and you serve the goals of the house on its terms. You don't have to work directly for the Big Casino. You can work for other gamblers, but there is still a casino element in finding this work, and their ability to reward you is proportional to how well they have succeeded in the Big Casino. Two people who have never served the Big Casino either directly or indirectly have no property to reward each other with. Until you have earned your independence, by satisfying the Big Casino's terms, you are its subject; your need for the means of survival forces you to accept its work and serve its goals, at its pay and under its conditions. The laws of your state make you a nominally free person, but the property rights regime maintained by the state forces you to serve at least one member of the ownership group; the laws effectively put you into involuntary servitude as much as if you were born in debt to the Big Casino.

Although you can ignore any one of its constituent parts, you cannot ignore the whole. You are not bound to any one master, but you are effectively born in servitude. No one would feel injured if you choose to starve on the street. But you will not choose to starve; you will give them your labor as surely as if you were in their debt. The freedom to serve or die is the same kind of freedom experienced by serfs and slaves. Although you have a choice of masters, you are born to serve someone from the class of property owners. You are not free. You neither agreed to the laws and circumstances that brought about this situation, nor are you allowed to reject the role ascribed to you by it. You did not choose to create it, and you cannot choose to ignore it. The Big Casino neither follows from nor preserves your freedom.

Eventually, a band of philosopher-legislators starts a nonviolent, democratic revolution. They take over the Big Casino and rebuild it as the Big Cooperative in which everyone works together for democratically chosen goals. They intend to build a democratic Big Cooperative that distributes its products fairly according to what they believe to be an ethically sound theory of social justice, which might be equality of income, the difference principle, welfare egalitarianism, resource egalitarianism, meritocracy, or one of many others.

Unfortunately, the philosopher-legislators find that the gambling tables are infused into every part of the economy and that removing them is costly. Although removing some casino elements is purely beneficial, removing many of the casino elements either decreases the economy's ability to turn effort into welfare or decreases freedom (by decreasing the choice of goals and actions available to individuals). They also find that no possible structure eliminates the casino element. Even a system of strict egalitarianism, in which everyone does identical work for identical rewards, implies good luck for those who like that work for those rewards and bad luck for those who don't. And even that ideal is imperfectly achievable. The philosopher-legislators have to make trade-offs. The Big Cooperative prohibits many of these things people did in the Big Casino, to the resentment of everyone who liked to do those things and to the benefit of many who were burdened by those things, but no matter what they do, the Big Cooperative is still, in part, the Big Casino.

The philosopher-legislators have to decide not only what goals to pursue but also which of the casino elements to trade off for the purpose of achieving their conception of fairness. To some extent the Big Cooperative still rewards luck and irrelevant characteristics, and still stacks the deck in favor of the house. However, the democratically chosen philosopher-legislators decide that the Big Casino is good enough and fair enough for everyone who does not want to starve to be obliged to work for it. No one has access to the resources they need to maintain their existence unless and until they work for the Big Cooperative. Depending on its rules and your luck you might eventually be able to earn your independence in several years, or it could take a lifetime.

Unfortunately, you are one of the people who don't fit in. Perhaps the Big Cooperative is meritocratic, and you're an egalitarian. Perhaps it's the other way around. Whatever the goals of the cooperative project, they are not your goals. You don't like the work, the terms, the rewards, your place in the hierarchy, or the lack thereof. If you can't command better terms, you'd like to be left alone. You go to see the

Cooperative Complaints Review Board, but ahead of you in line is one of the people least advantaged under the old Big Casino regime.

The review board tells the least advantaged person, "Congratulations, you are no longer exploited! You would have been right not refuse to participate in the old Big Casino. But the New Improved Big Cooperative Casino is reasonably fair and shares its fruits with you. All jobs are good jobs. Your reasons for wanting to quit have all been eliminated."

The disadvantaged person replies, "Maybe you shouldn't tell me, as a disadvantaged person, that I'm no longer exploited. I'll tell you. You show me the jobs, and I'll tell you when they are good enough.,"

The Cooperative Complaints Review Board replies, "We're not interested in your individual opinion of justice; we're interested in true justice. We've made the determination in terms of abstract, objective principles of social justice that have been endorsed by the democratic process. We've imagined what your perspective is like and we've given your position top priority as we formulated the imaginary contract upon which the Big Cooperative Casino is based. We created a list of great job opportunities for you to choose from. Therefore, you must choose one of them."

"If you're so much on my side, why do you want to force me to work for you just as much as the bad guys did? If you really want to help me, why not let me decide?"

"Society is based on mutual obligation. Now that your exploitation has been eliminated, you have a duty to reciprocate to others. We appreciate your disadvantages, but if you won't participate, you must just be lazy."

Seeing how things went for your less-advantaged brethren, you drop your case. You find that, like the Big Casino, the Big Cooperative doesn't directly force you to serve. If you don't want to serve, the Big Cooperative will leave you alone, but without food and without a place to sleep at night. If you want to be left alone with enough resources to build a decent life for yourself and to follow your own goals, you have to fulfill their understanding of your obligation to serve their goals first.

You cannot ignore the Big Cooperative any more than you could ignore the Big Casino. You are not free. You are not free to pursue your own goals until you have made it in the interest of the Big Cooperative to part with enough property to let you be independent. The laws of the state say that you are a free person, but the property rights structure and system of social duties enforced by the state force you to serve at least one member of the ownership group; the laws effectively put you into involuntary servitude. The philosopher-legislators represent the majority and act on what they believe to be fair principles, but they are not you, and you are still bound to their service. You neither agreed to the decisions that brought about these circumstances, nor are you allowed to decline the role ascribed to you in this situation. You are still unfree. Your position neither follows from nor preserves your freedom.

The revolution failed to make you free because it failed to deal with the root cause of your unfreedom in the Big Casino—propertylessness. When resources are owned (privately or publicly), individuals without property are obliged to work for at least one member of the group that controls property before they can achieve even their bare subsistence, much less a decent life. Whether that group is a capitalist class or a democratic majority, you are its subject. As long as there are people without access to enough resources to maintain independence, there will be people who are unfree.

What kind of revolution would make you free?

Suppose you and I become part of a democratic majority coalition that wins control of the Big Casino and wants to make people who live there free in the most meaningful way possible. We must try to avoid imposing things on others against their will. So, we will have to allow everyone who lives in the Big Casino to participate equally in the decision-making process that governs it, but we cannot hope to get everyone's agreement. Decisions that obtain the agreement of some are likely to cause others to withdraw their agreement. Therefore, we have to seek both the widest possible agreement and the minimum negative impact on those who are disadvantaged by or who dissent from our agreement.

We have to make the Big Casino more like the Small Casino. To the greatest extent possible, we must allow people to ignore the Big Casino if they don't want to participate. As much as we try to ensure that the Big Casino is good for everyone, we are only a majority coalition; service to the Big Casino is only assuredly service either to the coalition that governs it or to the individuals who own pieces of it. We must not force anyone to serve us unwillingly. We can't make it possible for individuals to ignore the rules that protect others and make the Big Casino work, but we can compensate people for what we impose on them, and we can make it possible for them to refuse active service to the Big Casino. We have all the resources and output of the Big Casino with which to create positive rewards for voluntary participation. As long as meaningful freedom is our priority, these are the only tools we can use.

That is, we need to recognize and respect every individual's independence, and attempt to build a society on voluntary participation of willing individuals. We invite everyone to share in the benefits of participation, but we compensate individuals for the burdens we impose on them before we ask them to serve us, and the least we can leave for any individual—even if they are unable or unwilling to participate—must be enough to meet their basic needs.

The democratic coalition that sets rules in this way says to its disadvantaged and to its dissenters, "Our system of social cooperation is as fair and mutually beneficial as we know how to make it, but it is up to you to decide whether it is fair and beneficial enough to earn your participation."

The goal of this book is to examine and make the case for this view of how an organized society should treat individuals.

CHAPTER 1

Introduction

We're all stuck here for a while. Let's try to work it out.

—Rodney King
in his Can't-We-All-Get-Along speech
trying to quell the 1992 Los Angeles Riots

The prologue's representation of the economy as a casino is partly derived Milton and Rose Friedman's example of "an evening at baccarat." He concedes that a capitalist economy contains unfairness and leads to inequality, but justifies it on grounds that many such differences follow from choice and people ought to be free to choose what they do.[1] Using the example of the Big Casino, I concede that freedom has the potential to justify a great deal of unfairness and inequality, but I hope to illustrate how a modern economy (both in practice and in the visions of many political theorists of different political views) fails to deliver sufficient freedom to be justified on the grounds of choice or anything else. All economies (that we know how to create) contain what we might call a casino element: they are persistently affected by systemic unfairness, such as nepotism, brute luck, irrelevant requirements, and odds stacked in favor of people with past advantages.

The solution I propose can be put simply. If you can't make the game fair, you can't force people to play. By the end, I will go further—even if you can make the game fair, only in extraordinary circumstances can you force someone to play.

Reducing the unfairness of the system is not my most central concern, partly because we simply don't have the information or the moral certainty to eliminate unfairness. Unless everyone with a dollar spends it according to some universally agreeable principle of fairness, and everyone has the perfect knowledge necessary to make decisions consistently with that theory of fairness, the casino element will remain. Better rules might reduce that casino element, but there is very little hope that society can eliminate the casino element to everyone's satisfaction. The economy is not fair, and neither you nor I know how to make it fair. This is no reason to be unfair; we must try to make it as fair as we can. But our inability to be fair is a reason to be magnanimous to people who object to what we've done. If we force anyone to take part, we force them into an unfair system.

Egalitarian political philosophers have expended a lot of energy on the difficult task of devising the principles and institutions of a just economic system without the casino element. Property rights advocates have responded by asking: What's wrong with the voluntary exchange of goods and services among free people?[2] If consenting adults want to play a game with a casino element, forcing them to stop seriously inhibits their freedom. The libertarian ideal (that freedom as the absence of force is important for everyone) is appealing, but capitalism, as offered by right-libertarians, does not deliver that ideal. It is not simply a system of unforced voluntary exchange among free people. An appeal to freedom can't justify the unfairness of the political system in a world where people assert ownership of natural resources without the consent of or compensation for those without.

The central point of the story is not that the Big Casino is a casino but that it is big—too big to ignore—and its size threatens freedom in two ways. The system of property ownership in most existing and many proposed versions of capitalism, welfare capitalisms, or socialism neither follows from nor preserves liberty. A system that forces people into the position in which they must serve property owners to meet their basic needs cannot be said to preserve freedom. Such a system also can't be said to follow from freedom, because its most onerous duties are forced onto people, not freely accepted by them. An egalitarian attempt to eliminate the casino element but to retain forced participation misidentifies the problem in the modern economy. We cannot eliminate that casino element, but we can avoid forcing people to participate in an economy with a casino element or with any other features to which they might reasonably object.

Sections 1 and 2 below discuss the arguments that the modern economic system neither follows from nor preserves freedom. But the main goal of this book is not to point out problems, but to propose a solution. Section 3 outlines the theory of freedom that is examined and argued for throughout this book. Section 4 briefly discusses how the solution proposed here relates to other theories of justice. Section 5 includes a chapter-by-chapter summary of the book.

1. Failure to Preserve Freedom

The claim that modern economies fail to preserve freedom relies on the observation that, in a world where resources are not freely available, those without property must meet conditions set by at least one person who controls access to resources needed to attain even their basic survival, much less a decent life. This observation is not new.[3] Although the atmosphere, the oceans, and some lakes and rivers are still freely and unconditionally available to everyone, the land and everything we make out of it is not. Private landowners and governments dominate resources by putting individuals in the position in which they do not have enough access to resources to meet their basic needs, without meeting conditions set by others. For the argument here, it doesn't matter whether governments or private individuals and institutions dominate resources or whether the group that dominates resources is large or small, coordinated or uncoordinated. It matters only that whichever group dominates resources puts individuals in the position in which they must serve at least one member of the dominating group to meet their basic needs.

It is helpful to define a few terms. "External assets" are all assets external to the human body. External assets include natural resources and everything the current and past generations have made out of them. I usually use "resources" synonymously with natural resources (external to the human body), but the distinction between natural and other resources is not usually important to the argument, because all external assets embody natural resources.

People are "propertyless" if they lack independent access to a sufficient amount of resources to meet their basic needs. It does not mean that they literally own nothing. People who own their own bodies and some external assets but do not own enough to meet their basic needs (either by direct use of those assets or by trading the external assets they hold for the goods they need) are propertyless in this sense. But being free from propertylessness does not necessarily mean that a person owns any property. None of us are propertyless in terms of the atmosphere. Although we don't own any portion of it, we have sufficient access to the atmosphere to meet the needs it can satisfy. Before landownership developed, no one was propertyless in terms of land. Early hunter-gatherers had no exclusive property rights in land but they had access to a sufficient amount of it to meet their needs.

People who are in the position in which they must toil to meet their needs (as subsistence farmers do) are therefore not propertyless. But people who are in the position in which they must work *for* someone to meet their needs (as tenant farmers, sharecroppers, peasants, serfs, and proletarian laborers do) are therefore propertyless. Selling one's labor without force does not make one propertyless. Many people who own substantial amounts of property choose to trade their labor as well.

Propertylessness and resource domination are reciprocal terms. If one person is propertyless, some other person or group dominates resources; if some person or group dominates resources, they force at least one person to be propertyless. However, there are multiple ways to avoid dominating resources: people can leave a sufficient amount of external assets unowned and freely available so that no one else is propertyless. People can divide external asset ownership in such a way that everyone owns a sufficient amount. Or, a group of people who would otherwise dominate resources can pay compensation so that otherwise propertyless individuals can buy what they need.

The effect of propertylessness on freedom is clear. Human beings have needs that can only be satisfied by external assets or the resources with which to produce the needed goods. Human beings who are unfree to meet their needs are unfree to live or to live a decent life. Rules of property regularly put propertyless people in the position in which someone will interfere with any efforts they make to satisfy their needs on their own or with other propertyless people, indirectly forcing them to serve at least one member of the group that dominates resources. Direct force might be only applied to the control of resources, but it is an effective force nevertheless.

2. Failure to Follow from Freedom

The prologue also illustrates that propertylessness does not follow from voluntary interaction between free people. Supporters of strong private property rights often characterize the market as the embodiment of liberty because people are free to exchange their property rights, once they have them. The *exchange* of property rights does not often threaten freedom; the threat comes from how property rights are defined, assigned, and enforced. A property right in an external asset is the legal right to interfere with other people who might want to use that external asset. Had the propertyless chosen to grant control of the earth's natural resources to the propertied in exchange for some benefit, one could fairly say that propertylessness followed from their exercise of the freedom to make that choice. But the decision to enforce property rights in external assets is imposed on the propertyless without their agreement, and therefore cannot follow from their freedom.

Other property rights regimes are possible. For example, external assets could remain in common or be publicly owned; property rights could be defined in a way that entailed a responsibility on the part of owners to compensate nonowners for the duties they impose on them. The freedom of the propertyless is inhibited by the continual decision to enforce a property-rights regime that creates propertylessness, not by the exchange of titles under that regime. The voluntary aspect of trade is merely the exchange of the right to interfere with people who have not chosen the duty to be subject to that interference. The ownership of property and the right to trade property does enhance the freedom of the holder by granting them external assets that they can use without fear of interference by others, but that freedom has to be balanced against the reduction in freedom that property rights imposed on others. That balance is an important subject of the book. The freedom-inhibiting aspect of property rights is an important consideration of justice that has been too often ignored.

The effect of propertylessness on freedom is substantial. As argued in section 1 above it puts individuals in the position where they are effectively forced to enter the marketplace and serve others. If that decision is not voluntary, much of what follows from it cannot be said to follow from freedom either: the wages and working conditions one accepts are forced, not free, if one is unfree to reject them. Their choice is reduced from whether to serve the group that dominates property to which member to serve.

Once one group has no choice but to serve members of another group, the freedom to choose which member to serve is not sufficient to remove an aristocratic, or even feudal, element to that relationship. By feudal, I mean an economy in which one group of people is born in servitude (whether to a person, to a uncoordinated group, or even to an organized democratic collective). When people take loans, they promise to work for someone else's benefit. As long as they enter the debt voluntarily and have the ability to declare bankruptcy rather than face debtors' prison, debt does not have to threaten their status as free people. But a person born without individual access to property is as unfree as if she were born in debt without means of default. The feudal period was characterized by rigid class distinctions and with subjects born owing specific duties to specific members of the aristocracy. Today, the aristocracy is somewhat fluid. People are not subject to any one master. Many working people accumulate property throughout their lives. But one critically important element of feudalism remains: some people are born in servitude to another group of people because continually enforced rules put someone else's property rights between them and the resources they need to survive.

Given this understanding of the cause of propertylessness, freedom is not a constraint on the redistribution proposed in this work but the motivation for it. The problem is not the voluntary aspects of trade but the involuntary aspects of capitalism as currently constituted. Supporters of contemporary capitalism apply the principle of voluntary agreement selectively—to the *exchange* of property rights but not to the *assignment*, *definition*, and *enforcement* of property rights. One goal of this book is to suggest how to balance the freedom-enhancing and freedom-inhibiting aspects of property rights.

3. A Proposed Solution

What shall we do? When I use the term "we," I mean you and I, two citizens discussing what rules we think we should live under. The solution proposed in this book can be summarized by saying that, as much as possible, we have to make the Big Casino more like the Small Casino. We have a duty to try to stay out of each other's way. If we can't stay out of each other's way, we have to seek accord with others who are affected by what we do. If we can't reach accord with everyone, we have duties to seek accord with the largest possible number of people and to minimize the negative impact on those who can't be brought into the accord.

This book contains a very tentative exploration of a theory of justice and more detailed exploration of the corresponding theory of freedom. I will call the wider theory *justice as the pursuit of accord* (JPA) because it rests on the belief that people have a responsibility to strive for agreement in a world in which unanimous agreement is usually impossible to achieve. Agreement plays a central role in this theory, both in the interaction of individuals and in the creation of the basic structure of society, but the theory neither pretends that agreement has been achieved when it has not (as some contractualist theories do) nor sets up one-sided conditions prior to agreement (as property rights-based theories do). It assumes that the closest approximation of justice that society can reach is to maximize the number of individuals brought into agreement and to minimize the negative impact on those who are disadvantaged by or who dissent from the social agreement.

I hope to explore this theory of justice over a series of at least two books. This first book focuses on the freedom-related aspects of this theory. It culminates in an argument that whoever controls external assets has a strong duty to provide unconditional support to the poor and the disadvantaged. The duty to stay out of each other's way corresponds to a negative conception of freedom. We might also have a duty to help each other. However for the purpose of this book, I both accept the existence of duty to help each other and refuse to rely on that assumption to support my argument for redistribution. This starting point sets a difficult bar for my argument. I argue for redistribution without relying on a duty to aid, and I argue for unconditional redistribution without denying the existence of a duty to aid.

An entailment of staying out of each other's way and of minimizing the negative impact on others is to respect each other's freedom in the most important and substantive way. Beginning with the familiar idea of negative freedom as noninterference, the book builds a theory of the most important freedoms not to interfere with. I call a theory that identifies the most important freedoms a theory of status freedom: the effort to identify the difference between a free person and an unfree person. The book proposes a theory of status freedom that requires personal independence along with familiar civil and political rights. For reasons discussed in chapter 2, I call this particular theory of status freedom: freedom as effective control self-ownership (abbreviated as ECSO freedom). It is the effective power to accept or refuse active cooperation with other willing people—in short—freedom as the power to say no. To respect another's ECSO freedom you must avoid forcing them to do anything for you, and avoid directly or indirectly forcing them into a situation in which others can force them to do things for them. This entailment is a major concern of the theory discussed in this book.

Independence does mean people actually choose to live independently; it means that they participate actively in projects with others only if they have voluntarily chosen to do so. If all individuals choose to participate, when they were free to do otherwise, everyone is independent, but no one lives independently. The central independence-based complaint with many theories of justice (including some liberal, egalitarian, welfarist, contractualist, and property rights-based theories) is that they effectively endorse a mandatory-participation economy in which the propertyless have no other reasonable choice but to serve whichever group controls property. This book argues instead for a voluntary-participation economy in which each individual has a reasonable alternative to active participation. Respect for independence demands that we do not force individuals into a state of material deprivation in which they have no effective power to refuse participation.

The concern for independence and voluntary participation makes arguments for freedom from propertylessness central to this book. Propertylessness is a persistent characteristic in most economies in the world today. Many people enter an economic interaction without property of their own, holding nothing with which to produce their own goods to satisfy their own needs unless and until they serve someone who controls property. Propertylessness prohibits individuals from using the earth's resources to meet their needs. It forces people to accept forms of service that they would otherwise reject. Sometimes it forces people into both service and poverty.

I tentatively call the ideology that follows from JPA "indepentarianism" because of the importance that support for personal independence plays in the theory. It has some relation to left-libertarianism, republicanism, sufficientarianism, liberalism, and liberal-egalitarianism. It is most distinct from these in the respect it places on personal independence and the stress it places on material deprivation as a threat to freedom. The preservation of independence does not eliminate the casino element from the political and economic system; it only makes individual participation in that system voluntary. Individual interactions follow from freedom because individuals have the effective power to choose whether they actively participate in projects with others.

This book does not elaborate the parts of JPA that have to do with property rights and territorial rights, but I will give a quick preview here of the constraints on building an accord to manage resources and any other assets people make out of resources.[4] The requirement to seek accord means that such decisions must be made democratically with the widest possible participation. But unanimous agreement is unlikely to be possible. Imposed authority must have a minimum impact on those who dissent from it. Therefore, the agreement must (to the greatest and most equal extent possible) respect individuals' ECSO freedom and equal claim to overall freedom from interference, which includes everyone's equal claim to freedom from interference with their efforts to make use of resources. Therefore, the decision should be thought of as an agreement by which those who want to get to use resources their way compensate those who want to use resources another way.

The theory implies that the greatest (or most important) equal freedom for all requires a property-rights regime with more limited property rights than the traditional Anglo-American understanding of full individual property rights, and it contains a different justification of the right to private property than is usually proposed. The payment of a tax (such as a wealth or resource-value tax) for the purpose of compensation to the propertyless is not "interference" with property "rights" but is part of the purchase price of property. The justification of private property in resources (and any external assets we might make out of them) is the payment of taxes for distribution to those who have less to compensate them for interfering with whatever use they might make of those resources. Under this theory, compensation must be sufficient to preserve each individual's status as a free person and to make it in each otherwise propertyless individual's interest to support the greater shares of property held by others. This policy will increase the negative freedom of the propertyless and eliminate the problem of people whose independence is threatened by economic deprivation without interfering with those who want to obtain relatively large shares of property any more than a seller interferes with a buyer when she demands payment.

Both the property rights argument and the status freedom argument of JPA support a "basic income guarantee" (BIG): a government-provided, unconditional assurance that everyone has a regular cash income large enough to meet their basic needs. The income is "unconditional" in the sense that it is not limited by the imposition of requirements that individuals perform (or show willingness to perform) some kind of work or service in exchange for it. The income is "regular" in the sense of it being paid daily, weekly, monthly, or often enough to ensure stability. There is an enormous literature on the basic income guarantee, and therefore a detailed explanation of the working of it is not necessary here.[5]

The basic income guarantee has two principal forms, "basic income" and the "negative income tax." Basic income gives a small income to everyone, regardless of their private income. Negative income tax gives income only to those whose private incomes fall below a certain level. The important connection between the two is that they both unconditionally assure that no one's income falls below some minimum level—both are guarantees. Most of the recent literature on the topic (especially in political theory and political philosophy) focuses on basic income, and so I will sometimes focus on basic income as well, but the arguments presented here do not substantially deal with the issue of whether the basic income guarantee should take one form or the other.

Although the property rights and freedom arguments both support basic income, they are different in terms of the size of the basic income they imply. The status freedom argument in this book supports a basic income not less than an amount enough to provide for each individual's basic needs. The indepentarian property rights argument to be elaborated in a future work supports a basic income not less than an amount enough to make it in the interest of individuals at the bottom of the distribution of property to accept the property rights of others (and/or to compensate them for imposing rules to which they might reasonably object). Therefore, JPA overall supports a basic income set at the larger of the two levels.

To summarize in more exacting language, indepentarianism is the name I give to the theory of justice as the pursuit of accord (JPA); it has three central ideas.

1. People's first duty is try to stay out of each other's way. This duty entails respecting each other's need to maintain core well-being, and their equal entitlement to the most important liberties—to status freedom,
2. When it is not possible to stay out of each other's way, people's duty is to seek accord, to seek an agreement in which each party literally accepts the sacrifices they make in exchange for the sacrifices others make on their behalf.
3. When universal accord is not possible—and it is usually not possible—people's duty is to seek both the widest possible agreement and the minimum negative impact on dissenters (i.e., those who cannot be brought into agreement).

JPA implies the following rules for a social agreement to create property rights in natural resources. Of all sets of rules that could be established over resources, the just set attains majority support, respects everyone's status as a free individual, and interferes least (in the least substantive ways) with those who are disadvantaged by or who dissent from the agreement. Democratic governments set rules by which individuals may purchase (or lease) property rights; these rules involve some form of compensation for dissenters and for the disadvantaged, and that compensation must be distributed unconditionally.

4. Alternative Solutions

This section gives a brief preview of how JPA fits in with other theories of justice. This book is critical of the way in which many theories of justice use agreement both at the individual level and in the creation of the basic structure. At least since Thomas Hobbes,[6] most versions of social contract theory have relied on the assumption that legitimate government requires universal agreement. But they have also relied on questionable arguments that such consent actually exists. At least since David Hume,[7] critics have argued that universal consent does not exist. I assume here that universal agreement would be the first-best justification, but it cannot be expected to exist. Different people will want different systems. Any group that sets up a system (including anarchism) interferes with people who would prefer that another system existed on the same land. The justification (under JPA) for one group imposing its system on others is both that the group that gets its way has majority agreement and that it interferes less (i.e., in less substantive ways) with those who do not get their way than any other system.

Rawlsian constructivism doesn't necessarily assume agreement to a social contract but uses the device of an imaginary contract to justify *how* government authority is organized.[8] This device can be useful, but the same constraints apply. No one's power to imagine a contract is perfect. The view of justice adopted by the ruling coalition will reflect the beliefs of its members, but it might not sufficiently take into account the positions of disadvantaged and dissenting minorities. Therefore, the ruling coalition must seek majority support and interfere as little as possible with dissenting minorities.

Theories, such as right-libertarianism, that rely on a natural right to private property insist on agreement at the individual level—once property rights are established. Robert Nozick, for example, sums up his theory writing, "Ignoring acquisition and rectification, we might say... From each as they choose; to each as they are chosen."[9] He thereby invites us to ignore and to remove from the realm of consideration the tremendous amount of coercive force right-libertarianism necessarily imposes on the propertyless and the effects that propertylessness has on a person's ability to make unforced choices. No adequate theory of freedom or justice can ignore these issues. Although voluntary exchange will cause some inequality, and although the application of social control over property is also a potential threat to freedom, the most important causes of unfreedom and inequality are the ones that defenders of unrestricted private property invite us to ignore.

JPA reflects skepticism both with the idea that resources naturally belong to the community as a whole and with the idea that they naturally belong to some private individuals and not others. Without individual access to resources, theories based on either one of these ideas can put individual freedom in jeopardy.

This view of resources gives indepentarianism a clear relationship to left-libertarianism, which Peter Vallentyne defines very broadly, "Left-libertarian theories of justice hold that agents are full self-owners and that natural resources are owned in some egalitarian manner."[10] In these terms, indepentarianism is essentially a left-libertarian theory.

However, JPA's version is quite different from the more standard version of left-libertarianism, which I take to be that all people have claim to an equal share of the ownership of natural resources and that this claim is best secured by an equal share of the current market rental value of natural resources.

The view of resources in JPA is not based on any belief about a natural right to resource ownership on the part of individuals or the community as a whole but on the belief in equal freedom from interference, including equal freedom from interference with the uses people might make of resources. The establishment of any property regime involves interference with someone. Devoting resources to private uses, devoting resources to public use, and maintaining an open-access commons makes people freer to do some things than others. There is no simple answer to what mix of resources should go to what sort of use and no natural price for the interference created when that decision is made. Ideally the various sides would negotiate and either agree to all uses or agree to a price at which those who get to use resources their way compensate those who do not. The JPA property theory is an attempt to approximate such an accord when universal agreement is unattainable. Status freedom acts as a constraint on that agreement.

JPA or indepentarianism is critically concerned with the issue of status freedom. Therefore, this book's main complaint with other theories of justices is the endorsement (or tacit endorsement) of a mandatory-participation economy through resource domination (or any other means). Not all theorists clarify their position on this issue, and so throughout the book, much of my criticism need to be considered as criticism of a particular version or a particular interpretation of the theories in question.

Egalitarians have tended to focus on the unfairness of contemporary capitalism rather than on the unfreedom it imposes on the propertyless. The central problem in the market economy is not that people choose to play games with rules that do not meet a certain standard of fairness; the problem is that rules that make natural resources into private or collective property force people to play games that are not of their own choosing. Yet, many egalitarians have argued for mandatory participation in an economy that meets some standard of fairness. But this solution leaves an individual with the same unfreedom as the propertyless under right-libertarian capitalism—compelled to serve goals chosen by someone else at whatever terms those others demand, whether or not the individual voluntarily agrees. Without the power to refuse participation, an individual has only as much control over the terms and goals of her work as the group in control allows. An egalitarian project that leaves the propertyless in this state of unfreedom has left them to the mercy of the powerful. The possibility that the powerful will be a democratic coalition does not relieve the propertyless of their individual powerlessness in a world of disagreement where not everyone is a part of the ruling coalition. The primary motivation for an unconditional basic income (if that proves to be the best method) is to ensure that no individual is at the mercy of others: not at the mercy of an individual, a class, a system, or a state.[11]

One offshoot of left-libertarianism, Philippe Van Parijs's "real libertarianism," makes the delivery of basic income central to its proposed solution. Van Parijs focuses on "real freedom," which he defines as the freedom to do whatever one might want to do. He justifies the highest sustainable basic income, because it maximizes the freedom of the least free individual and that sense.[12] Van Parijs's policy conclusions (at least on issues of taxation and redistribution) end up being similar to those proposed here. However, the argument for them is very different. The primary "real libertarian" (and left-libertarian) argument for basic income is that people should have unconditional access to an equal share of resource rents regardless of whether such access meets their basic needs or gives them power in their interaction with others. Whether the level of basic income is sufficient to secure the power to opt out or whether control of resources gives one group power over other people are inconsequential to real libertarianism, while they are centrally important to indepentarianism. As noted above, JPA involves concern for the equalization of rents, but securing a level of need and a certain status in relationships are more central concerns.

Civic republicanism (at least in Philip Pettit's version) is concerned with status freedom as non-domination or the freedom from any potential arbitrary interference.[13] The conception of freedom outlined below has some important similarities to non-domination, but later sections will argue that non-domination does not capture impersonal, systemic, or nonarbitrary threats to status freedom.

5. Preview of This Work

This book proposes, defends, and examines the ramifications of the theory of ECSO freedom. Chapter 2 defines ECSO freedom as the effective power to accept and refuse active cooperation with other willing people. It derives ECSO freedom from the more familiar concept of self-ownership, but shows that ECSO freedom is a separate concept. It is broader in some ways and narrower in other ways. This chapter discusses how ECSO freedom can be understood as a theory of status freedom, and argues for the need for a theory of status freedom. The most important feature of this definition is its focus on individuals' *effective power* to control their interactions. One can interfere with another's ability to refuse both directly by forcing them to do something and indirectly by denying them access to the resources they need to live a decent life until they do something. ECSO freedom requires "personal independence" or "an exit option," unconditional direct access to resources to maintain individuals' effective power to refuse unwanted service to others.

Chapter 3 discusses some of the implications of understanding status freedom as ECSO freedom or independence. It addresses issues such as the alienation of status freedom and the complexity of freedom and unfreedom. It argues that independence requires unconditional access to sufficient resources to maintain a threshold of human need. The chapter examines several theories of human need to identify that threshold and argues that the best way to maintain that access in a modern industrialized economy is through an unconditional basic income guarantee.

Chapters 4, 5, and 6 argue for the importance of respecting and protecting independence. Chapter 4 frames the issue. Two very different aspects of independence are important: freedom from deprivation and the freedom from being forced to serve someone often by the threat of deprivation. The argument hinges on forced deprivation being a significant loss of liberty both in itself and because it can lead to forced service to others' projects. There are two obvious contrary positions: the belief in a social responsibility to work and the belief that private property rights to natural resources must be upheld even though doing so forces one group of people to work for another. The chapter considers three ethical models of human interaction (trade, pure voluntarism, and mutual obligation), all of which are appropriate in different situations. It also considers three mechanisms for getting humans to interact (trade, pure voluntarism, and force). The argument for independence laid out in subsequent chapters involves arguing that trade and voluntarism models are appropriate in most situations and that the trade and voluntarism mechanisms are often superior to force even when mutual obligation is appropriate.

Chapter 5 makes several first-best ethical arguments for respecting personal independence. It argues that individual consent is a constituent part of what makes most social and economic interaction just, that the trade or voluntarism model is appropriate for most economic interaction, and that respect for human integrity entails respect for individuals' decisions on when and whether to participate in projects with others. It suggests that there is a great deal in the economic system that gives individuals reason to object and that an important justification for any economic system should be that participants literally choose to participate.

Chapter 6 makes a second-best or indirect argument for the importance of respecting independence. The chapter shows that independence is an important mechanism to protect vulnerable individuals from poverty and exploitation both in their market and nonmarket interactions. It concludes that even if we completely disregard the possibility that participants' agreement has a direct bearing on whether the social project is just, the requirement to obtain each participant's agreement is an extremely powerful tool to ensure that the goals, methods, and terms of cooperation are good, fair, right, or just and not one-sided in favor of the ruling majority (or any other powerful group).

Chapter 7 briefly recounts the recognition of indirectly forced labor in the history of political thought. It then considers the theory of ECSO freedom in relation to several prominent theories of freedom. Protection of independence does not necessarily conflict with protection of most conceptions of freedom considered, most of which are theories of scalar freedom rather than status freedom. The chapter argues that theories of freedom would be stronger if they incorporated respect for independence. It also discusses indepentarianism's relationship to sufficientarianism, left-libertarianism, and real libertarianism. Indepentarianism has a similar view of natural resource ownership as left- and real libertarians, but it connects these concerns with resources and sufficientarian concerns for a threshold of need to a theory of status freedom. The focus on status freedom gives indepentarianism a significantly different perspective from left- and real libertarianism.

Chapter 8 examines the indepentarian view of freedom in relationship to liberal-egalitarians theories of justice, arguing that theories that do not respect the independence of the poor are insufficiently egalitarian. It examines Rawlsian arguments that can be used both for and against an enforceable obligation to contribute to social production, and gives several reasons in both ideal and nonideal theory to support the power to refuse for the least advantaged and for everyone.

Chapter 9 considers the question of duty. It assumes that there are some situations in which individuals have an enforceable obligation to contribute to a joint project and the extent to which such an obligation is a limitation on the arguments in this book. It presents this question in the context of the reciprocity or exploitation objection of basic income. It concedes that there may be such duties but argues that these duties cannot do the work basic income opponents would like them to do: ground a lifetime obligation to participate in the labor market. The chapter concludes that duty could at best ground a temporary national service that would be equally onerous for all participants.

Chapter 10 summarizes and concludes the arguments in this book placing the respect for independence as a requirement of the basic respect for human dignity. Without it "egalitarian" theories are insufficiently concerned with equality and "libertarian" theories are insufficiently concerned with liberty.

CHAPTER 2

Status Freedom as Effective Control Self-Ownership

This whole program is voluntary.... The men don't have to...if they don't want to. But we need you to starve them to death if they don't.

—*"Milo Minderbinder," Joseph Heller,* Catch-22[1]

What does it mean to be a free person? Consider an answer given by someone who experienced chattel slavery. Garrison Frazier was the spokesperson for a delegation of former slaves called "freedmen" (although many were women) who met with General Sherman on January 12, 1865, before the end of the US Civil War.[2] When asked what he understood by slavery, Frazier replied, "Slavery is, receiving by *irresistible power* the work of another man, and not by his *consent*." He defined freedom as, "taking us from under the yoke of bondage, and placing us where we could reap the fruit of our own labor [and] take care of ourselves." Asked how best to secure their freedom, Frazier said, "The way we can best take care of ourselves is to have land, and turn it and till it by our own labor."[3]

The story of what happened after the meeting has come to symbolize broken promises to African Americans. Sherman distributed land seized from former slave owners to freedmen in a large area of the southeastern coast, sometimes along with surplus army mules. Rumors spread that all freedmen would receive 40 acres and a mule. Less than a year later, the federal government reversed Sherman's order, restored the prewar property rights of former slaveholders, and forcibly evicted the freedmen,[4] many of whom had to work for their former masters, taking the least desirable jobs and the lowest pay. Some descendants of slaves continue to serve the holders of those property rights to this day.

The discussion at the meeting is illustrative of another important issue. The significance of Frazier's request for land is not that freedom requires the opportunity to become a subsistence farmer; it requires the freedom from indirectly forced labor. Frazier recognized that legal self-ownership is not enough to make a person free. It does not free an individual from the "irresistible power" to do the bidding of others. Individuals who are prevented from working for themselves alone (and not sufficiently compensated for being denied that option) are forced to work for someone who controls access to resources. Forced labor is unfreedom whether that force is direct or indirect. The freedom from indirectly forced labor is a liberty that propertyless people in the world today lack. This chapter develops a theory of freedom that incorporates the freedom from indirectly forced service as a centrally important liberty.

This chapter proposes a theory to identify the most important liberties to protect. It asks the question, under what conditions is an individual free enough to be called a free person? This question uses the word "free" in two different ways. Although we do not have different words for these two senses of freedom, the distinction is well understood in ordinary English. One common definition of freedom is the absence of impediment, restriction, or interference.[5] I call this "scalar freedom" or "freedom as a continuous variable," because in this sense freedom is a matter of degree as on a scale or a continuum. Another common definition of freedom is the absence of slavery, detention, or oppression.[6] I call this "status freedom" or "categorical freedom," because in this sense freedom is a distinct state of being. Freedom in the status sense is the distinction between the status of a free individual ("freedom") and the lack of that status ("unfreedom"), or the difference between a person who controls her own life and a person who lacks that control (such as a prisoner, a slave, or a subject of a totalitarian state).

Although status freedom reflects a common usage that has clear importance for practical politics, political philosophers have focused more of their attention on scalar freedom. Without an adequate theory of status freedom, political philosophy cannot answer two questions that laypersons and practitioners find comprehensible and important to politics: What does it mean to be a free person? How can we ensure that everyone is free? This chapter attempts to answer those questions, or to put the goal of this chapter in simpler terms, it attempts to identify the most important liberties.

Section 1 clarifies the relationship between status and scalar freedom and discusses the need for a theory of status freedom. Section 2, the main body of the chapter, puts forth a theory of status freedom, deriving it in relationship to the familiar concept of self-ownership. It develops, "Freedom as Effective Control Self-Ownership" (ECSO freedom) as the effective power to accept or refuse active cooperation with other willing people. It creates only a slight risk of oversimplification to call it *freedom as the power to say no.* Section 3 argues that ECSO freedom requires "personal independence" or "an exit option," unconditional direct access to resources, and shows how exit options have been closed off by the coercive interference of other people.

1. The Concept of Status Freedom and the Need for a Theory of It

Status freedom and scalar freedom are both made out of the same stuff. A person could hardly be enslaved, detained, or oppressed without being somehow impeded, restricted, or interfered with. I use the word "liberty" for the absence of any particular restriction.[7] A theory of scalar freedom identifies a continuum of liberties. On that continuum, a theory of status freedom identifies the core liberties—the most important liberties. Liberties that don't affect status freedom are secondary liberties. It identifies a person who has the most important liberties as free and a person who lacks them as unfree. Like bass and treble or light and dark, freedom and unfreedom identify ranges on a continuum. A theory of status freedom identifies a threshold on that continuum separating freedom and unfreedom, but its most important job is to identify the most important liberties.

If it is important not only to maximize the scalar freedom of the average person but also to ensure that every citizen has the most important liberties, we need theories of both scalar and status freedom. We need a theory of scalar freedom to understand the way particular liberties affect overall freedom whether or not those liberties affect an individual's status as a free person. We need a theory of status freedom to identify when particular liberties crucially affect a person's status.

Some liberties, such as a release from prison, directly affect status freedom. Restrictions on some liberties, such as access to places to stand, affect scalar freedom in small amounts and status freedom in large amounts. Some liberties affect scalar freedom without affecting status freedom at all. For example, if a prisoner is given videos, she is freer in the scalar sense, but she is no less a prisoner and no less unfree in the status sense. Access to an infinite number of videos would give her an infinite number of liberties, but it would not make her free. The continuum of liberties is multidimensional and not all dimensions are equally important. We cannot determine whether someone is free by counting liberties; we must consider the value of those liberties.

If status freedom is a coherent concept, respect for an individual's status as a free person must be a crucial duty.[8] It is, therefore, surprising that political philosophers have not paid more attention to this concept. There are a few theories of status freedom (under various names) but a large majority of philosophical attention has been to scalar theories of freedom.[9] The lack of attention would be justifiable if status freedom were incoherent or obvious, or if the maximization of freedom as a continuous variable necessarily assured status freedom as well. We cannot be sure that an effort to maximize scalar freedom for the average person also delivers status freedom to everyone because any society will deliver different liberties to different people. We need a theory of status freedom (or some way to prioritize liberties) to know whether the restrictions imposed on some to promote the freedom of others are justifiable.

One might think it is obvious that people who are not imprisoned or enslaved have status freedom. But this claim does not survive scrutiny. Certainly, people subject to a totalitarian government are also unfree. African Americans in the United States between emancipation and the civil rights movement were not as unfree as slaves, but they faced such extreme oppression that it is inaccurate to point to their status as an example of what it means to be a free person. This book is particularly concerned with the issue of people who face economic destitution: those with no place to sleep, bathe, or urinate; those who have to eat scraps they find in garbage cans; or those who are forced to accept whatever wages and working conditions are available to avoid such conditions. A theory of status freedom should explain why destitute people should or should not be considered free.

Before advancing a theory of status freedom, I need to make five remarks about what shape such a theory should take. First, although any theory of status freedom must identify a threshold that divides freedom and unfreedom, that threshold does not need to be a fine line. There is likely to be a large area of restricted freedom or threatened freedom in between full freedom and full unfreedom. To insist on a fine line would be to assert the black-and-white fallacy. For example, gradually adding molecules of black paint to a white paint slowly changes it to grey and to black. No nonarbitrary line divides white from grey or grey from black, but it is fallacious to conclude, therefore, that white and black are essentially the same thing or that they do not identify meaningful or meaningfully distinct categories.

We should expect the threshold between freedom and unfreedom to be a large grey area of restricted or threatened freedom.

Second, not all (un)free people are (un)free in the same way. Not all free people experience the same liberties or the same amount of scalar freedom; not all unfree people experience the same restrictions or the same amount of scalar freedom. A person whose alternative to doing X is to be tortured to death has less freedom than a person whose alternative is a year of detention, even if neither is fully free. People have faced many different kinds of unfreedom throughout history. Roman slaves, African American slaves, African Americans between emancipation and the civil rights movement, medieval serfs, Ming Dynasty harem members, Victorian proletarians, women before the equal rights movement, and Soviet citizens were all unfree in different ways. It is far less useful to develop a rank ordering of the various kinds of unfreedom than it is to develop a strategy to ensure that everyone has full status freedom. This book argues that destitute people today are unfree. This argument does not imply that they are unfree in the same way or to the same extent as all unfree persons. It only implies that they have not reached a crucial threshold required to be a fully free person.

Third, not everyone is capable of having status freedom. Children and people with certain kinds of mental disabilities are either not capable of being free or not capable of making good use of that status. This book does not address the question of what level of mental ability is necessary to make a person capable of being free, although the power to identify that ability and the power to supervise people who lack it are both vulnerable to abuse.

Fourth, I have implied above that a theory of status freedom requires a theory of scalar freedom. I will use Isaiah Berlin's simple definition of negative freedom as the absence of other people's interference with what one is able to do.[10] Because freedom is about making choices, any interference or threat of interference that reduces a person's choice set ought to be understood to reduce their negative freedom, even if they might not have chosen that option were it available. I do not believe that negative freedom is all there is to scalar freedom or that the case for ECSO freedom necessarily relies on that distinction. I use it to establish a difficult bar for a theory to pass. I wish to show that we have stronger duties toward the disadvantaged than commonly recognized, and I intend to show this by using the same definition of freedom as many who argue that we have few duties to the disadvantaged. Thomas Pogge uses negative freedom similarly. He argues that negative duties are more compelling than positive duties. The argument that we must take greater action to aid the disadvantaged is more difficult to make and more compelling when made, if the duty to take action was generated by our failure to avoid interfering with the disadvantaged. He also argues that it is not necessary to resort to a theory of positive liberty to show that greater distribution toward the disadvantaged is justified, because so much of the poverty in the world is largely attributable to interference with the people living in poverty.[11]

Fifth, by a free person, I do not mean a person with absolute or complete freedom. In the negative sense, complete freedom would be achieved if other human beings did not restrict anything a person was capable of doing. For example, they would not interfere with her if she tried to kill another person. By that definition, only people in very unusual or undesirable circumstances could be completely free: a person having no contact with other human beings, an omnipotent dictator, or a person with severe physical limitations on her abilities. Therefore, complete freedom is neither desirable in abstract nor worth striving for in practice.

2. Derivation, Definition, and Discussion of ECSO Freedom

Self-ownership is not a theory of status freedom, because it is not a threshold concept. It provides a good, familiar starting point from which to derive ECSO freedom, but this section will show that it is too broad in some ways and too narrow in others to capture what it means to be a free person. Although I use self-ownership for reference, the two concepts are independent; the endorsement of one does not necessarily imply the endorsement or rejection of the other.

Self-ownership might be too quickly dismissed because it appears to commodify humanity. John Locke did not intend this when he proposed the idea that people have property in themselves. He meant only the people have *rights* in themselves.[12] Self-ownership is merely a way of specifying what rights persons have in themselves. Self-ownership, at least if it is seen as inalienable, does not imply that freedom entails treating yourself like a commodity; it implies that freedom prohibits anyone else from treating you like *their* commodity. According to G. A. Cohen,

> [T]he thesis of self-ownership...says that each person is the morally rightful owner of his own person and powers, and, *consequently*, that each is free (morally speaking) to use those powers as he wishes, provided that he does not deploy them aggressively against others.[13]

To have full self-ownership is to have full ownership rights in over all of the assets internal to one's mind and body. Call these "internal assets," and call everything else "external assets."[14] External assets include natural resources and everything humans make out of them (except other humans). Tony Honoré identifies full liberal ownership as a bundle of 11 incidents (i.e., rights and duties). These are the rights to possess, use, and manage income, capital, and security as well as the properties of transmissibility, the absence of term, the duty to prevent harm, liability to execution, and residuary character. Self-ownership, therefore, is the possession of these rights and duties over all of one's internal assets. Self-ownership alone says nothing about ownership of external assets.

Some proponents of freedom such as self-ownership have taken it to extravagant lengths, arguing for example, that it is violated even if an already wealthy person pays an income tax.[15] Many trivial restrictions are, therefore, violations of self-ownership, and the theory of self-ownership provides no guidance to identifying the most important violations. Many proponents of self-ownership ignore the inability of the legal or nominal right of self-ownership to ensure that individuals actually do control their own lives if they are unable to meet their needs. Therefore, I will discuss to refinements of the concept.

A. Control Self-Ownership

Self-ownership is too broad to be a theory of status freedom. John Christman argues that freedom cannot be equated with *all* aspects of self-ownership. Citing Honoré's list, Christman argues that each incident of ownership requires *separate* justification.[16] According to Christman, it would be inappropriate to argue that because *some* of these incidents are essential to freedom, we must therefore understand freedom as *all* of them. He argues that the most important aspects of freedom are captured by the four incidents concerning control rights (the rights to use, possess, manage, and capital). "The central idea of these rights is that the owner maintains primary say over what is to be done with the thing insofar as this affects only the owner."[17]

Christman argues that income self-ownership is not a central incident, because income is not the right to *x* dollars from a trade, it is the right to bargain with others for some undetermined amount of income. These rights depend on the pattern of trade, the willingness of others to trade, and the rules under which trade takes place; "preventing me from reaping increased benefits from trade does not necessarily prevent me from controlling my life."[18] For example, he argues, the respect for freedom that makes us reject a rule forcing a sighted person to donate one of her eyes to a blind person, does not necessarily make us reject a rule preventing a sighted person from selling one of her eyes to a blind person.[19]

B. Effective Self-Ownership

Self-ownership is also too narrow to capture what it means to be free. Many authors have argued that even the full right of self-ownership has little value if it is not supported by an effective power.[20] At least since Thomas Paine, many philosophers have recognized that the assignment of property rights in external assets can lead to some form of forced service.[21] A property right is the legal right to exclusive use of something. It is not only the right to use that thing but also the right to interfere with anyone else who might want to use that thing. If A owns all external assets, A is authorized to interfere with any use of external assets B might make. If B is a human being who needs resources to stay alive, B needs A's permission to stay alive; B is effectively forced to work for A. If group A controls all external assets, they collectively coerce each member of group B to trade their self-ownership to at least one member of group B. For self-ownership to be effective, people need not only the legal right to refuse to sell their labor but also sufficient freedom from interference with uses they might make of resources to give them the genuine power to refuse.

An unforced person must be free not only from an imminent threat of death but also from significant deprivation. Using a sense of force derived from Serena Olsaretti: A is forced to do *x* if A has no acceptable alternative to doing *x*; and A's choice to do *x* is unforced if she has an acceptable alternative to doing *x*.[22] As Cohen argues, "When a person is forced to do something, he has no *reasonable* or *acceptable* alternative. He need not have no alternative at all."[23] Stuart White interprets Cohen's understanding of force as follows, "[A]n alternative is unacceptable if it is 'thoroughly bad' in an absolute sense; if, say, it would push the individual below the threshold of core well-being."[24] To say that an alternative is unacceptable is not to say that everyone always refuses it. There were slaves who chose death to servitude, but their choice did not make other slaves unforced employees. We cannot say that homelessness is a reasonably acceptable alternative to employment simply because some people actually accept it.

Michael Otsuka defines "robust self-ownership" incorporating effective power as follows:

> [I]n addition to having the libertarian right itself, one also has rights over enough worldly resources to ensure that one will not be forced by necessity to come to the assistance of others in a manner involving the sacrifice of one's life, limb, or labour.[25]

Robust self-ownership contains the central aspect of Frazier's request for land to avoid the "irresistible power" of forced labor for others, but it also includes *all* incidents of self-ownership, and it is, therefore, too broad to capture what it means to be a free person.

C. *Effective Control Self-Ownership*

"Freedom as Effective Control Self-Ownership" (ECSO freedom) combines Christman's narrowing with Otsuka's broadening of self-ownership. ECSO Freedom is *the effective power to accept or to refuse active cooperation with other willing people.* It is the genuine power to exercise the rights entailed by control self-ownership including the rights to use, possess, and manage oneself. Individuals with ECSO freedom are not subject to external control—from a person, a class, a system, or a state. They have control over the direction of their lives, the goals they pursue alone or with others, and the terms of cooperation they will accept. ECSO freedom is freedom from being subjected to an alien sense of value; it is violated when people are subjected against their will to terms or goals of social or individual cooperation that they oppose.

The basic idea of ECSO freedom is that forced service is inconsistent with freedom—whether that force is direct or indirect. If one group does anything to force unwilling people to participate in their projects, they deny freedom in its most basic sense. There might be great emergencies that justify forcing individuals to serve some project, but any such force involves the sacrifice of an individual's standing as a free person, at least for the time they are forced to serve. Freedom is about making choices. Freedom is not about being subject to force—even justified force.

The power to cooperate with other willing people is secured by familiar rights of freedom of association, expression, movement, political participation, and so on. The nominal right to refuse unwanted interaction is well recognized in the laws of most democracies by the protection of the nominal right of self-ownership. Military conscription is a substantial exception. Other exceptions tend to be either trivial (such as jury duty, subpoena power, and mandatory voting) or motivated by self-protection (such as the imprisonment of criminals) or by the belief that the individual is incapable of being free (noted above). Like the power to define mental competence, the powers of conscription and imprisonment are vulnerable to substantial abuse and reasonable disagreement, but I will not address these issues here.

Because formal self-ownership is normally well respected, my attention falls on the one component of ECSO freedom that is not widely recognized: the effective power to refuse unwanted active cooperation. This component requires an "exit option" or "personal independence." That is, unconditional, independent access to sufficient external assets to secure core well-being. Respect for independence requires one of two things. People must leave everyone else alone and leave alone enough resources or external assets so that they can maintain independence, or people must compensate others for not leaving resources alone, and that compensation must be unconditional and sufficient to protect their core well-being. That is they must avoid resource domination or compensate others sufficiently to preserve independence. When a person lacks independence, she is a *forced servant*, not in the sense that she works in the service industry or for a particular person, but in the sense that she must serve the interests of someone who controls resources, or she will be unable to maintain core well-being.

Access to resources is not merely instrumental to securing freedom from forced service. A person is unfree if other people force her below the threshold of core well-being out of indifference without giving her any option to attain resources. It doesn't matter whether one group dominates resources with the intension of forcing the propertyless to do something or if they do so out of indifference to the needs of others. It doesn't matter whether assets are dominated by an individual or a group or whether that group's actions are coordinated or uncoordinated, intentional or unintentional. If any person or group takes actions that collectively threaten a person's access to a sufficient amount of resources, they threaten her life, her core well-being, and her independence.

ECSO freedom is, in short, *freedom as the power to say no.* To avoid oversimplification, this summary definition requires two clarifications. First, the power to accept interaction with other willing people is as important as the power to refuse unwanted interaction. Second, ECSO freedom does not involve the power to refuse anything one might not like but only the power to refuse within a defined sphere of personal activity ensuring core well-being and free association. It is logically impossible for all people at the same time to have the power to refuse any rule (including rules against imposing rules on others), but it is logically possible for all people at the same time to have the power to refuse active cooperation.

The power to say no is the power of independence. The following section discusses that concept more fully.

D. Independence

No one, aside from an omnipotent dictator, can be independent of all rules set by other people, but people can be independent in a meaningful way. Passive cooperation (such as traffic laws and the designation of public and private spaces) is required just to keep out of each other's way. Mandatory rules ensuring passive cooperation are unavoidable as long as people might want to make different uses of the same resources or the same space at the same time. As long as these rules are not one-sided, are truly designed only to keep everyone out of each other's way, and do not threaten core well-being, they need not threaten status freedom in the way that rules mandating active cooperation in some project inherently do.

My use of the term "independence" applies only to independence from *active* participation on others' projects. Therefore it relies on the distinction between passive and active cooperation. Although passive (or negative) commands can be phrased actively (or positively), there is a substantive difference between active and passive obligations.[26] The command "don't come over here," which is phrased negatively, can be used equivalently to the command "stay over there," which is phrased positively. Yet, there is an important, substantive difference between the two following commands:

- "Pick up that hammer and help us pursue this project."
- "Don't hinder our project here; pursue your project there," when there is a place where the subject can pursue his project.

The second part of this book discusses the effect of passive duties on scalar freedom even if those rules don't threaten status freedom, but a theory of *effective* freedom must identify when passive duties are excessive. In terms of ECSO freedom, passive duties become excessive when they threaten core well-being and/or effectively force people to perform active duties. The theory must show the point at which an individual is not able to respect those passive duties and remain reasonably free to reject active participation in others' projects.

Using the theories described above, that point is the one at which a person has no reasonable or acceptable alternative to participation in other's projects. That is, passive duties are excessive if the alternative of both respecting one's passive duties and refusing active participation is thoroughly bad in an absolute sense.[27] Independent individuals need an exit option with access to enough external assets to live a decent life on their own or with people of their choice. This access frees them from (directly or indirectly) forced active cooperation with others not of their choice. Individuals must also be free to cooperate with others of their choice, and they must not be forced to cease interaction with people of their choice to gain access to the resources necessary to maintain core well-being. Chapter 3 discusses this issue in more detail, examining theories of need to determine an acceptable exit option and to consider policies for maintaining it. But I will consider a couple of simple examples here to illustrate the idea.

Example 1: Art enforces ownership of a small part of the atmosphere by blowing up a bicycle tire and forcing Bob not to interfere with the tire or with the air inside it. Bob's duty not to interfere with the air inside the tire is passive or negative, and it is not excessive, assuming the rest of the atmosphere is available for whatever uses Bob might make of it. If Art goes on to tell Bob that he can't use his tire or the air inside it unless Bob does X, Bob clearly has the power to refuse X. He has no duty to do X either passively or actively enforced. Art might give Bob good reason to choose to do X, but he hasn't indirectly forced Bob to do X.

Example 2: Art takes control of the entire atmosphere either by strangling Bob or by asserting ownership of the entire atmosphere by pumping it into a giant bicycle tire for safekeeping. No matter how Art controls the atmosphere, Bob has the same negative duty as in example 1: he has to respect Bob's ownership of some amount of air. The difference is that the amount is excessive. If Art now says that Bob can have access to the air if he does X for Art, Bob has no reasonable alternative but to accept. Thus, he has an active duty to do X for Bob. In the case of strangulation, Bob has an active duty directly enforced: Art assaults Bob's person unless he does X.[28] But in the case in which Art simply asserts ownership of the atmosphere, Bob's duty to do X is indirectly enforced. He is nominally free to say no, but he can't refuse to do X and maintain his passive duty to respect Art's ownership of the atmosphere without suffocating, which is thoroughly bad in an absolute sense. He has no exit option.

Thus, there must be some amount of resources (such as air, land, water, and so on) that one group can take control of without effectively forcing everyone else to do something for them. But this amount becomes effectively forceful if it puts the other group in a position in which their alternative to active service is unacceptable.

Similarly, an independent person must continually have access to an acceptable exit option. To say that one had an exit option at the age of 25 and chose dependence does not mean that the person at the age of 35 is independent or in accord with her current social arrangements. The need to maintain independence constrains both social rules and individual interaction.

Independence must obviously be understood at the individual level. Spouses or members of any other formal or informal group must retain their status as free persons against each other as much as they retain it against anyone else. Therefore control over a sphere of personal activity cannot be sacrificed because of group membership. Otherwise groups could create dependence.

The independent status argued for here requires only the *existence* of an exit option. It does not mean that people have to *choose* that option. The goal of respecting ECSO freedom is not to ensure that people live independently, but to give all people this one crucial aspect of equality in status so that when they cooperate, they come together as equals—not equals in all sense, but equal in status freedom. The alternative is that some will enter cooperation dependent on others. Independent people can come together to form a community, and people can choose to maintain a community even as they preserve and respect each other's right to choose independence.

Freedom from *forced* interaction does not imply the *absence* of interaction, and it certainly does not imply that unforced interaction is undesirable. ECSO freedom is important not because people should live independently but because *the potential value of social interaction is no excuse for one group to impose its idea of desirable goals, methods, and terms of interaction on others.* Neither a democratic majority nor a group of property owners has the moral authority to force others to serve them. Life without human interaction is terrible, but a life of forced interaction is also terrible. My concern here is not to determine which is worse but to determine how we can make sure interaction is voluntary.

To equate freedom with independence is not to stress independence as a virtue. If one argues, "Interaction is good or just; therefore I may force another to interact," one inherently opposes freedom. But if one argues, "Freedom is good or just; therefore no one may force another to interact," one does not oppose interaction; one merely limits the methods by which interaction can be promoted.

Consider sex as an example. Freedom from forced sex is not freedom from sex. I do not advocate celibacy as a virtue if I advocate securing for each individual the power to refuse *all* potential sex partners. A person does not have sexual freedom if others compel her to have sex with one of a prescribed list of potential sex partners while denying her the power to decline to have sex with all of them. Sexual freedom exists only when every individual has the effective power to accept and to refuse sexual contact with other willing people. Free interaction in all realms should be seen in the same way. Labor market freedom exists when all people have the effective power to accept and refuse labor market cooperation with other willing people. If cooperative labor is good for people, and I believe it is, there are ways to get people to choose it without resorting to force.

A prohibition on forced active cooperation does not prevent society from soliciting active cooperation. It just means that society must solicit cooperation in an independence-respecting manner. Independence does not ensure someone can refuse social cooperation and have access to all the external assets they want; it only ensures enough for a minimally decent life. The potential benefits of social cooperation (and people's desire for more than a minimally decent life) give social cooperators great ability to elicit participation even while respecting independence. ECSO freedom implies little about property right beyond a claim to unconditional access to a sufficient amount of external assets to maintain independence, and this book does not put forward a full JPA property theory.

Once an individual has access to a sufficient amount of external assets to maintain independence, they have ECSO freedom even if they must perform active duties for others to obtain larger amounts of external assets. People who have unconditional access to an acceptable minimum cannot say that their status as free individuals is infringed because they must work for someone else to get more. Similarly property owners cannot claim that they are denied ECSO freedom because they must perform a positive action to maintain control over a larger than sufficient amount of property in external assets. Any such issues have to do with *property* ownership, not with *self*-ownership—effective or otherwise.[29]

E. Independence and Negative Freedom

This section explains how a theory of status freedom as ECSO freedom can be built on a theory of scalar freedom as negative freedom.

Under negative freedom, defined as the freedom from interference, ECSO freedom implies that each person has the duty not to interfere with other people in ways that might limit or make it impossible for them to maintain their ECSO freedom. This obligation is the most important entailment of the duty to stay out of each other's way.

If ECSO freedom is built entirely on a base of negative freedom, others have no necessary obligation to take positive action to help others maintain their ECSO freedom. Such an obligation might be incompatible with preservation of the power to access or refuse for everyone. But a positive obligation is not necessary to justify the needed actions. This book attempts to justify significant and unconditional redistribution of property from people who control resources (i.e., private property owners and governments) to the propertyless based solely on property holders' failure to fulfill their duty to stay out of other people's way.

Negative freedom can be best understood by drawing a distinction between positive and negative rights and duties. Negative rights directly imply only passive (or negative) duties on the part of others. Positive rights imply active duties on the part of others. The right not to be murdered is negative because it implies only that others must refrain from murdering you. The right to police protection is positive because it implies that at least some other person has to take action to investigate if someone tries to murder you. Negative liberties rely directly on negative rights only; they directly imply only negative duties on the part of others.[30]

As argued above, respect for ECSO freedom requires the duty to refrain from both directly and indirectly forcing someone else to do something. Refraining from the direct force requires the duty not to interfere with or threaten to interfere with other person's bodies. Refraining from indirect force requires the duty not to interfere with or threaten to interfere with a sufficient amount of resources so that others can meet their needs. Both duties are negative. Therefore, ECSO freedom can be built on negative freedom.

The use of negative freedom here is very much the same as the one Jeremy Waldron employs in his argument that the homeless are unfree in the most liberal negative sense. He points out several things that the homeless could do for themselves if left alone. They are not unable to do these things; they are unfree to do them. Waldron argues that such interference causes them great difficulty in modern society, although he does not discuss the issues of whether the denial of access to resources forces people to work for others or of the extent to which the propertyless could meet their needs on their own without positive aid from others.[31]

Waldron employs a Berlinian notion of freedom in areas where Isaiah Berlin himself did not employ it. Berlin argues incorrectly, "Men who are half-naked, illiterate, underfed, and diseased need medical help or education before they can understand, or make use of, an increase in their freedom." This claim is not entirely true. Although many propertyless people might be in need of positive aid from other people, there are many things that they could do for themselves if propertied people would stop interfering with them. They could build shelters and attempt to secure their own clothing and food. They could even help to educate each other. The extent to which any particular homeless person or group of homeless people could meet their needs on their own is an open question. But when one considers the richness of the Earth's resource base, the value of external assets left by past generations, and the volume of information in the public domain, it becomes clear that interference by other people with what the propertyless could do for themselves makes their position substantially worse than it would be if we did not fail so badly in our duty to stay out of each other's way.

The use of negative freedom here is not quite the same as the one G. A. Cohen employs in his book, *Self-Ownership, Freedom, and Equality*. His version of negative freedom appears to be the freedom from *all* interference rather than freedom that requires only negative rights. Cohen uses the example of a poor person who is capable of getting on a train and riding it and that people would typically *interfere* with her to stop her from doing so. Therefore, this action is in his sense a denial of negative freedom.[32] Interference is certainly involved, but a person needs something more than just freedom from interference to take a train. She needs the positive aid of others to build, run, and maintain the train. Without that aid the person in his example would be unable to ride a train even if no one interfered with anything she might try to do on her own.

Although Cohen elsewhere appeals to the power of the narrower use of freedom from interference,[33] his broad use of the negative freedom concedes too much to the opponents of redistribution. As Pogge argues, it is not necessary to employ a right to positive aid from others to show that many disadvantaged people around the world are made unfree by the interference of others.[34] It is also unnecessary to point out that one must interfere with someone to prevent them from consuming the products of others to show that the propertyless are subject to a great deal of interference. There are many things that propertyless could do for themselves (either alone or in groups of their choosing) to maintain their well-being, if others would stop interfering with things they are capable of doing for themselves. The problem is not (or is not solely) that people fail to provide positive aid to the propertyless; the problem is much more directly that people have not fulfilled their duty to stay out of the way of the propertyless. This problem has strong implications for the assignment of property rights.

ECSO freedom requires an exit option, which in turn requires access to resources. A property rights advocate might say that ECSO freedom is essentially positive by arguing that ECSO freedom requires someone else to provide the individual in question with the required amount of property.

Property rights' advocates have created confusion on this issue in two ways. First, some of them have characterized negative freedom as the "freedom from" and positive freedom as the "freedom to." As McCallum established decades ago all liberties are both the freedom from something and the freedom to do something.[35] If there is a meaningful definition of negative freedom that is consistent with common understanding, it must be the freedom from interference by other people with what one is able to do. Land and natural resources were here before all of us. All you need to use resources is for others to refrain from interfering with you while you use those resources.

Second, property rights advocates have confused this issue by ignoring the effect of the assignment, definition, and enforcement of property rights on the negative freedom of nonowners. As mentioned in above, property is merely the legal right to interfere with other people. If I say this land should be mine, I say that I should be able to interfere with your use of it. If you say it should be yours, you say that you should be able to interfere with my use of it. If someone else says it should be a commons', they say that someone should be able to interfere with anyone who would use it in some ways so that we can all use it freely in other ways. All of these requests involve negative duties only. A theory of freedom that takes a set of property rights as given is not a theory of negative freedom. A large part of the reason (if not the whole of the reason) people do not have the exit option they need to secure independence is the interference of other people who dominate resources. A person factually does not need aid from other people to use the land and minerals of the Earth. If negative freedom is the freedom from interference by other people, any theory of negative freedom has to take into account how the establishment, definition, and maintenance of property rights in resources involves interference and coercion with nonowners.

To illustrate, I'm using the atmosphere right now much the way our ancestors used land. I take what I need from it without claiming any portion of it as my property. If some other group of people enforced property rights to the atmosphere, they would have the legal power to interfere with my breathing. Certainly, my demand to breathe is a demand for negative freedom. When I breathe the atmosphere my ancestors breathed, all I need from others is the purely negative duty to stay out of my way. When propertyless individuals attempt to meet their needs by using the land and resources of the Earth, they ask for a freedom that is negative in the very same way. If it seems different, it is only because people have been interfering with the propertyless in this way for so long that we have come to accept it as natural. It is not. Property rights do not exist in nature. It is a socially created institution that humans lived without for hundreds of thousands of years.[36]

The argument here is not against property; it only seeks to recognize the significance of the unfreedom of being a nonowner of any owned external asset and to balance the freedom one gains by establishing property against the freedom another loses by being subject to the duty to respect others' property.

One could concede that the denial of access to resources is a limitation of negative freedom without accepting the claim that ECSO freedom can be secured by negative freedom alone. Although the argument from pure negative liberty would seem to imply that we should deliver raw natural resources to the propertyless, chapter 3 argues for securing independence with an unconditional basic income in cash, with which people can buy whatever active services they want from others.

The connection between the duty to stay out of each other's way and the provision of basic income is made by replacing an unfulfilled negative duty. That is, the respect for independence can be fulfilled by replacing the negative duty (of leaving resource alone) with an active one (of providing compensation). The provision of compensation makes the right itself no less negative. In the same way, my negative right that you not break my leg can transform into an active duty that you pay my medical bills and lost wages if you have been unable to avoid breaking my leg. The active nature of your fulfillment of your duty, in no way reduces the negative nature of my liberty to control my leg. If we as a society have dominated resources and we find it more difficult to make an adequate amount of resources available than it is to make an adequate level of basic income available, we can fulfill the substantive part of our duty to respect ECSO freedom by providing the basic income instead.

One might suppose that an argument based solely on negative freedom provides support for basic income for the able-bodied only. There are people, such as children and those with certain kinds of mental disabilities, who are incapable of having status freedom. The issue here is not about people who are incapable of holding that status but of people who have disabilities that are severe enough to make them unable to provide for themselves without positive aid from others but that are not severe enough to prevent them from making competent use of freedom once they have it. Identifying such a group might be trickier than it sounds, but I concede the possibility. Members of this group would be entitled to the same freedom from interference as everyone else, and therefore, at least to the same compensation for loss of that freedom as everyone else. So, the group at issue becomes the smaller set that could attain status freedom only with additional positive aid. I believe that there is good reason for extending the power necessary to maintain ECSO freedom to this group as well, but I do not argue it here.

One might argue that no person is capable of living independently because all people need other people to help maintain core well-being. The following two sections deal with different aspects of this issue.

F. Dependence and Interdependence

This section argues that whether or not humans are interdependent, the institutional structure we live under is not one of interdependence but one in which one group is dependent on another. Although a person might become rich by selling services only to the poor, one cannot become propertied without somehow serving people who own property. Consider an example that might be supposed to show the opposite. Joe is a destitute person who finds a rag in a trashcan. He uses it to shine the shoes of minimum-wage workers. His customers are the poorest working people in society who live paycheck to paycheck and accumulate no wealth throughout their lives. Gradually, Joe builds a successful business with hundreds of employees always serving the same clientele.

There are three reasons why this example does not refute the argument that the propertyless must benefit people with property to become propertied. First, there is no way one person or a group of *destitute* people can support themselves. If Joe's clientele were destitute, rather than minimum-wage workers, no amount of service to them would have won Joe any property. Joe's ability to support himself by serving minimum-wage workers is indirectly dependent on their ability to serve people with more property in exchange for their wages. Serving them he indirectly serves their employers.

Second, opportunities to become rich by serving others are proportional to how much property they have. The more property a person has, the more ability they have to reward people who want to serve them. This is why the economy doesn't behave like an interdependent system: investors direct huge amounts of resources toward producing goods and services to make the already well-off better-off and very little investment (or thought) toward getting basic nutrition and other services to the world's destitute.

Third, once Joe earns money, from whom will he buy a house, land, and anything he wants? He must go to the propertied class. Even if his customers are made up entirely of impoverished workers, he is the customer of the propertied class. He cannot attain the goods without trading the fruits of his labor with the propertied class. Any resources he might want to use are owned by someone else, and he must find some way to make it in their interest to part with those resources voluntarily. This discussion illustrates how, in a market economy, although it is possible to become propertied without benefiting the poor and the destitute, it is impossible to become propertied without benefiting someone who is propertied. In these three ways, the propertied class is entitled to benefit from the labor of the propertyless, as much as if they were born in debt to the property-owning class. Legally, we are not born interdependent on one another; one specific group among us is born dependent on another group among us.

The ownership of resources by a social democracy would not create an interdependent social structure either. Instead of one group being dependent on another, everyone would be dependent on the decisions of the majority. Even if people are dependent on other people, it is not true that propertyless people are dependent on the group that dominates resources whether that group is a capitalist class or a democratic majority.

I can't imagine a way to create a workable and genuinely interdependent social structure in a modern society. We could create interdependence by giving everyone a veto over all decisions, but that rule would be unworkable. I don't know how to prove this statement, but it seems to me that any rule denying independence creates dependence of some on the group that dominates resources. Even if people are naturally interdependent, the choice of social structure seems to be between independence and dependence. The question, then, would seem to be whether rules creating independence were more supportive of freedom, equality, and human flourishing than rules creating dependence. Later chapters discuss this issue in more detail, arguing for the benefit of the protection of ECSO freedom in protecting the vulnerable. For now it is sufficient to say that interdependence does not imply that people are dependent on any *specific* group of other persons or any specific set of goals, methods, and terms for social interaction, any of which could provide legitimate reason for rejection of the project.

G. *Interdependence and Independence*

Despite the argument above the question of whether anyone can be truly independent even with access to resources is relevant. One could use an argument from interdependence against my claim that the ECSO freedom can be sustained by a negative liberty. On might also use an argument from interdependence to support the conclusion that independence does not need to be respected. Perhaps on the basis that majority rule over a joint social project (to which everyone is obliged to contribute) is the best approximation of and best response to interdependence. This section addresses the possibility of independence with concern for its factual and normative relevance to the issue.

Many simple observations support interdependence. Most of us, if we found ourselves alone in the wilderness, would probably be dead in a short time. Particularly skillful people might be able to survive for a while, but eventually they would need someone to take care of them when they are sick or disabled. We all needed someone to take care of us when we were children. And apparently, we all need human interaction to remain sane. Therefore, it is fair to say humans are interdependent as a species.

This view of interdependence involves a misconception that might be easily drawn from the argument in this book so far. The book argues for the freedom to accept and reject interaction with other willing people, and it argues that people need independent access to resources to have this freedom. An individual needs an exit option so that if current arrangements are oppressive to her, she can pick up her resources and go elsewhere, or she can go elsewhere and find resources available there. If humans are interdependent in the sense described above, any such individuals will have to look for other people wherever they go—or at least they will *eventually* have to look for other people. The likely truth of this conjecture does not invalidate my argument, but it will take some background to make this point.

To the extent humans are interdependent we are not interdependent on the whole of the species or any particular social project with any particular set of rules. It must be possible to create smaller circles of interdependence. People have lived in very small polities in history, some with very little interaction with the rest of the world. When one group, even a majority group, dominates resources they interfere with any smaller circles of interdependence that people might like to form. That is, they prevent people from making arrangements with other willing people and force them to participate in a system that they might object to. Thus, even if we can't say that individuals are capable of providing all their needs on their own, we can say that resource dominance by any particular group interferes with the liberties that ECSO freedom requires.

There are millions of propertyless people in the world who must be capable of forming viable communities if only they have access to the necessary resources. Such a group could do anything from hunting and gathering to forming a fully industrialized society under alternative rules. Typically, propertyless people can't get access to a sufficient amount of resources until they serve members of the property-owning group in such a way to make property owners willing to turn over ownership of those resources. Even if we are interdependent on some number of people, we need independent access to resources to have the ability to form whatever group we might want to form.

It is probably impractical to allow every group that might want to do things differently access to the resources they would need to form fully autonomous communities. But my point is not that we *should* allow all such groups to break off and form their own groups. My point is only that we should recognize that the only thing preventing them from doing so is our interference. If we then deny them access to resources until they participate in our project, we force them to participate in our project, when they could do otherwise if we more effectively stayed out of their way. That is, even if humans are interdependent, we deny ECSO freedom (the power to accept or refuse voluntary cooperation with other willing people) by denying negative freedom to individuals. If it is impractical to stop interfering with people in a way that denies their independence, we might be obliged to do something else to restore that status.

Another difficulty with connecting the claim of interdependence to an obligation to serve the group that dominates resources exists because that group can't take credit for all that every individual has gained from all others, nor hold them in debt for things they gain or learn from others. The independence at issue here is material independence. Humans' emotional interdependence is not necessarily related to their ability to be materially independent. One person does not have to work for (or even with) another person to meet their emotional need for human interaction.

Children are dependent on adults, but it would be difficult to use this fact to justify making one group of adults materially dependent on another group of adults. Children are not capable of having ECSO freedom. Another realm of justice must apply to them. I simply assume that when they reach adulthood and are capable of independent decision making, they don't carry with them enforceable debts from childhood that would justify keeping them in a state of dependence throughout their lives. Children are not capable of giving voluntary consent to take on such debt.

Although I have argued that the kind of independence defined above can exist even though people are to some extent interdependent, it is important to realize that individuals might be capable of meeting many more of their needs individually than we realize. We live in a complex, global, industrial or postindustrial economy, in which millions of people contribute to each person's consumption. It is hard to conceive how different things could be. Yet, the main thing people need to feed, shelter, and clothe themselves is not aid from other people; they need resources, or more accurately, they need other people to stay out of their way while they use resources that were here before any of us.

At the time of the US revolution, a large majority of Americans were subsistence farmers, who produced most of what they consumed with simple farming technologies. In the early 1700s, Alexander Selkirk supported himself alone on an island for more than four years without any special training.[37] For most of the time humans existed, they lived in small foraging bands of less than 60 people. Some groups had less than 10 adults and some broke up into nuclear family units for large parts of the year. Membership in such bands was fluid. Individuals were free to join other bands or to attempt to live on their own for as long as they wanted to try.[38] There are people living in shantytowns in South America today who grew up in small groups of hunter-gatherers. Many propertyless people maintain themselves by foraging in the garbage cans of more fortunate people, because someone else has interfered with all the possibilities for better foraging. In most places today, if 1, 100, or 100,000 propertyless people would like to support each other, they are denied the option to try.

If there is any doubt whether people are capable of living independently, the argument from interdependence is a poor justification for denying individuals access to resources with which they could try to meet their needs and with which they could meet many of their needs. It is paternalistic, in a self-serving way, to say, "We think you will fail to support yourself. So, we'll stop you from trying and force you to support our project." If we actually stopped interfering with people as they attempt to use the Earth to meet their needs, we might find that they could meet many or most of their needs without labor market participation—especially if we leave the most useful resources alone for those who might not wish to serve people who control property. Some areas of the Earth, such as the Northwest Pacific Coast of North America, once had such abundant foraging that a person could support herself with extremely minimum effort.[39]

The poor and disadvantaged could do many things to support themselves that they are prohibited from doing by the laws governing resources. One of the most pressing needs that sends people into the labor market is the need for housing, but housing is not that difficult to provide for oneself, given access to the right resources. Most of the homeless people in the United States today are not incapable of building *some* kind of shelter, but they will be subject to interference if they try. There are no shantytowns in United States, because there is no place where the homeless are allowed to build shanties. Many disadvantaged and dissenting people might be able to do much better than to build a shanty. Henry David Thoreau famously chronicled how easily and cheaply he built a sturdy house. He also claimed that maintaining himself mostly by his own efforts was easier and less time-consuming than the things people have to do to maintain themselves in an industrializing economy.[40] We could only find out whether people would like to build a house like Thoreau's, if we'd let them try.

Few people today know how to forage, farm, herd, or build their own shelters, but they are not any less capable of learning how to farm, herd, or forage than their ancestors. Today, people have no reason to learn these skills because any chance to use these skills has been blocked by the interference of other people. People have learned skills that are useful in the existing economic system and not other skills, because there is no alternative to participation in the prevailing system. If individuals' dependence on the prevailing system is caused by the dominance of that system, that dependence cannot be used to justify that system.

One might suppose that *no one* would want such alternatives, if they were available. In a world in which some of the most prosperous economies have desperately poor people who forage through other people's garbage or live on the streets, and dissenters voice strong disapproval, this claim is hard to believe. If people were allowed access to resources without interference, perhaps many of them would scramble to learn the relevant skills to live in many very different ways. Even if it were true that no one wanted the alternatives, it would not give reason to deny them the power to ask. The provision of an exit option is one way to call the bluff of anyone who would justify social arrangements by the supposed agreement of all participants. Only a society that gives its citizens the power to reject participation can claim that it has the willing participation of all participants.

It might be more plausible to claim the opposite: so many people would want to live in alternative ways that we could never make enough resources available. This claim could be used to *justify* interference with people who would like access to resources, but it cannot be used to argue that doing so is something other than interference. Indeed, it would seem to accept as true that there are large numbers who are able to live independently if the rest of us were able to stay out of their way, and it would fit in well with an argument to provide an exit option by replacement through basic income or some other strategy.[41]

One might respond that even if individuals or small groups are capable of providing for many of their direct needs, society can seldom, if ever, put groups of people fully outside of its benefits. They will still benefit from defense and police protection, and they might eventually appeal for medical care, disaster relief, or something else. One could also make a moral argument for interdependence: we all have a duty to help others who need care, just as all others have a duty to help us if and when we need care. I cannot rule out this argument, because I am not basing my argument for unconditional redistribution on the denial of all active duties to aid others.

This section has not ruled out the possibility that people are to some extent interdependent, but it has shown that propertyless people face a great deal of interference that makes them much less independent than they would otherwise be. The rules of property in natural resources do not establish a circle of interdependence; they make the propertyless dependent on the group that dominates resources. The dependence of this group on that ground is caused by coercive interference; it neither follows from nor preserves the freedom of the propertyless. Chapter 9 considers the possibility of duty of active participation. For now, I will assume that people are largely capable of existing outside of any particular social project.

3. Conclusion

Protection of ECSO freedom requires the protection of free expression, free association, political participation, *and* personal independence. Individual start with at a minimally decent level before they interact with others, ensuring that their interactions with others are genuinely voluntary, and they retain the right to a decent minimum throughout their lives. The individual starting point here is very different from many political theories on the Left and Right. Theories supporting strong private property rights often ignore that the property rights system is a system of social cooperation and that it effectively forces the propertyless to participate. Liberal egalitarian theories often tacitly or explicitly assume that all people are dependent on a system of social cooperation—apparently for *all* of their consumption.[42] The protection of ECSO freedom does not conflict with building a market. Nor does it conflict with building a democratic community that helps the needy and pursues shared goals. It only conflicts with certain methods of doing these things. Respect for ECSO freedom means that the methods by which the community can do those things have to rely on voluntary rather than forced participation of each member of the community.

CHAPTER 3

Forty Acres and a Mule? Implications of the Duty to Respect Personal Independence

> *[Milo Minderbinder] raised the price of food in his mess halls so high that all officers and enlisted men had to turn over all their pay to him in order to eat. Their alternative, there was an alternative, of course—since Milo detested coercion, and was a vocal champion of freedom of choice—was to starve. When he encountered a wave of enemy resistance to this attack, he stuck to his position without regard to safety or reputation, and gallantly invoked the law of supply and demand.*
>
> —*Joseph Heller,* Catch-22[1]

Respect for ECSO freedom implies limits on how people can go about building community and on the powers government and private individuals can assert over individuals and resources, but it does not conflict with the desire to build a community or a government. The challenge of indepentarianism is to build a community in an area while respecting the personal independence of everyone who happens to be stuck together in the area. This chapter discusses a few of the implications that follow from the respect for ECSO freedom.

As argued above, a group of people fails to fulfill the obligation to stay out of each other's way if their actions (individually or collectively; directly or indirectly; intentionally or unintentionally) prevent another person from maintaining core well-being. Indirect force takes up most of this discussion because it is less well recognized by most modern democracies or most political philosophers than the other rights necessary to secure ECSO freedom. Most of what we need to do is to ensure that everyone is free is to leave them alone with access to a sufficient amount of external assets to live a decent life. Some circumstances call for more, but most people most of the time would be just fine with that. I will argue for the duty to do more primarily by in compensation for our failure to stay out of each other's way. I argue below that we have failed in the duty to stay out of each other's way to such an extent that it is easier and more effective to provide positive compensation for that failure than it is to cease interference. Thus, to the extent I argue for the duty to something more than leave other people alone, it is in compensation for our failure to leave them alone.

To respect another individual's status as a free person is to recognize that other people have needs and not to prevent, interfere with, or put conditions on their efforts to meet those needs alone or with willing partners. If some group cannot avoid dominating resources, they can maintain respect for ECSO freedom by compensating individuals sufficiently for the lost access to resources that they are forced to accept. That compensation could come in the form of goods or cash income sufficient to maintain a person's core well-being. Whether direct access to resources, in-kind compensation, or cash compensation is an appropriate strategy for safeguarding the effective component of ECSO freedom might vary depending on the institutional makeup of the economy. But this chapter argues that the most reasonable way to secure the effective component of ECSO freedom in a modern, industrial society is with some form of unconditional basic income guarantee.

A society that respects personal independence has a "voluntary-participation economy"; one that does not has a "mandatory-participation economy." Maintaining a voluntary-participation economy is a simple and not terribly demanding obligation, but most modern democracies and most theories of justice fail in it. Right-libertarians, who claim to be so concerned with freedom, fail in it, by allowing one group to use indirect force to get another group to serve them. Many liberal-egalitarians, who claim to be so concerned with the disadvantaged, fail in it by using indirect force to serve the social project. Most forms of capitalism (even those with generous but conditional welfare systems) have mandatory-participation economies, as do feudal, socialist, Leninist, or absolutist societies. Some forms of left-libertarianism or basic income capitalism have voluntary-participation economies, as did most hunter-gatherer and simple agrarian societies.[2] The mandatory-participation economy has become so ubiquitous in recent centuries that it is hard to imagine an alternative. But most people lived in voluntary-participation economies until chiefs and kings gradually began claiming the right to deny people access to resources. The transformation began perhaps seven thousand years ago, and there are still remote parts of the world with traditional voluntary-participation economies.[3]

Sections 1–5 clarify and discuss implications of the theory of ECSO freedom. Section 6 makes the connection between ECSO freedom and basic income.

1. To Say No to What?

ECSO freedom includes the effective power to say no to active cooperation. As noted above, it *does not* include the freedom to hold a title to all the resources you want *and* refuse conditions set by the people who will have the duty to respect your title to those resources. ECSO freedom includes unconditional access to enough external assets to meet basic needs, but it does not include the power to say no to taxes and regulations on people who wish to hold more than the minimum amount of external assets.

For the most part, people in Western democracies are free from active participation in others' projects except when they are effectively forced by propertylessness. A propertyless person can legally attempt to attain what she needs to survive by performing a service for someone who has property (work), by marrying or remaining married to someone willing to support them, by receiving gifts, by begging, by scavenging in garbage, or by meeting conditions imposed by a charity or a government agency. All of these, except scavenging and receiving gifts (if given unconditionally), are forms of active cooperation with others, and ECSO freedom is the power to refuse to do any of them. The primary focus of the argument here concerns forced labor market participation,[4] both because work is a significant part of people's lives and because it is what the propertyless are usually expected to do.

However, work is not always the most significant thing that propertylessness can force a person to do. Marriage to the wrong person can be more onerous than many jobs. The arguments for the importance of ECSO freedom apply just as much to the freedom from any other conditions that could be put between the propertyless and the means of survival. Freedom from forced labor can be seen as an example for the freedom from all the things propertylessness might force a person to do.

One reason to focus on employment is that it has a central importance in most people's lives. Labor can take up nearly half of a person's waking hours for most of her adult years, and the concern with it fills up much more time. If people are unfree to decide when, how, whether, and under what conditions to join the labor market, they are unfree over such an enormous portion of their lives that their freedom to control their interactions in their off-hours can seem insignificant by comparison.

Another important reason for focusing on employment is that political philosophers are more likely to find it acceptable to force the propertyless to work than to force them to do other things such as marry or perform religious rituals. Unfortunate side effects of our societies' uses of propertylessness to coerce individuals to participate in the labor market include some people's resort to begging, prostitution, foraging through garbage cans, and remaining in abusive marriages.

2. Dissent and Disadvantage

This section clarifies my use of the terms "dissent" and "disadvantaged." I use the term "dissenter" for a person who (for whatever reason) does not want to participate in the economy or the social project designated by whichever group dominates resources. There must be a difference between a dissenter who merely objects to the social project and wishes to be left out and a parasite who wants to benefit at the expense of others or a criminal who wants to harm others.[5] The term "dissenter" includes many different people, some having better complaints than others. A dissenter might be a potential worker who finds the rewards for participation too low, the goals objectionable, or the conditions overbearing. A dissenter could also be many other things: someone who simply does not want to take orders from others; a care giver or a volunteer worker who believes that such unrewarded work should count as a contribution; an ethnic minority who believes society is too racist; a racist who believes society isn't racist enough; a pretender who believes she is the legitimate monarch; an oppressed individual who does not wish to support her own oppression; and so on. Most reasons for dissent are moral or personal objections to the goals, methods, or terms of the social project. Probably everyone objects to at least one aspect of the social project, but few have objections so strong that they would refuse to participate if the rewards are appealing.

By disadvantaged, I mean anyone whose attributes are such that they are unable to participate or their options for participation involve low pay, low status, poor working conditions, lack of respect, and so on. Disadvantage might be one reason for dissent, but not all disadvantaged people are dissenters, even if more of them should be. There is a great deal of overlap between the two and no great reason to determine which category an individual fits into.

The theory of ECSO freedom is an attempt to determine the minimum level of decency with which society should treat dissenters and the disadvantaged. The main thrust of the argument in this book is that society needs to have greater respect for the disadvantaged than many egalitarians propose and greater respect for dissenters than many "libertarians" propose. Society can deny dissenters many of the fruits of the joint project while respecting the ECSO freedom, but it cannot force dissenters to participate by denying them all access to the external assets they need. A society that respects ECSO freedom may use positive reward for participation, but only after everyone's needs are met unconditionally.

3. The Complexity of Separating Freedom and Unfreedom

Freedom and unfreedom are complex concepts. Although a theory of status freedom identifies a threshold separating freedom and unfreedom, it is not possible to draw a fine line stating that a person with X number of liberties is fully free and a person with X minus one liberties is unfree. There is a large area of restricted or threatened freedom in between the two. As argued in chapter 2, to insist on a fine line would assert the black-and-white fallacy.

The effective component of freedom must be obviously seen as a matter of degree,[6] depending on the liberties people have and the penalties for exceeding them, but the same is true for most liberties. The more onerous the duties people are held to, the more their freedom is threatened. The greater the force applied to people who fail to comply, the more their freedom is threatened. Restrictions on some liberties threaten freedom more than restrictions on others, and nearly all liberties can be threatened by degree.

A person in prison serving a life sentence is unfree, and a person outside is free. But suppose Skipper is sentenced to spend 6 days and 23 hours each week in jail for the rest of his life but to be released for one hour each week. Suppose he is sentenced to spend half the week in jail or half the week out, or one hour in jail and the rest of the week out of jail. These situations fall into the murkier area of restricted freedom. When he is in jail for only one hour per week, he is close to being a free person even though one of his core liberties is restricted.

Time is not the only important determinant of whether a liberty is core or secondary: whether and how much an individual objects to what she is asked to do is also as important. Suppose Ginger opposes the death penalty on moral grounds. Suppose the vast majority of people in her country believe that the death penalty is the morally correct way to punish criminals, and every citizen has a duty to spend one hour every five years performing the unpleasant but necessary job of executing criminals, and they enforce this rule with the death penalty. Most people think nothing of complying with this rule. The amount of time that Ginger is forced to put aside is trivial, but what she is asked to do during that time is not trivial to her, and therefore, her freedom is seriously restricted (even if it is a trivial restriction in the opinion of everyone else). The same would be true if laws forced her to spend a trivial amount of time performing a significant religious ritual or anything else that is objectionable beyond merely the lost time involved.[7]

Not all liberties affect a person's freedom in the status sense, as chapter 2 argued with the example of the prisoner with access to DVDs. The same effect can be seen in a free person. Suppose Mary Ann is a free person. An authority (sentencing her for some infraction) denies her access to some frivolous luxuries.[8] This action makes her less free, but it does not threaten her status as a free person as making her a part-time prisoner would. The continuum of freedoms is multidimensional and not all dimensions affect ECSO freedom. Some dimensions of the continuum of liberties do not appear on a scale that measures freedom and unfreedom. This fact does not mean that those liberties are wholly unimportant, just that they don't affect this distinction.

ECSO freedom can also be lost and gained temporarily. A detainee is unfree for the time she is detained, but she regains her freedom as soon as she is released. A torture victim might not regain full freedom as soon as the torture stops if it creates lingering trauma. A labor contract in which the employer gained the power to keep the employee from quitting by physical force would temporarily sacrifice ECSO freedom, but one in which the penalty for breaking the contract involves only financial sacrifices that do not threaten core well-being creates no sacrifice of ECSO freedom.

Remember that ECSO freedom is the power to refuse active cooperation in the projects of others, and it brings with it the responsibility to respect everyone else's ECSO freedom. It requires control over some minimum amount of worldly resources, but ECSO freedom alone says nothing about anyone's claim to more than that amount of resources[9] or about tradeoffs among secondary liberties. ECSO freedom is not immunity to all involuntary interaction with others, or the power to say no to anything one might object to. Therefore, some prohibitions, such as a restriction on a person's ability to impose something on someone else, can reduce her freedom without reducing her core liberties or threatening her status as a free person.

For the most part, we will have to consider reductions of core liberties that do not make a person entirely unfree, but that do threaten her status as a free person and move her into the area of restricted freedom. If ECSO freedom requires an independent option that is not "thoroughly bad in an absolute sense," the question becomes: How bad does an alternative have to be before it becomes thoroughly bad? That question is the subject of section 6. The same problem of drawing a fine distinction between black and white exists when drawing a distinction between "acceptable or reasonable" and "thoroughly bad in an absolute sense." There is an important difference between force and the absence of force, even though there is a large grey area of partial force in between them. If a person's independent option is thoroughly bad, her social participation is forced, and she is unfree. If it is reasonable or acceptable, she has ECSO freedom. But there is a large grey area in between, where her freedom is restricted or threatened. Like black and white, light and dark, or bass and treble; freedom and unfreedom identify ranges on a continuum. The goal is not to find a nonarbitrary cutoff point (which is impossible) but to find an area in which an arbitrary cutoff point would lie safely in the light grey area away from any serious threat to (or restriction on) individuals' ECSO freedom.

4. Alienation of ECSO Freedom

The issue of so-called self-alienation of self-ownership applies to ECSO freedom as well. The question is whether a person can sign a contract sacrificing their self-ownership, by selling themselves into slavery or indentured servitude. This issue has wider implications for ECSO freedom because it applies not only to authorizing direct force but also the authorization of indirect force: to whether a person can mortgage their claim to the resources they need to maintain core well-being.

According to Arthur Kuflik, Kant, Locke, Rousseau, and Spinoza all oppose self-alienation for various reasons and to various extents.[10] John Stuart Mill and John Gray also argue against self-alienation.[11] Those who are sympathetic with the potential validity of self-alienation usually justify it on the basis of some right of contract[12] or something like a right to waive rights.[13]

The term "self-alienation" is a misnomer. No one can alienate their status freedom by themselves. They can sign a piece of paper declaring the intention to alienate their freedom, but if they change their mind, *someone else* has to *force* them to make that declaration into the genuine alienation of their status as free individuals. A person can choose to do everything another person says but that is not the alienation of status freedom. It is merely the exercise freedom for the benefit of another. To genuinely alienate freedom, a person must put herself in the situation in which she is no longer free to choose. That is, to alienate status freedom, she must find an authority to interfere with her ability to choose in the future, if and when she changes her mind. The authority is what alienates her freedom, and it only acts to restrict her freedom when she disagrees. At best, "self-alienation" should be called "self-contracted alienation."

Under JPA, the government's primary duty is to protect people's most important freedoms from interference, to protect their status freedom. The promotion of positive opportunities is a secondary goal. The ability to sign an enforceable contract is a positive opportunity. A government completely dedicated to nothing but the protection of negative freedom would enforce no contracts at all. Pure caveat emptor would then be applied to all contracts. Parties are free to sign any contracts they want, but if they know from the outset that no contracts are enforceable, they have no claim to say that anyone "interfered" with them by breaking a contract.

It would probably be foolish to prioritize negative freedom to the point at which the government enforced no contracts, but expanding people's positive opportunities is a lesser priority than protecting their core freedoms from interference. Therefore, the government must not take positive action to enforce unconscionable contracts including those alienating status freedom. Nor should it reduce its protection of people from the interference of others by allowing a private authority to interfere with them on the grounds that in the past they signed a contract alienating their status freedom.

Some authors argue that the refusal to enforce a contract alienating one's self-ownership is somehow paternalistic. The refusal to enforce slavery contracts has nothing to do with paternalism but with a consistent application of the protection of core freedom from interference. A slavery contract is not in the same category as a law against smoking designed to prevent a person from harming herself. The future harm from smoking is a natural effect of smoking. Contracts have no natural effects; they only authorize the use of force. When the government considers whether to use that force, the choice is not between freedom and paternalism but between two freedoms. The choice for the government is which freedom is more important to protect: the freedom to have made an enforceable contract in the past, or the freedom from coercion now. Which is the government's greater responsibility? The answer depends on the importance of the liberties in question, not the order in which the actions occur. If the government's greater responsibility is to protect people's status as free individuals, it has a duty to avoid using its power to coerce people to fulfill an agreement alienating that status. There is nothing paternalistic about the refusal to force an unwilling person to be a slave.

If the above argument holds, government must not enforce any contract setting ECSO freedom aside, whether it was a marriage, service, or financial contract. Applying this argument about self-alienation to ECSO freedom implies that any contract alienating personal independence is also unenforceable. Individuals would have the right to declare bankruptcy while keeping enough property to secure their ECSO freedom—bankruptcy without fear of destitution. Assuming that a basic income is in place and set just at the level that secures a person's basic needs, it could not be used as collateral for a loan, and would be a protected asset in the event of bankruptcy (with possible exceptions noted below). However, if the basic income is set higher than that level, a portion of it could be used as security for a loan and could be seized in the event of bankruptcy.

This argument does not prohibit all possible denial of status freedom. Self-defense might justify imprisonment of aggressors. Negligence, accidental bodily harm, and paternity also might be grounds for an obligation for one person to work for another's benefit. This book does not explore these issues, but clearly an application of JPA would imply that any such enforcement be the minimum necessary for self-defense and maximally humane.

5. Moral Duty and Status Freedom

Although this book puts off a detailed discussion of active duties until chapter 9, this section briefly argues that the enforcement of active moral duties restricts a person's status as a free individual. That enforcement might well be justified, but we need to recognize the sacrifice it involves.

Without saying where moral duties come from and how they are justified, suppose that there is a moral duty and a person is ethically obliged to perform it whether or not she is willing to do so. For example, suppose a person has a moral obligation to save a child from drowning.[14] Forcing her to fulfill this duty restricts her status as a free person, even if it is for ethically justified reasons. For example, an infant begins to drown. Just then, by coincidence, Bob reaches the age and maturity level at which he is capable of being a fully responsible adult. Bob is the only person who can save the infant. A bystander, who is not physically able to save the child herself, and who has neither time nor ability to explain the gravity of the situation to Bob, forces Bob at gunpoint to save the child. One second after Bob fulfills his obligation, by another coincidence, he dies of a brain aneurysm. What role did freedom play in Bob's adult life? None: freedom is about making choices; Bob made no unforced choices. His life was entirely determined by some other moral value. His short adult life was morally valuable and well spent, but freedom played no part in it. The fulfillment of his obligation to save the child took all of the time he would have had available to make adult choices. Therefore, even if his forced participation was justified, it must have come at the expense of his freedom. Enforcement of moral duties involves a sacrifice in freedom.

There are at least two ways to justify the duties that restrict ECSO freedom. One is the argument that a competing value (such as respect for life, fairness, or the obligation to help the needy) is more important than the restrictions that duty imposes on a person's status as free. Another is Kagan's argument that greater actual freedom might be achieved by holding people to some duties.[15] For example, suppose the jury system was the only mechanism capable of preventing the government from imposing arbitrary imprisonment. If so, the small restriction on persons' status freedom (a few days every few years on jury duty) is necessary to prevent a larger restriction of persons' status freedom (arbitrary imprisonment). However, the power to force people to do things is extremely vulnerable to error and abuse. It should be applied rarely, minimally, and only when clearly necessary.

It might be impossible to have a society in which everyone's core freedoms are completely unrestricted, but we have to be aware that, as much as we search for accord, there will be disagreement over many basic issues. Enforcement will involve one group forcing another to serve its goals. If we understand the sacrifices involved, we have good reason to minimize restrictions on core freedoms and to take every sacrifice seriously.

6. From Human Need to Basic Income

Personal independence requires unconditional access to a sufficient amount of external assets to meet one's basic needs. This section examines what policies are necessary to secure that access. This question breaks down into two more: How much do people need, and what method should we use to ensure they have what they need? Section A addresses the first question by examining prominent theories of human need. Section B examines the second question by considering three alternatives: distribution of raw resources, in-kind direct provision of goods, and an unconditional basic income guarantee. Although all three of these strategies are possible in some circumstances, I argue that only a basic income guarantee is a workable strategy to protect independence in a modern, industrial economy. Second C connects the argument for provision of cash and services with my contention that the theory of status freedom as ECSO freedom is built on a negative conception of scalar freedom.

A. Theories of Need

Good theories of need exist in the political theory literature. Therefore it is not necessary to advance a new theory of human need. This chapter simply applies the theories of human need by Martha Nussbaum, Len Doyal and Ian Gough, and Ingrid Robeyns.[16] Although the three theories take different approaches, they have a great deal of overlap,[17] and they imply similar level of need fulfillment. I have elsewhere discussed how these theories can be used to formulate the characteristics of an acceptable exit option. This section (along with section B) summarizes the argument from that article.[18]

Nussbaum's theory of need (called "basic human functioning" or "central human capability") is based on Sen's conceptions of "functionings" and "capabilities." Functionings are parts of the state of a person, particularly the various things that she manages to do or be in leading a life. Capabilities are the alternative combinations of functionings from which a person can choose.[19] Nussbaum specifies a list of basic capabilities that can be used to define a threshold of minimum acceptable human functioning or need.

In a series of works, Nussbaum has proposed and refined a list of ten basic human functional capabilities or central human capabilities:

1. **Life**. Being able to live to the end of a human life of normal length; not dying prematurely, or before one's life is so reduced as to be not worth living.
2. **Bodily Health**. Being able to have good health, including reproductive health; to be adequately nourished; to have adequate shelter.

3. **Bodily Integrity**. Being able to move freely from place to place; to be secure against violent assault, including sexual assault and domestic violence; having opportunities for sexual satisfaction and for choice in matters of reproduction.
4. **Senses, Imagination, and Thought**. Being able to use the senses, to imagine, think, and reason. Being able to use one's mind in ways protected by guarantees of freedom of expression with respect to both political and artistic speech, and freedom of religious exercise. Being able to have pleasurable experiences and to avoid non-beneficial pain.
5. **Emotions**. Being able to have attachments to things and people outside ourselves.
6. **Practical Reason**. Being able to form a conception of the good and to engage in critical reflection about the planning of one's life. (This entails protection for the liberty of conscience and religious observance.)
7. **Affiliation**.
   A. Being able to live with and toward others, to recognize and show concern for other human beings, to engage in various forms of social interaction; to be able to imagine the situation of another.
   B. Having the social bases of self-respect and non-humiliation; being able to be treated as a dignified being whose worth is equal to that of others.
8. **Other Species**. Being able to live with concern for and in relation to animals, plants, and the world of nature.
9. **Play**. Being able to laugh, to play, to enjoy recreational activities.
10. **Control over One's Environment**.
    A. Political. Being able to participate effectively in political choices that govern one's life; protections of free speech and association.
    B. Material. Being able to hold property (both land and movable goods), and having property rights on an equal basis with others; having the right to seek employment on an equal basis with others; having the freedom from unwarranted search and seizure.[20]

The argument in this book is not premised on the full acceptance of Nussbaum's reasoning. The only part of it I employ here is her identification of human need as these ten functional capabilities. Robeyns employs Nussbaum's approach with a slightly different list of basic capabilities. Doyal and Gough do not frame their discussion in terms of functional capabilities. Instead, they derive a list of basic instrumental goods necessary to secure two broad, basic needs—physical survival and personal autonomy. These needs are universal, but they must be satisfied in different ways in different cultures and environments. Gough observes that every item on their list has some equivalent on Nussbaum's list (and vice versa) except for play and concern for nature, which appear only on Nussbaum's list. Robeyns also remarks on the similarities, and so I do not go into the details of Robeyns's and Doyal and Gough's lists here.[21]

For my purposes, it is helpful to group these capabilities into three broad categories. This is not a new theory of need, but simply a categorization of the needs listed in these theories.

1. **Access to the goods or resources necessary to secure life and health**: nutritional food, clean water, protective housing, safe physical and work environments, appropriate clothing, a healthy environment, and appropriate health care (Nussbaum's 1, 2, 3, and 8).
2. **Access to noneconomic interaction with other willing people**: the need to form meaningful relationships with others (Nussbaum's 5, 7 and the sexual and transportation portions of 2).
3. **General access to resources**: being able to use the five senses; being able to imagine, to think, and to reason, being able to form a conception of the good and to engage in critical reflection about the planning of one's own life, being able to laugh, to play, to enjoy recreational activities, being able to live one's own life and nobody else's; being able to live one's own life in one's very own surroundings and context (Nussbaum's 4, 6, 9, 10).

If a person has these capabilities without doing someone else's bidding, she has the exit option necessary to secure personal independence. If she chooses to work for someone else from that starting position, she does so voluntarily.

The first of these categories is the need for the goods (or the resources needed to produce the goods) that secure survival and health. Importantly, none of the theories of need discussed above limits needs to the purely physical needs of this category. An alternative that provides just enough resources to meet one's physical needs, but makes it impossible or extremely difficult to form relationships with others, to plan a conception of the good life in one's own surroundings is thoroughly bad in an absolute sense. Although it may not be as immediately distressing as one that denies physical needs, it will eventually become very pressing. Such a default position would not provide an adequate exit option.

The intrinsic need to interact with other people is captured by the second category. Many, if not all, of the goods required by the other two categories of need can be produced better in cooperation with other people. Human cooperation is instrumental but not intrinsic to securing the goods to satisfy those categories of need. Satisfying the human need to interact with other people requires civil rights and access to goods such as transportation, communication, and public spaces. These goods are instrumental to forming personal relationships just as cooperative relationships can be instrumental to producing goods. The government can guarantee access to the goods necessary to facilitate personal interaction and the civil rights that allow willing people to interact, but short of paying people to be each other's friends, it cannot guarantee that others will be willing to interact. Therefore, the government can directly secure the first category of need, but it can only secure access to the second category.

This third category can be summarized as a person's need for resources to pursue her conception of the good life. It encompasses anything for which a person might need resources other than to secure her physical survival and maintain relationships with other people. This category of need introduces a difficulty, because a threshold is much less apparent in it than in the other two categories. The more resources a person has, the greater her ability to direct them toward her conception of the good life. Determining a cutoff point is difficult but not necessarily insoluble. The next few paragraphs propose a way to do so.

It would be helpful to be able to measure need in terms of money. Although money does not always secure the same functioning for everyone, Sen argues that the cautious use of the money measure can work if guided by understanding of the capabilities approach:

> As long as minimal capabilities can be achieved by enhancing income level...it will be possible (for the specified personal and social characteristics) to identify the minimally adequate income for reaching the minimally acceptable capability levels. Once this correspondence is established it would not really matter whether poverty is defined in terms of a failure of basic capability or as a failure to have the *corresponding* minimally adequate income.[22]

Sen warns that money is at best a rough measure of capability. Income will not necessarily reveal the lack of capability experienced by a disabled person or the lack of freedom experienced by disadvantaged groups. It is not money per se that a person needs but the specific capabilities that can be secured by a given amount of money.

Access to the first category of need can be measured fairly well in money. Access to the second requires civil rights and a few (often publicly provided) goods such as transportation, communication, and public spaces. The third category of need is difficult to measure in terms of money, even if it can be largely secured by money. However, once a competent adult assures her family's physical survival, she can direct any additional resources to achieving the third category of need. Therefore, an income that is safely beyond serious pressure on physical needs gives an individual at least some ability to reflect, play, and live her own life.

Mohammed Sharif examines the work behavior of families in less developed countries in a way that can be useful for a threshold that includes the third category of need. He finds a point of distress at which reductions in wages cause entire families including children to forego physical rest so that they can increase their hours of work to maintain consumption as wages fall. Total income, at the point where this behavior begins, "can be considered to provide an estimate of their subsistence—the lowest income free of distress"[23] As difficult as it is to determine an exact cutoff point, it is possible to say that a person who is constantly struggling to keep her family fed, sheltered, and safe does not have her needs met, and a person who has enough so that they are clearly not struggling for these needs has the ability to direct the surplus toward planning their conception of the good life. Thus, physical needs can provide a rough guide to the required level of income.

However, the money measured revealing safety from immediate distress is not everything. Quality is also important. Although people might not be desperate to obtain available housing and food, the quality of goods and food they can obtain could be so low that it fails to meet their needs. How can we be sure that the available goods are of adequate quality? For this problem, we would have to keep an eye on statistical measures. If a significant number of people have food and shelter but suffer from malnutrition, accidents, the cold, infant mortality, epidemics, and so on, their needs are not adequately secured.

Therefore, we could get an estimate of the necessary cash income by looking at the prices of a few basic commodities. Assuming the assessment is done in a country that follows the prevailing conventions among industrialized nations of providing free education, health care, thoroughfares, and public spaces; normally abled individuals would require enough money for the rental of a basic but safe house or apartment, an adequate diet, basic clothing, reasonable transportation, plus enough extra so that they do not exhibit signs of economic distress. Those with disabilities or special needs would require something more.

B. *Capability in Cash, Kind, or Raw Resources*

If section A correctly identifies the minimum capability level of an adequate exit option, the final question is what policy best secures that level of capability? An exit option requires *unconditional* access to resources. Arguments throughout this book indicate that a guaranteed government job might provide an exit from the *private* labor market, but it would not provide an exit from mandatory service. Unconditional access could be provided by benefits in cash or in kind or by direct access to raw resources. This section tentatively argues that some form of basic income guarantee is the best policy to secure an exit option in a complex industrial economy.

There is an enormous literature on the basic income guarantee, and therefore it is not necessary to go into it in detail here.[24] Economists often argue that cash transfers are Pareto superior to in-kind benefits, and therefore at least potentially better for both the payer and the recipient than in-kind benefits.[25] Pareto superiority does not imply that they should always be preferred to in-kind benefits, if some important value is at stake. At least some of the goods on the list need to be provided in kind, such as childhood education and public spaces. Most nations provide healthcare in kind, perhaps because of market failure.[26] However, most of the goods necessary to secure life and general access to resources are difficult to supply in kind. Living one's own life is personal; it is different for everyone. The individual might decide to make do with slightly worse housing for slightly better food or slightly worse of both to use resources to achieve some other centrally important goal. A rigid system of in-kind benefits would keep individuals from making those decisions and reduce their ability to control their lives.

In-kind benefits have also been criticized for segregating or stigmatizing recipients. Stigma may not be as problematic for securing a minimally adequate exit option as it is for redistribution based on other reasons, but stigma could be a barrier to forming human relationships. If the goal of redistribution is to allow individuals to refuse forced service, without punishing them for doing so, the possibilities of stigma and unnecessarily restricted freedom to live as individuals wish provide a reason to favor a basic income guarantee over in-kind transfers even if both can potentially provide the necessary exit option.

The argument for an exit option implies the need for freedom from forced work in the sense of one person being forced to serve another; it does not imply that people have any right to be free from the need to work in the sense of toil—applying effort to turn raw resources into consumption. The provision of raw resources is one way to provide an exit option and to satisfy people who believe that everyone (without sufficient wealth) must work for their subsistence. In some cases, access to resources may be exactly what those who are unwilling to join the prevailing economic system want. Colin Ward argues for an anarchist society with the right to squat in unused buildings; to self-build housing on available land; to produce food on allotments; and even mutual aid groups to provide for some of their own healthcare, education, and daycare. James Robertson argues for self-organized and self-controlled "ownwork."[27]

However, there are problems with the attempt to secure an exit option by the provision of raw resources. An exit option might prove to be far more expensive to provide in raw resources than in cash. Modern capitalism is both very hungry for resources and very good at turning resources into consumption products. Therefore, it is probably far cheaper for a capitalist society to secure an exit option by providing enough cash to buy goods than it would be to secure an exit option by providing enough resources for individuals to produce those goods themselves. This fact is capable of transforming a claim to resources into a claim to cash that can be used to buy goods and services from other people.

The land-demanding anarchists might prefer the larger amount of land to the smaller amount of basic income guarantee and might fear that if society provides just enough income so that an individual can attain their basic needs by purchasing the cheapest products, it makes only one lifestyle possible. To put it simply: if the basic income makes only one lifestyle possible, it is set too low. Recall that basic needs are not limited to physical needs, and one category of needs on the list above is general access to resources. If people have a basic income guarantee safely above the bare minimum they need to survive, they might not have enough to buy all the land they would want, but they would have the flexibility to put what they have toward alternative lifestyles and to combine it with other similarly situated people. It would be difficult to give people raw resources and give them great flexibility about how and where to use them without allowing them to turn the resources into cash. Money is flexible because money buys every good in the market. It might be possible to make resource grants at least somewhat flexible with the provision of some kind of resource voucher, but it would be simpler to skip that step and start with cash.

Two other problems with raw resources also give reason to provide cash instead. First, the provision of raw resources has the potential to be both punitive and stigmatizing. Second, the attempt to secure an exit option by the provision of raw resources might require a long-term or even a lifetime commitment on the part of the person who would like to make use of an exit option. A basic income guarantee allows people to move seamlessly in and out of the labor force as the need may be. Thus, although all three policies have the potential to secure the physical conditions of voluntary trade, the basic income guarantee is likely to be the most effective and least expensive.

C. The Negative Freedom Argument for the Basic Income Guarantee

I describe above the main argument connecting a negative conception of freedom to the positive provision of cash and services: cash and/or services replace direct access to resources. No group either private or public has a natural right to dominate resources in an area or worldwide. Any group that otherwise dominates resources takes on the responsibility to compensate others sufficiently to maintain their independence. This obligation is chosen: if they want to get out of the responsibility to pay that compensation, they may stop dominating resources. When a group dominates resources, it takes on a great deal of duties to those who dissent from or are disadvantaged by the rules made over resources. These duties are necessary to justify the enforcement of property rights and the laws that any ruling coalition imposes on everyone regardless of whether they support the coalition's power or are able to obtain a significant amount of resources under the rules it creates.

One might suppose that I have taken this argument further than it can go. One might get the impression from the negative freedom argument that the resource-dominating group in, say, New York has the responsibility to do no more than to provide a stretch of land in Alaska where one might eke out a living as a subsistence farmer or a hunter-gatherer. Even if this were enough, I don't think societies could provide it. There are six billion people in the world, perhaps a billion of them with extremely low living standards, including shanty dwellers in the lesser-developed countries and the homeless in developed countries. If there were land available in Alaska where a person might make a decent living as a subsistence farmer or hunter-gatherer, no doubt someone would take it. The United States forcibly stopped people from living as hunter-gatherers in the nineteenth century and it stopped making land available for new farmers to homestead in the twentieth century, not because nobody wanted the land but because the government didn't believe enough land was available.

But there are several reasons why land on the edge of human habitation is not enough. First, they are likely to be punitive. Simply making land available is a viable option in horticultural or hunter-gatherer societies that underuse their resources so that dissenters can simply walk out of the village to find available land, but not in a modern globalized economy where available land (if any) would be in a remote and possibly inhospitable location. Remember that the idea is to leave someone out of the social project, not to punish them or deprive them of their ability to meet their needs. Banishment is a punishment. It is the attempt to interfere with the second category of need: the ability to form relationships with others. Resource grants are punitive if they involve separating the receiver from other people who wish to associate with her. Forcing people to leave their home community in order to exit a joint project can have the effect of denying them access to the second category of need (access to noneconomic interaction with other willing people). It is one thing if all the other individuals decide independently that they are not willing to interact with someone who refuses to cooperate in a joint economic project, but quite another for the government to interfere with individuals' desire to interact.

Second, once banishment is ruled out, it becomes obvious that the provision of raw resources is prohibitively expensive. New York City could not grant direct access to local land to *even one* of the 40,000 people who seek beds at its homeless shelters every night. The rent on the amount of land necessary to support one person with direct access to raw resources would go a long way to supporting the income of nearly every homeless person in New York. However, it might be possible to grant people resources a little farther away while simultaneously granting them access to transportation so that they can maintain relationships with others.

Third, provision of raw resources might have the effect of putting people in the position of choosing *between* their ECSO freedom and social participation. It is important that people maintain independence throughout their lives; it is not enough that they have the option to choose to live independently once in their lives. Much of the economic distress that threatens people's independence in modern societies comes temporarily or at least unexpectedly during economic downturns. Such a worker would need access at least to temporary cash or in-kind benefits, but this argument doesn't necessarily preclude moving to a raw resource policy for a longer-term exit option.

Fourth, the freedom that an individual is being compensated for is not merely the freedom to live independently but the freedom to choose who they interact with and under what rules. There is no reason to limit what people might do with resources to subsistence farming or hunting and gathering. If we're going to grant people resources, we have to accept that they can combine and use them any way they wish. Given sufficient access to resources, dissenting individuals could provide things like education, transportation, and medical care for each other. Furthermore, establishing a certain kind of system (such as a market economy) makes certain things appropriate that would not be appropriate in a different kind of system. The kind of skills and knowledge a person needs differs in a post-industrial economy than it is in an industrial economy, an agricultural economy, or any other economy. To the extent to which these skills and knowledge are essential to maintaining basic human functioning in a given society, the group that dominates resources takes on the responsibility to educate people appropriately for the kind of society their resource domination has created. A similar argument can be made for appropriate transportation.

7. Conclusion

This chapter has discussed several implications of the theory of ECSO freedom. The last section discusses the policy implications of the effective component of ECSO freedom. It argues that in some circumstances, personal independence could conceivably be secured by in-kind grants or raw resources. But in a modern, industrial economy, this status is best secured by an unconditional basic income guarantee large enough to secure housing, food, clothing, and basic transportation, plus enough more that individuals do not display signs of economic distress.

Under this theory, the basic income should be thought of as compensation for what would otherwise be the failure to satisfy the duty to stay out of each other's way, transforming that negative claim into a positive claim to cash that can be used to buy services. In the same way a negative claim that no one breaks your leg can transform into a positive claim to cash if someone does in fact break it. Under this theory, the obligation to pay compensation runs from those who would otherwise dominate resources to those who are in some way disadvantaged or would otherwise have been made propertyless by resource domination.

CHAPTER 4

The Importance of Independence I: Framing the Issue

I'm working, but I'm not working for you.

—*Mac McCaughan*[1]

According to Amartya Sen, a man named Kader Mia went to a riot-plagued and hostile part of the city of Dhaka to find work during the civil strife near the end of the British occupation of South Asia in 1944.[2] His wife told him that it was too dangerous, but he went because he had no food for his children. He was stabbed and died from his wounds. "The penalty of his economic unfreedom turned out to be death."[3] What Kader Mia found in the labor market was unusual, but the unfreedom that compelled him into the marketplace was not. Hunger made Kader Mia unfree to refuse whatever employment happened to be available at the time. Billions of people worldwide face hunger if they refuse whatever employment is available. Most of them are not forced to accept an imminent risk of death in the marketplace, but many of them are forced to accept a lifetime of the worst working conditions, lowest pay, and lowest status in jobs that require them to serve the interests of at least one person who controls access to resources. Throughout history, economic deprivation has forced people to accept slavishly long, difficult, humiliating, dangerous, or low-paying jobs; to prostitute themselves; to beg; and to sell themselves into indentured servitude. Although some people have done some of these things voluntarily, economic deprivation has clearly forced reasonable people to do things they should not do and would not do if they had the power to say no.

This chapter and the two that follow argue for the importance of the elimination of this kind of unfreedom because putting people in such a position both leads to bad outcomes and shows insufficient respect for their humanity. The kind of unfreedom under consideration is personal independence or the effective component of ECSO freedom: unconditional access to the external assets (or resources) necessary to meet basic needs. The power to say no is not only for people like Kader Mia who find themselves in extreme circumstances but also for everyone. Two very different aspects of independence are important: freedom from deprivation and the freedom from being forced to serve someone else through the threat of deprivation or any other means. Thus, I'm arguing that it is important to eliminate propertylessness because forced deprivation and forced service in others' projects is a significant loss of liberty. Forced service is a threat to freedom no matter how a person is forced to serve, but I focus on indirectly forced service because it is the most common means by which people force others to serve them.

There are two obvious contrary positions: the belief in a social responsibility to work and the belief that private property rights to natural resources must be upheld even though doing so forces one group of people to work for another. The argument here is compared primarily to the position that people have a social responsibility to contribute to a mutually beneficial joint project underpinning an enforceable duty to work. Chapter 9 addresses the question of what to do if independence is unsustainable or if mutually enforceable obligations exist. The ensuing chapters argue both that there are times when it is best to respect individuals' independence despite the existence of a potentially enforceable contributive duty and that there are many situations in which there is no such contributive duty.

1. The Social Responsibility to Work and Its Discontents

"Poverty" (or "deprivation") is the state of having insufficient resources to maintain decent life and health. "Destitution" is extreme or complete poverty. The effects of poverty are severely damaging and well documented.[4] Whatever other duties we have toward each other, it must be wrong for one person to force another person to experience poverty or destitution. People can bring poverty on themselves, but earlier chapters argue that enforcement of the current property-rights regime causes many people to experience propertylessness, poverty, and destitution. Although people can access property by working for those who control it, there is often no assurance that doing so will get them out of poverty. A destitute person is in no position to demand above-poverty wages. Some people who start propertyless end up with a good standard of living. Others spend their lives meeting the conditions set by people who control resources and still live in poverty.

Of course, personal independence is not the only alternative to poverty. Many egalitarian philosophers believe that support for the poor should be conditional on the willingness to contribute to the social project.[5] A mandatory-participation economy could conceivably eliminate poverty by separating those who can and cannot work, assuring well-paying jobs for those who can work, and providing various forms of support for those who cannot work (such as disability, unemployment insurance, and old-age pensions). The welfare systems in most Western industrialized countries rely on some variation of this strategy, although they vary significantly in their generosity. Informational problems, market failure, and government failure make it unlikely that such a traditional welfare state could completely eliminate poverty (at least while maintaining fully mandatory participation for all able-bodied), but some of the more generous conditional welfare systems have greatly reduced poverty.[6]

Many authors who support a social responsibility to work argue that the refusal to work asserts nothing more important than the freedom to be lazy, which cannot be an important component of freedom or anything of concern to society.[7] The argument is presumably: *one would have to work to live by her own efforts; social cooperation makes possible greater returns to work; therefore, it is reasonable to require everyone to make a social contribution by working.* One could argue that if sufficient opportunities are available, poverty in a mandatory-participation economy results at least partly from the failure to work. Even if people have access to whatever resources they want, the natural consequence of the refusal to work is the inability to consume. One might conclude, therefore, that a generous, conditional welfare system with mandatory participation simply makes the work that we all naturally have to do more pleasant, more rewarding, and less risky.

Even some authors who support the right to refuse employment or a claim to unconditional access to external assets accept this characterization.[8] Van Parijs's argument for sharing employment rents equally between those who do and do not wish to accept employment seems to imply that society should be neutral between people who do and do not have a taste for living off the efforts of others.[9] Arguments for basic income on these kinds of grounds are vulnerable to the criticism that it promotes laziness or parasitism.[10] These arguments for basic income concede too much.

This section argues that an individual's choice of whether to participate in an economic system is far more complex than the labor-leisure trade-off. Once work becomes a social activity, the choice to participate incorporates many issues about which reasonable people might disagree. Dealing with those disagreements complicates the question of whether work should be considered a social responsibility, and the best way to resolve those agreements is not obvious.

The argument about work in italics above conflates two very different meanings of the word "work." The words "work" and "labor" are used to mean many different things.[11] Five senses of the word work are important here—"toil," "employment," "service," "time spent making money," and "social contribution." To toil is to put forth effort to achieve a goal such as chopping wood to build a fire. A person can toil individually, cooperatively, or subordinately. One connotation of toil is that the activity is unpleasant, or that it is not as pleasant as other uses of time, or at least that it takes some discipline to learn to appreciate toil.

Employment or service means to put forth effort toward someone else's goals in exchange for pay. This definition of employment includes the self-employed: shopkeepers and independent contractors work for the goals of their customers even though they usually have more control over the terms, methods, and goals than most employees. Sometimes I substitute the word service for employment to emphasize the wider context in which I use the concept. However, I use service in the more narrow of its two common uses, defining it as, *to be in service to* or *to be a servant of.* This excludes parents who serve a child or volunteer workers who serve the homeless, because these people give to others without being under the command of others. They serve in a sense, but not in the sense in which servants serve their employers or masters. Employment in the sense of service captures most but not all time spent making money. It excludes independent traders who buy and sell financial assets without following anyone else's direction.[12] But few people are in this position, and I believe no otherwise-destitute people are in the position to support themselves in this manner.

Social contribution can be understood either as a productive effort that improves the welfare of others or as participation in a recognized activity. The difference between the two depends on what society recognizes as a contribution and what actually constitutes a contribution. Stuart White defines social cooperation as a decent productive contribution to the community,[13] amounting to a basic work expectation, proportional to talent.[14] In practical proposals, social contribution is usually defined in one of three ways: (1) time spent legally making money or looking for work, (2) the first, plus time spent caring for children and the infirm, and (3) the second, plus time spent doing an approved list of volunteer activities.[15]

Work is an ambiguous word in political philosophy, because it is often unclear whether the author means employment, service, toil, time spent making money, social contribution, all five of them, or some combination. The argument for a mandatory work obligation from above first uses work in the sense of toil and then uses it in the sense of employment, service, or time spent making money: *one would have to work (toil) to live by her own efforts; social cooperation makes possible greater returns to work (employment); therefore, it is reasonable to require everyone to make a social contribution through work (employment).* Toil and employment are very different things. Usually a social responsibility to work means the social responsibility to accept employment. The individual must find an employer, and follow some employer's orders for 8 hours per day, for 200 or so days per year, and for 40 or 50 years in a lifetime.

The person who performs individual toil is limited only by nature; she chooses where, when, and how she will work, and what goals to pursue; she enjoys all the benefits of the total product of the activity with no need to consider the relative size of her contribution and the contribution of the resources she uses. Working cooperatively obviously creates the possibility of overcoming many of the limitations of nature, making greater returns to toil possible, but it also introduces a whole new set of limitations. As the earlier chapters stress, the domination of resources by one group not only prevents propertyless individuals from working for themselves but also prevents them from working in groups of their choosing. The cooperative social project could pursue many different goals, by different methods, under different conditions, and at different rates of sharing the benefits. All of these conditions are things to which an individual might object without objecting to toil or asserting laziness.

Consider the following reasons why a person might object to social participation (or accepting employment). This list is not meant to be exhaustive.

1. **An objection to the goal or some of the goals of the joint project or of a specific task**: One person might believe that the economic system is wrong, because she believes (even if heavily regulated) that it is too materialistic and detrimental to human well-being. Another person might believe that the economic system is wrong because it is overly regulated, too

concerned with environmentalism or with solidarity, and not concerned enough with the flourishing of the strong.

2. **An unrecognized or unrewarded contribution**: Some individuals do things that benefit the community but go unrewarded (e.g., caring for children, volunteering, and producing art); others might think they benefit the community when they do not. Some people might choose to fulfill care responsibilities rather than recognized contribution without considering whether it should count as a social contribution.
3. **Insufficient pay (under-recognized or under-rewarded contribution)**: Some people might have access to jobs they would be willing to do if the pay or the recognition was reasonable to them, but do not find the jobs offered to them to have sufficient rewards. Anyone might think they are underpaid, but only some (probably mostly those near the bottom of the income distribution) object so strongly that they would rather live off a social minimum than accept employment.
4. **Difficult or unpleasant working conditions**: Laborers might object that their contributory obligation requires them to perform relatively difficult work, while others are (for whatever reason) allowed to satisfy their contributory obligation with more pleasant possibilities.
5. **Unfulfilling opportunities**: People whose only job opportunities are relatively boring, low-status, or unfulfilling might decide to refuse unless they are offered something better.
6. **Insufficient opportunities and unemployment**: Some people might want to contribute in a way that is well rewarded by the community, but for whatever reason can't get that job. Some people might have lost their job or be unable to find the kind of job they are looking for. Some might lack the required ability, and some might simply lack recognition of their ability.
7. **Improving skills**: Some people would like to drop out of participation temporarily to improve their skills or to begin a project that will allow them to reenter with more desirable opportunities. Society might recognize some improvement of skill as a contribution, and so for this to be considered a refusal to cooperate the individual must be improving her skills in some unapproved or unrecognized manner.
8. **Objection to hierarchy**: Some people might be perfectly willing to perform the functions they are offered but might object to the hierarchical structure in which those jobs are placed.

But of course, it is always possible that someone might object that the structure of society is not hierarchical enough.

9. **Objection to the specific place in a hierarchy offered to an individual**: Some people might not be opposed to hierarchy in general, but object to the low position in the hierarchy that their functions place them. Individuals might have good or bad reasons for believing they merit a higher place.
10. **Objection to the standard of fairness of the system (including the role of luck, discrimination, nepotism, social advantage, etc.)**: Any system with different roles for people and an imperfect ability to give maximal opportunities to everyone will run into somebody with a legitimate complaint about bad luck. Discrimination and social disadvantage are not simply bad luck; they are socially created arbitrary factors. They create similarly arbitrary outcomes that could inspire a similar unwillingness to participate. There might also be people who accept only unfairness in their favor, such as racists who are not willing to cooperate in any project that includes other races. Society might try to reduce these problems, but it is unlikely that they will have the ability to eliminate them.
11. **Objection to the required level of effort**: A person might believe that the effort demanded of her is larger than necessary even if others work just as hard. Or, she might believe that no one else works hard enough or that her extra efforts are not rewarded sufficiently.
12. **Grievance**: Someone might refuse social cooperation because she believes that she or a member of her family had been wrongly punished or wrongly deprived of rights, property, or privilege.
13. **Insufficient range of options**: A person might refuse to participate just because there aren't enough varied choices of how to participate. I hesitate to include this objection, because presumably most people who object to the range of options have some specific objection to each offer in the range of options. However, it is conceivable that someone might refuse an option they genuinely like just because they believe they have too few options to choose from.
14. **Mental or physical disorder**: Some people who appear to be lazy, gaming the system, or weak -willed might actually suffer from depression or some other mental disorder that inhibits their ability to interact with others and hold a position. Physical disorders (whether recognized or not) might have a similar effect.

15. **Weakness of will**: Some people might be much better-off in the long run if they worked for society's rewards but lack the self-discipline to do it.
16. **Gaming the system**: Some individuals might believe they benefit from the system and might feel they, therefore, have a duty to contribute actively to that system, but willingly take advantage of the system to get the benefits without fulfilling the duties.
17. **Laziness**: Laziness is in the eye of the beholder. When does a legitimate objection to insufficient pay or any of the terms offered become simple laziness? Possibly the term "lazy" is too vague and doesn't add much to insufficient pay, weakness of will, gaming the system, and mental disorder.

A few of these reasons for refusal involve the mental or physical state of the dissenter. The rest are objections that fall into four broad categories: to the goals of the project, to the methods of the project, to the fairness of the system, and to the desirability of the terms. By "terms" I mean (relative and absolute) pay, position, and working conditions. The 17 reasons don't necessarily fall neatly into any one category. For example, it is hard to tell whether an objection to terms is an objection to the fairness or to the desirability of those terms. Bob decides the wage is too low; he might think it is unfairly low, or he might think it is a legitimate offer that happens not to be desirable enough to deserve acceptance. Conversely, he could think the wage is unfair but still be willing to accept it. Each of the reasons for refusal might be overcome by some level of pay. Even weakness of will and gaming the system might be overcome by higher pay and more desirable working conditions. Even people with moral objections to the fairness or the goals of the system might be persuaded by some level of pay to participate notwithstanding their objections. If one accepts the postulate "everyone has a price," then all objections overlap with objections to the rate of pay.

Each reason that people might refuse to work is complex, involving usually three issues: the individual's opinion on whether it is a good reason, the enforcement authority's opinion on what is a good reason, and whether it is in fact a good reason—to the extent that it is a factual issue. If it is not a factual issue the question is which side's opinion should matter. Is it legitimate for individuals to refuse participation in a joint project because in their opinion they have good reasons, or is it legitimate for the ruling coalition to force individuals to participate against their will because in the majority opinion, these individuals do not have good reason? This question is an important concern for the discussion below, but the list demonstrates that the issue is much more complex than the characterization of the refusal to work as laziness or a greater preference for leisure implies.

This list reveals the importance of the equivocation in the word work in the above arguments justifying the duty to contribute and conflating the refusal to work with laziness. Working *for* a person or a group project introduces many issues that don't exist when one toils alone and that can provide reason for legitimate objections. Most of the objections on this list are potentially legitimate, ethically justifiable reasons to refuse labor market participation under the right circumstances even if people are interdependent and have a potentially enforceable duty to contribute to the social project.[16] It is unreasonable to dismiss the refusal to participate in a joint project as nothing more than laziness.

Stuart White gives an example showing that the refusal to work is the inability to consume. After a shipwreck, Alf and Betty find themselves on an island. More than enough fishing equipment coincidentally washes up on the shore. Although both are equally able, Betty spends the day fishing, and Alf does not. Clearly Alf's equal claim to the fishing equipment does not give him claim to her catch.[17] Notice in this example that resources are not dominated. Work is nothing more than toil. Notice also that there is nothing morally wrong with "laziness" in this example. If Alf and/or Betty want more fish and less sleep they can fish more and sleep less. If they want less fish and more sleep they can sleep more and fish less. They have no obligation. They also have complete ECSO freedom, and so this story doesn't make an analogy for a modern economy whether organized under capitalism, socialism, or any other system. There is no joint project. There is no boss. There is no employee. There are no orders to follow and no work expectations to meet. Reasons 1–13 in the list above (the reasons a reasonably mentally healthy person might object to "work") don't exist in this example. These reasons only come into play when some group dominates the fishing equipment or other resources. But this is also when people tend to claim that there is a social responsibility to work.

In all but the most giving environments, the natural consequence of the refusal to toil is the inability to consume, but there are no natural consequences to the refusal to spend time making money—only socially imposed consequences. If the rules of access to resources were different, individuals could attempt to meet their needs in different ways with different people and without subordination to any particular group or any particular social project. People who have not been excluded from resources (subsistence farmers, hunter-gatherers, and asset owners) might not always live well, but they do not experience destitution and homelessness. It is unreasonable to characterize the refusal to serve someone else's project under the terms and using the methods they designate as laziness or merely as the pursuit of leisure or the refusal to toil to meet one's own needs.

Who decides whether an individual's reasons for refusing participation are good enough? Or to put it more simply, why should someone go to work in the morning? Should I go to work because I like the pay, because I want to volunteer or because I have an obligation to my community? If there is disagreement, who should decide; should it be up to the individual or to society as a whole (through the democratic process)? The next section considers three different models of how this decision should be made.

2. Three Models and Three Mechanisms

I put forward the hypothesis that we tend to view human interaction through at least three models, all of which are appropriate in different situations. These models can be used as moral guides to determine when it is ethical to interact. They do not always correspond to practical mechanisms for governing human interaction. Different practical mechanisms might also be appropriate in different situations. The question that I am getting at, of course, is which model and mechanism is appropriate for active, individual participation in the economic system.[18] This chapter clarifies the issue before the next two chapters argue about it.

A. Three Models

Call the three models of human interaction the trade model, the pure voluntarism model, and the obligation or mutual obligation model. The trade model is appropriate when the justification for interaction is that all parties will benefit. If someone down the street wants me to invest in a business with him, because I will benefit from it, I *should* decide based on whether I think I will benefit from this decision. If an employer wants to hire you because he will profit from doing so, perhaps you should accept only if you profit from doing so. The trade model is also appropriate in some situations we do not think of as trade. If an acquaintance at a pub suggests I might enjoy a game of pool, I should also decide based on whether I will in fact enjoy playing pool with him. When the trade model is appropriate, people should contribute to a joint project if and when the organizers of the project make it in their interest to contribute. The answer to whether the goals, methods, and terms of the joint project are fair, desirable, and just is determined by the agreement of the parties.

Under the pure voluntarism model, people may decide to act or not interact, but they should neither seek (formal) reward for contributing nor be subject to (formal) punishment for not contributing. Perhaps they should seek no reward at all and be subject to no punishment at all, but clearly there's a continuum between trade, voluntarism, and obligation. So, I think we should consider some minor informal rewards and punishments for action as still fitting into the model of pure voluntarism. I use the term "pure voluntarism" to distinguish this model from the sense in which the trade model involves another concept of voluntary interaction. For an example of a situation in which pure voluntarism is appropriate, consider a college student studying in her dorm room when another student asks her to participate in a campus beautification effort. She may do it; she may not. It's up to her. If she does it people might say "good job," or even give her a good citizenship award. But if she does it *because* she thinks she'll get a good citizenship award, we therefore tend to view her actions as less praiseworthy.

Some of our interactions are morally driven by obligation. If my young child asks me to play pool, my decision is not quite the same as if an acquaintance in a pub asks me to play. We have obligations to children, the infirm, and people in emergency situations, such as a Peter Singer's drowning infant or even a drowning adult. Whether or not we agree some authority should be empowered to force us to interact in these instances, most people agree that the question of whether we *should* interact in these instances is not well modeled by trade or voluntarism. I should save Singer's drowning child if I can, even if I don't want to volunteer and have nothing to gain from it personally. It is probably wrong even to ask to gain from it personally. But these obligations are also one-way rather than mutual. In these examples, the obligation was justified because one party had great need and the other had relatively great ability.

But I am most concerned with mutual obligation among equally abled people. These occasions can exist. A flood is coming. Everyone in the village will surely die unless 90 percent of the available,[19] able adults go now to pile sandbags on the levy. Again whether or not one believes that a forced mutual obligation is the right mechanism to employ in this kind of situation, most people, I hope, agree that the right thing for me to do is to pile sand bags on the levy. Although the town can survive with up to 10 percent free riders, there is something morally wrong with being one of them. We can model many apparent one-way obligations as mutual obligations: when we are able, we all have an obligation to ensure that help gets to those who are in need (whether they are children, infirmed people, drowning adults, etc.), and we are mutually entitled to help when are in need. Of course, many people disagree about when the mutual obligation model applies. I'm not trying to resolve the disagreement, only to point out the differences in these ways of modeling interaction.

There are other possible models: the hierarchical obligation model, for example, in which lesser people owe one kind of obligation to their betters, who in turn owe different obligations (if any). Such models were popular in feudal and slave-holding societies at least among those at the upper end of the hierarchy, but hopefully, few people take hierarchical obligation seriously anymore.

It's not always easy to determine which of these models is appropriate at any given time. There might be times when I *should* play pool with an acquaintance in a pub, because he really needs a friend. Philosophers have written a great deal about if and when mutual obligations exist, but the issue is still controversial. We are likely to disagree about which model is appropriate under what conditions, and even when we agree that obligations exist, we might disagree about whether and how they should be enforced.

B. Three Mechanisms

These ethical models don't necessarily translate into practical mechanisms. Usually when the trade model is appropriate as a moral model, it is also appropriate as a mechanism. But market failure might be able to cause exceptions. The same probably goes for pure voluntarism. If it is an appropriate moral model, it is also the appropriate mechanism—in all or most cases. Few people think pure voluntarism is a workable mechanism for the bulk of contributions to the modern industrialized economy. Although Marxist literature asserts that voluntarism will work once we reach the highest stage of communism,[20] I haven't found any literature arguing that voluntarism is workable here and now. However, I've been surprised to read about the extent to which hunter-gatherer bands relied on voluntarism for a large amount of their jointly shared consumption. In most bands, people had no obligation to hunt, but if an individual or group caught a big game, it was treated as property of the band as a whole. The hunter was even expected to downplay the value of the contribution.[21]

The mutual obligation model has no directly corresponding mechanism. If a group unanimously agreed to enforce the same obligation on everyone, it would have a mutual obligation, mutually enforced. But unanimous agreement rarely, if ever, exists. In the absence of consensus, democratic enforcement is not the same as mutual enforcement; the ruling coalition forces everyone (supporters and dissenters alike) to uphold the obligations designated by the majority.

The question of whether obligations should be enforced is not so much a question of whether mutual obligations exist but who should decide whether all the conditions necessary for a person to be held to an obligation are in place. If the majority makes that decision best, then perhaps enforcement is best. If the majority is prone to error, perhaps the voluntarism or trade mechanisms are better.

Laws rarely enforce obligations directly and mutually. Mandatory voting and jury duty are two of the few cases where governments tend to force the same level of duty on people. Even the military draft is not usually enforced as a mutual obligation but as a hierarchical obligation. Military conscripts are often put into a hierarchy and forced to do very different duties with very different levels of risk and difficulty. A uniform national service, in which everyone did equally onerous duties would at least be enforced mutually if not agreed mutually. But this institution is rare.

Even if mutual obligations exist, it is not obvious that majority-enforcement of those obligations is the best mechanism to employ. In fact, even in the strongest cases of mutual obligation, societies often employ other mechanisms relying either on trade or volunteerism. I doubt that towns facing floods often force every able citizen out to the levies to stack sandbags. More commonly they would ask everyone in town to come out and help (volunteer mechanism) or call in a professional emergency management team (trade mechanism). Most of the regular activities we normally think of as mutual obligations are usually turned over to professionals (doctors, police, teachers, judges, etc.). Some communities rely on volunteer firefighters, some on professionals. Most communities rely on volunteers to give birth to and to take care of the next generation of children. Although many countries pay benefits to parents, I don't think any of these reimburse the full cost of caring for a child, much less constitute a wage for parents. If birth parents are unable to take care of their children, communities usually rely either on professionals (such as orphanages) or volunteers (such as adoptive parents) to care of the children.

Of course, the community is obliged to pay taxes to support the professional fulfillment of obligations, but in the JPA theory, taxation as an entirely passive obligation. Because taxes are a tax on the holding of external assets, they cannot count as an active contribution. If an individual wants more external assets, they pay taxes to obtain them. They don't work to contribute. They work because they want assets. Individuals, if they so choose, turn existing resources and external assets into more valuable forms in exchange for the right to own more external assets than they would have otherwise. For example, Gilligan's island needs a well. Everyone will die of thirst unless the stranded castaways dig a well. They could all get together and dig the well (mutual obligation model). They could call for volunteers to join in the digging of well (pure volunteerism model). Or they could pay someone to dig the well (trade model). Suppose the majority agrees to pay Mr. Howell to dig the well by himself in exchange for a larger share of the island's resources. The majority taxes away a little bit of each person's individual land (or designates Mr. Howell as owner of formerly common land). Mr. Howell agrees to dig the well at that price, and everyone is better-off. The obligation gets done with only one person fully paid for their contribution while everyone else contributes passively. No one in the story seems obviously to be exploited. So, it is at least possible to employ the trade model ethically when mutual obligations exist. Perhaps many mutual obligations can get done equitably without forcing anyone to contribute actively.

When mutual obligations exist, each of the three mechanisms has advantages and disadvantages. Although nothing seems problematic with the trade mechanism in the story of the well above, the trade model seems to invite people to look at the fulfillment of their mutual obligations as a chance for selfish gain. Pure voluntarism could allow free riders to take advantage of contributors. Trade might make free riding possible as well, if contributors are systematically underpaid. The majority enforcement mechanism seems like the closest approximation of the mutual obligation model, but forced labor necessarily involves ethical difficulties. Once one group forces others, all of the objections to participation discussed above become potentially legitimate. Individuals might object to the goals, terms, methods, and fairness of whatever system of mutual obligation the majority enforces. Enforced active obligation necessarily involves a sacrifice of ECSO freedom.

3. Modeling and Mechanizing Individual Economic Participation

Many political theorists refer to something like the mutual obligation model to justify an enforceable duty for individual participation in the economy. This idea has been extremely important in debates over basic income.[22] Many egalitarian political theorists view the economy as a mutually beneficial social project or a system of social cooperation. Some argue that individuals have a fulltime enforceable obligation to contribute (actively) to that project, as long as it is sufficiently fair and mutually beneficial. All or most of the active obligations a person might have are subsumed into one enormous duty to participate fulltime in the economic system until one can save up enough money to retire. Thus a dishwasher in a fancy restaurant indirectly fulfills his active duties—to help the sick, protect people from violence, ensure good schooling for the next generation, and so on—by making sure that people out for a fine meal have clean plates.

As the argument in section 2B above implies, forced participation in the modern economy is not an enforced *mutual* obligation; it is an enforced *hierarchical* obligation. Some people are eligible for well-paying jobs with pleasant working conditions and others are only eligible for poorly paid jobs with poor working conditions. Some give orders. Some must take orders. Enforced participation in the economic system is also a strange mix of the mutual obligation model and the trade model. Employers may hire workers for their own private gain, but workers must accept jobs as part of a "mutual" obligation. Only participation is modeled as an obligation; the goals pursued by firms, the products people buy, and so forth are all modeled as self-interested trade. The system of social cooperation is often justified by a hypothetical social contract in which every act of social cooperation makes everyone better-off, but reference to a mutually beneficial contract is also a reference to the trade model.

Right-libertarians claim to be extremely skeptical about the enforcement of any active duties, preferring only negative (passive) duties, but they are inconsistent. They endorse passive duties that are so strong that they indirectly force the propertyless to actively serve the interests of property holders. So, they endorse extremely onerous active duties, as long as they are indirectly enforced. Ignoring the effective unfreedom problem, most right-libertarians argue that only the trade or pure volunteerism mechanism are morally permissible. Even if mutual obligations exist, individuals should decide what they do, and by giving individuals secure property rights, they supposedly make individuals free to decide whether to act according to the trade model or the pure voluntarism model. Individuals may work or invest their property for their own benefit or for the benefit of others as they see fit. Right-libertarians deny that they have a social project; individuals are free to use their bodies and their external assets to further their own projects. However, right-libertarians do have a social project—the furtherance of the goals of property owners in proportion to how much property they own. And right-libertarians use the same indirect enforcement mechanisms as egalitarians who believe in mutual obligation—the denial of access to resources to propertyless individuals until they propertyless serve at least one member of the resource-dominating group. Right-libertarianism effectively enforces a hierarchical obligation, in which the propertyless have an obligation to work *for* the propertied and the propertied have no enforced reciprocal obligation even to hire the propertyless much less stay out of their way. Some right-libertarians endorse a proviso in which the economy must turn out to be better for everyone than a hypothetical alternative. Thus, right-libertarians also attempt to derive the obligation of the propertyless to serve the group that dominates resources by reference to the trade model.

It is interesting that although the hierarchical obligation model is discredited in almost all schools of thought in modern political theory, many political theorists somehow justify mandatory participation in a hierarchical economic system. It is also interesting to note how similar the steps are in the two theories described above:

1. Population begins low and resources are not dominated.
2. Some group comes to dominate resources (it can be a democratic government or an ownership class) without directly compensating the propertyless for the loss of liberty at this point.[23]
3. Destitution creates a mandatory-participation economy at least for the propertyless, who are indirectly forced to spend time making money.
4. The propertyless get jobs, and supposedly end up better-off than they were in step 1. Their wages (perhaps along with public goods and government services) not only compensate them for their labor but also double as compensation for the liberties lost in step 2.

Probably the most central idea of indepentarianism is the opposition to enforced hierarchical obligations. If people choose to form hierarchies, we would be wrong to stop them, but to force people into a subservient position in a hierarchy is a serious threat to their status as free individuals. Lost independence cannot be justified by an improved standard of living. Thus, we need to use the trade and voluntarism mechanisms as much as possible, limit the enforcement of active duties as much as possible, and when we must enforce them, apply them, as much as possible, on an equal and nonhierarchical basis. Consider an alternative to the four steps:

1. Population begins low and resources are not dominated.
2. Some group comes to dominate resources (it can be a democratic government or an ownership class).
3. Those who control property compensate the propertyless at least enough to maintain their independence. If there are any mutual obligations that must be enforced, they are enforced at this point on an equal and nonhierarchical basis.[24]
4. With all obligations on all sides fulfilled, and everyone's freedom protected, people enter a voluntary-participation economy. If they want, they may trade or volunteer.

Rather than mixing obligation into the trade system, the indepentarian ideal is to create a basic structure with a legitimate starting point so that the trade model is appropriate for an economic system based on trade. If a person's pre-trade starting point is legitimate, and the trade model is appropriate, there is no gaming the system. If a person has a legitimate claim to what she possesses without participating in the economic system and owes no further obligation to it, the refusal to participate is as legitimate as any other choice. If the alternative is more attractive than participation, individuals have no obligation to participate. If employers want employees to participate, they must make it in employees' interest to do so. If the market system is as productive and mutually beneficial as its supporters say, people will trade.

4. Conclusion

Now that this chapter has framed the issue in this way, the following two chapters make first- and second-best arguments in favor of respecting independence. Chapter 5 argues for the importance of respecting independence on ideal-theory grounds, arguing that for the vast majority of human interaction, unforced individual consent is one of the things needed to make that interaction just. The trade and pure voluntarism models are appropriate for most human interaction. Even when the mutual obligation model is appropriate, it does not always justify the enforcement of obligations at the expense of individual independence. Chapter 6 argues for the importance of respecting independence on nonideal grounds. Even if mutual obligations exist and are potentially enforceable, the trade and voluntarism mechanisms are good ways to protect the vulnerable.

CHAPTER 5

The Importance of Independence II: Freedom and Integrity

We don't want any part of the establishment, we want to be free to raise our children in our religion, in our ways, to be able to hunt and fish and live in peace. We don't want power; we don't want to be congressmen, or bankers... we want to be ourselves.

—*Grand Council of American Indians 1927*[1]

This chapter makes six first-best ethical arguments for respecting personal independence, arguing that individual consent is a constituent part of what makes most social interaction and economic interaction just. The final section responds to a potential criticism.

1. The Self-Evident Value of Voluntary Interaction

The argument for ECSO freedom relies on the simple, (and I believe) widely acceptable premise that a person who pursues goals she has chosen is free, but a person who is forced by others to pursue someone else's goals is not. One reason for stressing ECSO freedom is that the absence of force is inherently or self-evidently good: people with equal moral worth should be free to interact with each other on a voluntary basis. People are happier and cooperate better if they cooperate voluntarily. No one should force another to do something against her will. Perhaps in times of dire emergency or great need our concern for freedom might be overcome by some other important value, but not for our day-to-day economic interactions in an economy that devotes most of its effort to producing luxuries with a subjective value. Most of what we do is only worth doing because we choose to do it, but we create a situation in which many people have no power to say no to it. As a society, we usually don't tolerate overt force to promote some group's vision of desirable cooperation except for self-defense against criminals or in cases of extreme emergency. Certainly, a society built on the forced participation of every individual is less free and less respectful of the worth of individuals than a society built on the voluntary cooperation of everyone.

Most of these claims are usually not controversial, but they become controversial in the context of a propertyless person who is being denied access to resources until she performs a service for the group that dominates resources. Indirect force (by resource domination) is an extremely powerful way to coerce individuals. Most of what I ask here is that we apply restrictions that we take for granted when applying direct force just as seriously when we apply indirect force. Support for mandatory participation seems to be premised on a belief that work is a duty people will shirk if given an opportunity to refuse to their own detriment and to the detriment of society as a whole, or that work is good for people, but people (or *some* people) are unable to see it. If people are incapable of knowing their own best interest, the desirability of freedom in any sense of the word is called into question—as is the desirability of democracy. It is strange to advocate freedom in all other areas but not for the decision of what conditions make it worthwhile to join a cooperative project that requires 40 hours of service per week for 40 or 50 years.

Consider a more basic question: Why is slavery wrong? Is the wrongness of slavery contingent on how humanely the slaves are treated? No, slavery is wrong because of what it is—forced labor. Slavery is wrong no matter what the master asks the slave to do, no matter whether the master allows the slave choices about which forced labor to perform, no matter whether the master treats the slave humanely, and no matter how high the slave's living standard is in comparison to the master. If there is something deeply wrong with forced labor it should not matter what method of force is used: whether the method is interference with individuals' ability to breathe or with their ability to feed, clothe, or shelter themselves.

Imagine that the United States has a work obligation but meets every other standard for fair distribution of that obligation, fair distribution of its benefits, and fair input into group decision-making about what the obligation should be. Per capita GDP is higher in the United States than in the neighboring countries of Canada and Mexico. Therefore, participation in the US joint project can produce greater returns to work than remaining outside. Suppose the United

States captures Mexicans and Canadians who live within commuting distance of the border and makes them compete as equals in the US joint project. They have the same work obligation as every other American and the same share in the benefits of social cooperation; they have equal input into what the obligation will be and what goals the social project will pursue; and through participation they have access to a higher standard of living than before. They work a standard workday and can commute back across the border whenever they are not working. The one thing that they are not allowed to do is to refuse their work obligation and return to Mexico or Canada permanently before they save up enough to retire. That one thing is enough to make them forced workers. I think most people would agree that Canadian and Mexican workers in such a position are profoundly unfree. They are unfree because they are not free of a project they might not want to participate in.

One could respond that there is a crucial difference between forcing a foreigner to work—even as an equal—and forcing someone born in this society to work. The foreigner is not part of our circle of mutual obligation but the native or the willing immigrant is. This argument is fair, but it is a *justification* for unfreedom not an explanation that the American in this situation is any freer than a Canadian or a Mexican in this situation. In relation to contribution to the collective project, they experience the same unfreedom. Americans are born into the society rather than abducted, but with no access to resources until they have fulfilled a work obligation to a joint project, they are as unfree to refuse someone else's project as they would be if they were born somewhere else and forcibly brought in. If we can recognize that a Canadian forced to serve the American economic system is profoundly unfree, we should recognize that an American forced to serve the American economic system (or a Canadian forced to serve the Canadian economic system) is also unfree. If we recognize the level of unfreedom involved in effectively forced service, we should look at other methods to encourage participation. But as long as the self-evident value of ECSO freedom is not uncontroversial, an appeal to its self-evident value is less than decisive.

2. Why the Trade Model Is Appropriate for Most Economic Interaction

The mutual obligation model and the trade model represent different views of the reasons for economic cooperation, two different ways of asking the question: Why should I work? Why do I go into my job every day? Under the trade model, I should work if and when my employer makes it worth my while. The employer would not hire me unless I benefit her; I, therefore, should not work for her unless she benefits me. Under the mutual obligation model, I should work because I have an obligation to society, and people should pay me well because they have an obligation to me. I will not dismiss the idea that mutual obligations exist,[2] but I will argue that the mutual obligation model is a poor ideal for the whole of or even for most of society's economic interaction. There are things that we are obliged to do for each other, but little of our economic activity is devoted to such things.

The trade model of cooperation is appropriate because work serves wants. Work is only worthwhile if it produces something that is good for you or for someone else. Work is only worth doing if it produces something *someone* wants. Work must be in someone's self-interest or it is worthless. Suppose Gilligan is alone on an island; he may work as much or as little as he wants. He has no ethical obligations to do anything in particular. He may work on important things or on trivial things. How much time should he spend working and how much at leisure? As much as he wants. He should expend effort if, and only if, in his best judgment that expenditure of effort will make him best off in the long run. Similarly, if Gilligan is on an island with one million people who are like-minded and like-situated in every way, their thought process is the same. They should do what, in their best judgment, makes them better-off. They should expend effort only when it makes them better-off. Some of those wants are trivial, some of them are important, but as long as they do what they all want to do, they ought to be allowed to do it. The trade model replicates this situation at the individual level. If it is good for society that individual A does x, and if they can find a way to make it in A's interest to do x, then everyone is better-off. If they can put A in the position where she can't say no to x, they can make her worse-off than she would be on her own. Only disagreement about the value of interaction can justify departure from voluntary interaction, but force causes problems of its own, and the trade model has advantages even when objectives differ. There is value in people with differing minds coming to agreement, rather than one party forcing the other to do things their way.

There is a belief among egalitarians that the desire to base human interaction on voluntary agreement rather than mutual obligation is somehow conservative—something that primarily benefits the wealthy lord who wants to ignore a starving peasant. But JPA does not appeal to the mutual obligation model to derive the wealthy lord's responsibility to pay taxes to help the starving peasant. It appeals to the trade model. The lord owes the peasant because the lord imposes duties on the peasant by claiming ownership of natural resources. By establishing a voluntary-participation economy, and letting the disadvantaged choose the trade model or the voluntarism model, society ensures that every participant is a willing participant, protecting the disadvantaged from the most significant injustices. Throughout history, the effective power to refuse participation in someone else's project has usually been what the oppressed—the Medieval serf, the Victorian proletarian, or the Soviet worker—lacked most. A mandatory-participation economy is for the disadvantaged. It does not give them everything they want, but it asks nothing from them unless they give it willingly.

The previous chapter mentioned that social contract theorists, egalitarians, and right-libertarians all refer to the trade model to justify the economic system. If we view the economy as a "cooperative venture for mutual benefit,"[3] we indicate that the trade model is appropriate. Suppose A, B, and C live in autarky, producing goods by their own efforts.[4] Suppose it is possible for them to create a more complex economy such as capitalism, welfare capitalism, or market socialism. As long as it is a project for mutual gain, what does it mean for this interaction to be fair, right, or just either in its terms or in its goals, other than that it was freely chosen by free individuals? A, B, and C should move to the new system and endorse its rules, if A, B, and C *want* to move to the new system. If the justification for any system over any other possible system is mutual benefit as the individuals see it themselves, individual agreement must be part of the justification for that system.

3. Agreement as a Constituent Part of Just Interaction

Whether the trade model, the pure voluntarism model, or the mutual obligation model is appropriate in any particular situation, this section argues that consent of participants is a constituent part of what makes interaction just. One contributing factor toward making it just for A and B to do *x* is that both A and B agree to do *x*. I will not argue that consent makes up the whole of what makes cooperation just, but I will argue that it is an inherently important factor, because people are moral agents with the ability to make choices. The freedom to make choices can be overridden in certain situations, but its intrinsic importance does not go away. Reasonable people are likely to disagree about the goals, methods, and terms of any joint project. One of the things that make a joint project worth doing is that those who choose to participate in it come to some basic agreement to do so.

The alternative to agreement being a reason why doing *x* is just would be to say that people choose to do things for reasons, and agreement is only instrumentally important to fulfilling those reasons. Is it the fact of agreement that makes the interaction worthwhile or is it the reasons for the agreement that make the interaction worthwhile? People choose *x* because *x* is worthwhile for some reason; *x* is not merely worthwhile because someone chose it. If so, agreement seems to drop out of the equation. One could argue on this basis that if society can determine the just principles for contribution and reward, it does not need to give individuals the power to refuse or even that it would be wrong for them to refuse. Many egalitarian philosophers downplay the role of agreement in economic justice, arguing that a fair or just obligation is determined by abstract principles largely independent of the literal agreement of the participants.[5]

There are situations in which consent is obviously central to just interaction. Chapter 2 gave sex as example. People choose to have sex with each other for reasons, but the fact that they choose to have sex is an essential component of what makes it worth doing. No amount of objective evidence for the mutual benefit of sex makes it right for a person, or a governmental authority, to force A to have sex with B against A's will, or to mandate a list of sexual partners (B, C, D, etc.), one of whom A must choose, even if A would rather not have sex with any of them.

Consent is less important in other situations, such as Peter Singer's example of a drowning child. A passerby is the only person close enough to save the child, and he can do so with minimal effort.[6] Most people, except for self-ownership extremists, agree that it is just for the passerby to save the child whether or not she agrees to do so, and that it is unjust for the passerby to refuse. One justification could be that the passerby's consent has no value, but a more compelling justification is that whatever harm the passerby suffers from the brief and insignificant loss of freedom is extremely small compared to the harm the child experiences from death. The value of consent is not gone; it is overridden by extraordinary circumstances.

These examples show that there are situations in which consent is and is not essential for just interaction, but it is the first example that generalizes for most of the situations we find ourselves in. Most of the decisions we make from the most trivial to some of the most important require consent to be just. Should you and I play cards together? Should we vacation together? Should we start a business together?

Should we get married? Should we have children together? None of these activities are worth doing unless we both agree to do them. The same is true for market transactions. Suppose you are walking through the market place. A vender sells trinkets at "the just price" for trinkets, and therefore, she says you must trade your labor for one. You don't want it. She calls a police officer, who carefully considers the evidence that the vendor's price is just and asks your reasons for refusal so that she can evaluate them for acceptability. You insist your reasons are not relevant; you don't need to subject them to evaluation. The mere fact that you do not want the trinket is sufficient.

A market does not generate an abstract "just price," only an agreed price. If the potential buyer and seller do not agree on a price, the offers are not wrong; the deal is wrong. I do not commit an injustice if I offer to buy a wealthy man's house for one dollar. I merely get turned down. He does not commit an injustice to me if he says he won't sell his house unless he receives 100 times the market value of the house. He merely gets turned down. Most market transactions (with initially just property rights and in the absences of fraud, coercion, externalities, etc.) have this character in which consent is all there is to justice.

Choice is important in all these examples because basic respect for other people involves recognizing their freedom to make their own choices. Even if the importance of consent might be overridden in an emergency, modern economies are more like the trinket seller than the drowning child. Most people intuitively respect the need for consent to justify almost all activities. The mandatory-participation economy creates one enormous exception to that respect: all people are obliged to contribute to a social project up to 40 hours a week, 50 weeks a year, 40 years of their lives whether or not they consent to the goals, methods, and terms of the project. This point of view is surprising when most of our economic activity is directed toward frivolous and often contradictory activities that can only hope to be justified on the basis that people choose to do them. We cannot simultaneously justify each particular economic activity by supposed consent and justify forced lifetime participation in the economy as a whole by a supposed emergency. Even most of those parts of our economy that are dedicated to fulfilling vital needs are not usually pressing emergencies like the story of the drowning child. Opportunities exist to use trade or voluntarism to fulfill the need.

Even ideas such as fairness and mutual benefit often flow from people's beliefs about what is fair and mutually beneficial. When people play games together, fairness is the adherence to mutually agreed rules. The rules of pool vary from country to country and region to region. There is no objectively correct way to play pool; an unfair pool player breaks the rules agreed by the other players. It is not unfair or wrong for a person to refuse to play anything but German-rules pool in the United States, as long as she doesn't mislead or force anyone to play with her. One necessary condition for making the rules of pool just is that both players are willing to play by those rules. To ensure that the rules of interaction have this feature for all individuals, we have to cede the power to refuse to all individuals.

It is ridiculous to suppose that this element has no application to an ordinary worker's decision to participate in economic interaction. But without independence, without the power to say no, the ordinary worker is subject to someone else's conception of desirable employment both in its goals and its terms. The most important injustices throughout history have not been that the powerful took a disproportionate share of wealth, but that the powerful took away the freedom of others and forced them to serve the powerful on terms chosen by the powerful. Carole Pateman quotes G. D. H. Cole as recognizing this point in 1919, writing "The wrong reply was usually given when people tried to answer the question of what was wrong with the capitalist organization of production, 'they would answer poverty [or inequality], when they ought to answer slavery.'"[7] The same problem exists with any method of organizing production that forces individuals to participate.

4. Integrity

One might respond that sometimes people's conceptions about the desirable terms and goals are wrong, and in those cases one might justify holding a person to a compulsory obligation. I address this position by referring to Ronald Dworkin's argument for the importance of an individual's integrity as an ethical agent. According to Dworkin, life cannot be good just because the person thinks it is; she could be mistaken about what is good, but it cannot be in her own interest to lead a life she despises. Ethical integrity is achieved when a person lives life according to her own convictions, and it is worth respecting even if some of her convictions are based on mistaken beliefs.[8]

Dworkin makes a distinction between experiential interests and critical interests. The first is the kind of interest we have in experiences for their own sake. There are many different experiences we might enjoy, but it is not necessarily a mistake to prefer one to another. The second is the deeper sort of interest we have about what makes life good that it would be a mistake not to value. For example, it would be a mistake to go through life without valuing friendship.[9] One could argue that participation in a social project is a critical interest; people need to care about and contribute to each other's welfare by sharing in social production. Suppose with good democratic institutions we can make our project fair and mutually beneficial enough that there are no great reasons to object, so that all objections are likely to reflect weakness of will or gaming the system. That is, people refuse to contribute because they are seeking the instantaneous pleasure of idleness; they seek an experience interest at the expense of their long-term critical interests.

I have argued for skepticism about the belief that in such a conflict the majority is necessarily right and the individual wrong, but suppose the majority actually is right. It is against the individual's critical interest to refuse participation. They have a weakness of will and regret awaits them if they are allowed to make that mistake.[10] Under these conditions, is there any reason to allow the individual to make this critical error? Integrity is one reason. We must consider another person's beliefs as data. By forcing them to go against their beliefs, we might be making them lead a life that is better in the abstract, but as long as their beliefs are unchanged, we are making them lead a life that is worse for them. As Dworkin puts it,

> If we give priority to ethical integrity, we make the merger of life and conviction a parameter of ethical success, and we stipulate that a life that never achieves that kind of integrity cannot be critically better for someone to lead than a life that does.[11]

A person might be making an error by choosing a certain life, and we might therefore want to persuade her to lead a better life, so that she can achieve ethical integrity at a higher level, but if we force her to lead what we believe to be a better life, we force her to lead a life that, for her, is worse.[12] We give her a life that is better in some ways at the expense of denying her integrity.

The priority of ethical integrity, as I employ it, does not prohibit encouraging people to make what we believe are better choices, but that we should do so with respect to their status as free individuals. We may encourage, persuade, and reward them for living a better life, but we cannot force them to lead a life that is not of their choosing. The protection of ECSO freedom does not in any way imply that people who refuse to take part in a joint project should share equally in its output, only that those who refuse to contribute to the project cannot be left in such a thoroughly bad state that they are effectively forced to contribute. This leaves great room to encourage people to make what we believe to be the right choices without violating their integrity. If we resort to force instead of persuasion, we harm mistaken dissenters as the people they are. We give them reason to feel less like a free contributor to a mutually beneficial social project and more like the forced servant of the powerful people in society.

5. Integrity, Freedom, and the Goals of the Joint Project

It is widely accepted that the government cannot force an individual to attend a church or tax her to support an organization promoting a particular conception of a good life. But if we deny the voluntarily unemployed access to a sufficient amount of resources, we put them in the position in which they must serve the goals of whichever employer comes along. Work serves wants, and in a market economy an employer can hire others to work for any goal the employer chooses. The worker serves these goals, whatever they may be. After she earns some money, she can begin to pursue her own goals. Social interaction in the market allows people to pursue many different goals, but a work obligation forces the propertyless to pursue goals they may not approve of. To someone who is willing to further those goals for that price, this is not a heavy burden, but to someone who objects to the goals she's asked to promote and who would rather have resources to work for her own goals, forced participation is a long, difficult sentence to fulfill.

To see the importance of this argument, imagine a society called Patriarchy in which the democratic ruling coalition enforces its belief that the good life requires a male breadwinner and female caregiver. It enforces that belief by forcing women into the position in which they must find and keep a husband or a face financial destitution. This might not be hard to imagine. Men have important reasons to desire a wife, but they can go on unmarried without facing the thoroughly bad alternative of propertylessness. Suppose society tried to solve any abuses that follow from the dependence of women by regulating marriage. They created a form of unemployment insurance for unmarried women provided that women remained ready, willing, and able to marry as soon as a marriage partner became available. Certainly, any such set of laws make women unfree. Women who do not share this vision of the good life would be made extremely unfree by these rules, but even women who do share this vision would be made unfree by laws that do not let them when and whether to begin pursuing their vision. As laws that threaten women who refuse marriage with destitution make women unfree in their marriage interactions, laws that threaten workers who refuse employment with destitution make workers unfree in their labor market interactions.

6. Integrity, Freedom, and the Fairness of the Joint Project

Anything as pervasive and complex as an economic system incorporates values not only about the good but also about the right. The terms of interaction reflect beliefs about what it means to be fair to other participants. Rawls argues for pluralism from the belief that reasonable people will disagree about what it means to live a good life,[13] but he hopes that reasonable people can reach an overlapping consensus about what is reasonably fair and proposes several rules for fair distribution of the benefits of social cooperation. An overlapping consensus can justify the social regulations necessary to ensure fair labor standards while still holding every individual to a mandatory participation obligation.[14] Nozick pointedly and simply responds that to say Rawls's theory of justice is reasonable is "hardly a convincing reply to anyone to whom it doesn't seem reasonable."[15] Other authors have pointed out the asymmetry of Rawls's claim. If we can expect reasonable people to disagree about the content of a good life, we might also expect reasonable people to disagree about fairness, rights, and justice.[16]

Reasonable people do seem to disagree about the fairness of an economic system. Some people believe that a person who correctly guesses which number will come up on a roulette wheel should get a large cash prize, as long as she bets on that guess beforehand. Other people believe this would be fair if the roulette wheel were not designed to give the house a small edge. Others believe all gambling is wrong. Some people believe that if two people work together they should divide whatever they produce equally or according to their effort, average product, marginal product, virtue, or need. One popular belief is that it is fair for a person to keep whatever she can get by trading with property owners. Some people believe that the terms are just if and when both sides freely agree to them.

A system that protects ECSO freedom works within the value systems of its participants who have differing beliefs about justice. It allows them to combine in any way they believe is fair, and if they do not find social cooperation fair, it allows them to live without actively supporting the system of social cooperation. They can use this leverage to negotiate a way of cooperation that is more acceptable to them, and if they don't get it, they don't have to participate. Therefore, with ECSO freedom protected, all participants participate willingly.

Without the power to refuse cooperation, an individual controls no aspects of cooperation. As Fabienne Peter argues, consent to take one job in the market does not imply consent to the market as a whole if there is no other alternative.[17] Others choose the goals, the terms, and the range of choices. The individual has as much choice as they allow her to have. Such a system can seek consensus through the political process, but the pressing political question in our world is what to do in the *absence* of true consensus. A system that asks for voluntary cooperation offers its citizens the opportunity to share its values without forcing those values on them. A system that gives every citizen unconditional control over some amount of external assets gives each citizen a sphere of control over her life and interactions. Within the sphere an individual controls, her values prevail unless she chooses to compromise to combine hers with someone else. Hopefully, people will find ways to work together that are good for both, but by not allowing society to force its values on individuals, society forces itself to find a way to make sure that all cooperation is consistent with the values of the people involved in cooperation and to respect those who do not fit in.

One could reply that some of those individuals will simply have bad values. Some people have racist, sexist, or otherwise destructive values. Is it really so important to give people with such values the power to refuse cooperation with a non-racist, nonsexist system? My first response to this question is another question: What feature of destructive value systems is most worthy of our objection? It is the use of force. One of the justifications for our system ought to be its avoidance of force. Sex again provides a good example: it cannot be just without consent, even if a person withholds consent for bad reasons. Suppose A refuses to have sex with B only because B refuses to join a hate group. No amount of objective evidence that sex is mutually beneficial or that A's refusal is badly motivated makes it right for B to force A to have sex. The minimal level of decency with which B can treat A requires him to free her from force sex and respect her autonomy over her reasons even if her reasons are bad. As a democratic society with a just economic system, there must be some level of decency that we must have for those who do not share our desire to be a part of it.

The best way to handle people with destructive value systems is not to force them to follow other values but to keep them out of positions of power where they can force their values on others. If a person's bad values lead her to go out and murder, steal, and oppress others, self-defense requires her to be stopped. But if a person's bad values—no matter how hateful and destructive—lead her to stay home and tend her own garden, self-defense does not require her to be stopped. Remember that people who refuse receive only a social minimum. They pay a price for their nonparticipation in that they will have to make do with access to fewer external assets than participants.

It is not necessarily the government's job to differentiate such a person from someone (such as a contemplative monk) who does the same thing for what we judge to be good reasons. We can try to encourage that person to adopt better values, but forcing her into a cooperative project that she despises is not the best thing for her or for social justice. A society that protects everyone's independence gives people the least possible power to impose their values on others and hence the best protection against destructive values. This strategy might not make people with destructive value systems see the light and the value of a pluralistic society, but it would make them much less dangerous should they get into a position of power.

7. Why Don't More People Feel Unfree?

If everyone who is forced by propertylessness to seek employment is unfree, many people in modern society are unfree. Why don't more people feel unfree? It would appear to be evidence against my claim that ECSO freedom captures what it means to be a free person, if so many people can be unfree in those terms without feeling unfree. I offer two replies to that argument: the type of unfreedom described here does not press on everyone, and those on whom it does press may not voice their complaints in these terms.

The lack of ECSO freedom presses significantly only on those who have undesirable options that they would refuse if only they had the power, but many people have good jobs that free them from material deprivation and that they would do even if they had the power to refuse. People in this position do not often feel the need for the power to refuse. Employment does not make a person unfree, forced or involuntary employment makes a person unfree. Cohen argues that being forced to do something does not necessarily entail doing it involuntarily.[18] For example, when I walk down the street, I have no desire to break every window I pass. I freely and voluntarily refrain from breaking windows. I know that if I were to try to break every window I pass, someone would force me to stop before I finished, but being forced to refrain from something I don't want to do anyway doesn't bother me. It's barely noticeable. My compliance is both forced and voluntary.

The unfreedom faced by people who currently have acceptable jobs is hard to envision: Am I vulnerable to losing my job in an economic downturn? Has my limited economic power reduced my leverage to demand better terms? Would the power to refuse increase my options of how I can live my life? These are not pressing day-to-day concerns for people in this group.

If everyone in society were permanently in the position in which they had no desire to refuse the available options, a basic income guarantee could exist without anyone choosing to live off it, which would be a very desirable outcome. If such an outcome is possible, the power to say no may not be essential for making everyone feel the benefits of ECSO freedom, but it is still important to protect that power. Denying people the power to say no on the grounds that we know that they will say yes is suspicious to say the least. We would be rightly suspicious of a society that had no mechanism to report rape on the grounds that men in that country did not commit rape. Even if I chose to say yes to such and such action I still have the right to control my actions, and therefore, the power to say no should still be protected. In other words, even if it were a fact that everyone would say yes given the opportunity to say no, no one has the right to put another in the position in which they must say yes. Protecting the power to say no is at worst superfluous, and eliminating that protection has enormous potential dangers against the most vulnerable. If there is any uncertainty at all, diligent protection is needed to ensure that the conditions we believe hold actually do hold and will continue to hold.

There are people who would refuse the options available if they had the power: the poor, the disadvantaged, dissenters who object to what they must do to comply with society's conditions, and those who do comply and still live in deprivation. Although the lack of ECSO freedom presses heavily on this group, they are likely to voice their complaint in other terms. Most of those who are hard pressed economically are too busy struggling to survive to think much about the issue of liberty or even to complain about their situation. People tend to accept the world around them. It's uncertain how often medieval serfs dwelt on their extreme lack of freedom rather than simply acquiescing to the inevitable, but their acquiescence did not make them free. Modern disadvantaged people have few personal targets to single out for complaint but merely an insensitive system that gives them the message that their position is their fault. When they do complain, some voice it in terms of freedom, but there are many other equally legitimate ways to voice a complaint about one's poverty.

People who live in poverty are regularly accused of laziness, and in response it might be prudent for them to direct their complaints toward working conditions and pay rather than toward the fact that they are forced to work. Independence gives a person the power to refuse a bad offer, but the hope is not that it ends there—with a large number of bad offers on the table and a large number of people refusing them. The power of independence is the power to refuse offers unless and until an acceptable offer arrives, and hopefully, if there are large numbers of refusals, offers will improve. Poor people who complain are not necessarily thinking about how they would enjoy the freedom from a mandatory work obligation but about the enjoyable terms of cooperation they could have if they could command them.

Certainly all theories of a just economic system, from right-libertarianism to socialism, hope that they will be able to build a system that is sufficiently good that everyone will contribute willingly. The goal of a society that protects ECSO freedom is the same. The difference between a society that protects ECSO freedom and one that does not is where they put the burden if that goal is not achieved. If a system that does not protect personal independence is unable to achieve this goal, it forces the disadvantaged to contribute anyway. If a society that protects independence is unable to achieve this goal, it allows the disadvantaged to refuse to contribute. The first-best argument for the power to refuse is that there are many aspects of the social project that people can reasonably disagree about; we should expect disagreement, and we should not force people into a project they disagree with.

For many of the disadvantaged, the thing they would most want is the ability to command better terms from the rest of society. This brings the discussion of ECSO freedom to its instrumental role in protecting the vulnerable.

CHAPTER 6

The Importance of Independence III: Market Vulnerability

If you lay duties upon people and give them no rights, you must pay them well.

—*Johann Wolfgang Von Goethe*[1]

I have conceded that there may be situations in which A and B have a duty to do *x* with or without consent, but this observation does not necessarily imply that giving a democratic majority the power to force individuals to do things is the best method to ensure that duties are done under just conditions. There is an important second-best reason to protect personal independence even if active duties exist. Mandatory participation is vulnerable to abuse and error, which are likely to produce unjust outcomes, because people are fallible, and no one has privileged knowledge of abstract morality. For the social project to be just, its goals, methods, and terms have to be just. Even if we completely disregard the possibility that participants' agreement has a direct bearing on whether the social project is just, the requirement to obtain each participant's agreement is an extremely powerful tool to ensure that the goals, methods, and terms of cooperation are good, fair, right, or just and not one-sided in favor of the ruling majority, property owners, or any other powerful group. Section A argues that the power to say no is useful to protect the vulnerable in a market economy. Section B argues that, to some extent, other social safeguards such as labor regulation, are deficient without it. Section C argues that independence is also a powerful tool in protecting individuals in their nonmarket interactions.

1. The Invisible Hand and Economic Independence

Michael Lewis and I have argued elsewhere for the efficiency advantages of an unconditional approach over the conditional approach.[2] I want to show here that even a perfectly working labor market does not necessarily work for the poor in the way we would want it to. Mainstream market theory is still based on Adam Smith's invisible hand theorem, which demonstrated that under certain conditions voluntary exchange benefits everyone.[3] This insight is the basis for what is now known as the first fundamental theorem of welfare economics.[4] As long as all parties involved know their own best interest, and as long as all trade is truly voluntary (perfect information and no fraud, theft, externalities, or extortion), neither side will engage in a trade that makes them worse-off. Under those assumptions, even if traders seek their own benefit, voluntary trade drives them, as if by an invisible hand, to benefit the other. The theory goes on to argue that competitive trade will exploit all possibilities to benefit both parties relative to their starting points.[5] If all markets for all conceivable commodities are characterized by "perfect competition" the economy will reach an efficient equilibrium at which it is impossible to make one person better-off without making another worse-off.[6] That is, it exploits all opportunities for gains from trade. The conditions necessary for the theorem to hold fully are seldom if ever present, but to the extent that it works at all it provides a guide to how, why, and to what extent trade is beneficial. And when it doesn't work it provides a way of understanding how markets fail.

Each party benefits from voluntary trade in the sense that they are better-off than they were with the initial distribution of property without trading, but nothing in the theory ensures they benefit in the sense of getting a fair share, what they deserve, or even a decent standard of living. If a trade begins with one party on the edge of starvation, the best the invisible hand can assure is that they are slightly better-off than that—perhaps one day away from the edge of starvation—but the invisible hand theorem does not assure how much better. Smith recognized that propertylessness and the need to get a job to survive could adversely affect workers' wages.[7] If the economy works perfectly, workers are paid their "marginal product," but they do not control their marginal product. The equilibrium wage (and therefore the marginal product) depends on a large number of impersonal market forces, one of which is workers' next best option to labor market participation. The worse the workers' next best option, the lower we can expect wages to be.

If people start with the ability to live by their own means, and the conditions of the invisible hand hold, trade ensures them something better than they could provide for themselves on their own. If we takeaway individuals' ability to provide for themselves and put them in the position where they must sell their labor to survive, trade does not assure that they will be even as well off as they would have done on their own. A "free" market without free workers—even under theoretically perfect competition—does not assure that they will finish better than they could have done on their own or that they will have decent wages, decent working conditions, decent housing, or a decent life. Workers who lack an exit option are inherently vulnerable.

Respect for ECSO freedom provides, in Robert Goodin's terms, the basic safeguard against market vulnerability, which is, in short, invulnerability through self-reliance.[8] The power to say no is not a perfect protection against market vulnerability. There could be a system in which an advantaged group left others with just enough to give them economic independence but seized control of everything else. The only cooperative opportunities they offer to the disadvantaged group are the worst forms of social participation in the sense of working conditions, pay, and hierarchical position. However, the power to refuse can be an important tool even in these circumstances. If the disadvantaged find the dominant group's project to be too unfair or not enough in their interests, they can refuse it. They won't live as well as they would in a fairer society, but they will live decently without contributing to the system that is being unfair to them, and the more people who refuse participation under such circumstance, the more upward pressure they put on wages and working conditions.

2. Regulation as a Substitute for Independence

An egalitarian who believes in a mutual obligation to contribute to a joint project might recognize the labor market benefits to disadvantaged individuals of having an exit option but yet seek another policy to achieve the labor market benefits without allowing people to avoid their social responsibility to work. I conceded above that a conditional welfare state might be able to eliminate poverty while maintaining a mandatory-participation economy with the following strategy. The government would have to separate those who can and cannot work; provide conditional benefits for those who can't work; and use market regulation, subsidies, or direct job creation for those who can work. All welfare states across the industrialized world use the conditional model, although they vary greatly in generosity and strictness. The ubiquity of the conditional welfare state indicates a popular desire to combine greater labor market fairness with mandatory participation.

Many liberal-egalitarians favor some version of this approach. Stuart White, for example, makes a thorough and explicit argument for a potentially enforceable duty to contribute to a mutually beneficial social project as long as the community provides a sufficient range of satisfying opportunities and a fair share of the social product.[9] In this context, we would like to reach an outcome in which three conditions are satisfied: people do their duties (*x*); people are not forced to do things that aren't their duties (*y*); and side constraints are met (*z*). In a first-best world, some infallible authority would ensure conditions *x*, *y*, and *z* are met, and everyone would comply without the need for force. In a second-best world, society must find the institutional arrangement most likely to approximate justice in *x*, *y*, and *z*. Under mandatory participation, a democratic government oversees the market to separate duties (*x*) from non-duties (*y*), to decide when side constraints (*z*) are satisfied, and enforces participation. The ruling coalition assumes power, at least over propertyless individuals, in all three areas. Under voluntary participation, after the ruling coalition sets rules determining *x*, *y*, and *z*, individuals respond by deciding whether they will participate under that set of rules. The ruling coalition may respond to people's choices by changing the rules. Therefore, *x*, *y*, and *z* are partly determined by a bargaining or a market process between those who have power over the social project (government and property owners) and individuals who have power over their own participation. Decision makers either find a way to elicit voluntary participation or tolerate refusal.

This strategy can be thought of as one to minimize the maximum possible injustice in a perfect world. Unjustly forced labor must count among the worst possible injustices—far worse than the threat that someone might get more than their fair share. We can eliminate the possibility of unjustly forced labor by eliminating all directly and indirectly forced labor. If we want to minimize the maximum possible injustice, and we recognized that the most vulnerable, the most disadvantaged people have been subject to the most severe injustices throughout history, we should take special care to minimize injustices against this group by not demanding anything from them. We restrain ourselves from taking advantage of vulnerable people by creating a basic structure in which support for the disadvantaged is unconditional.

This section argues that there is a significant trade-off between the goals of maintaining a mandatory-participation economy and improving the lives and living standards of disadvantaged individuals. The mandatory-participation economy leaves workers vulnerable both to market failure and government failure, so much so that a voluntary-participation economy might lead to better overall fulfillment of conditions *x*, *y*, and *z* than a mandatory-participation economy. Cession of the power to say no to the least powerful people in society is an extremely valuable tool to ensure better outcomes than granting the democratic majority full authority in all three areas.

Although market forces generally favor workers with the power to refuse employment, they can actually frustrate efforts to boost incomes of workers who cannot.[10] If redistributive policy employs lump sum grants, such as basic income, recipients benefit fully; that is, by the amount of the grant,[11] and the exit option can give workers additional power to command higher wages in the private market.[12] However, if redistribution is conditional on work, it gives employers an incentive to reduce private sector wages, partially counteracting the effort to increase the welfare of the disadvantaged.[13]

Government regulation of wages and working conditions demonstrates de facto recognition that workers are unfree to refuse exploitative jobs, but it is often an inadequate solution. The regulating authority can say that, in its opinion, there is no longer a need to refuse, but once we leave the realm of a voluntary agreement between parties who all have the power to refuse, we need more than an opinion; we need a strong assurance that force is being used to promote justice. The ruling coalition might fail to get *x*, *y*, and *z* right because it is merely a majority-sized group of fallible people, who might not have adequate concern for or the ability to protect the welfare of dissenters and the disadvantaged. To reach a desirable outcome without the consent of the participants, the regulating authority has to consider all of the 17 reasons a person might object to participation, decide which ones are legitimate and which aren't in all conceivable cases, and then find a way to eliminate all of the conditions that could give workers legitimate reasons to refuse. It is a difficult job. The potential for government error is great, and the burden on the disadvantaged will be substantial if the government fails. Experience shows that disadvantaged individuals have reasons to be wary of government programs bearing conditional benefits.[14] When the fully fair solution is not possible (because of imperfect information or market failure), the ruling coalition has to determine how closely they need to approximate it. The ruling coalition must rule on all of these issues with the confidence that they are not merely stating the ruling coalition's opinion about justice, but they are doing what is really just.

Because any ruling coalition is a fallible group of people in a complicated, hard-to-understand world, governments should seek mechanisms that empower individuals and/or institutions in ways that are likely to promote fair, just, desirable, and reasonable outcomes. The separation of powers between the legislature, the executive, and the judiciary is one such strategy.[15]

The power to say no is the ultimate separation of powers—the ultimate check in government—because it is the only power that can be effective at the individual level and that isn't dominated by some other power. The powers to speak, vote, organize unions, and so on are important powers to protect dissenters and the disadvantaged, but they are not powers that are effective at the individual level. Trade unions quite obviously get their power when working collectively. The right to vote can be exercised individually, but it only becomes effective when many people vote the same way. The power to speak can be exercised individually but it is only effective in terms of economic outcomes if other people change their behavior based on the individual's speech.

Consider the economic powers legally held by major groups in the market. The government has the power to tax, regulate, and redistribute property rights. Property owners have the power to decide whether and in what industry they will invest.[16] Propertyless individuals have the power to decide which job to take but not the power to decide *whether* to take a job.[17] The power to decide which job to take can be exercised individually and it can have positive effects, but it is dominated by governments' and investors' powers. If some group can effectively create a list of available jobs, the power to choose any particular job from that list is entirely dominated by the power to make up the list.

If every individual holds the power to say no, whatever other powers everyone else controls, every individual has one very powerful decision to make. This tool is valuable on its own, and it is valuable when used in concert with others whether or not those who refuse coordinate their decisions with each other. It might lead to more acceptable labor market conditions and even if it doesn't it frees individuals from being forced to accept unacceptable conditions.

Essentially, this argument applies a well-known game theory strategy to the labor market as a whole. Game theorists use the example of two people who have to decide how to divide a cake to examine the problem of finding an incentive-compatible strategy to ensure fair division.[18] The "cut-and-choose" rule has proven to be a robust and incentive-compatible solution. The first player is given the power to cut the cake and the second is given the power to choose which half of the cake she wants. The first player has the incentive to cut the cake as evenly as possible, because if one piece is obviously better than the other, the second player will have an incentive to choose the better piece.

The cut-and-choose strategy works because each participant controls something the other does not. It works almost perfectly for the simple problem of dividing a cake, because the two powers are equally valuable: the power to cut the cake is just as valuable as the power to choose the first slice. Therefore, each player has the incentive to act in a way that leads to equal division. The economy is too complex to give every player completely equal powers, and the labor market is far more complex and deals with many more issues at once than the simple cake division problem. Thus, we shouldn't expect to find any rule that works as well as cut-and-choose. But we can keep one essential characteristic of the cut-and-choose rule: ensuring that every player in the market controls something no one else does.

A society that respects and protects personal independence concedes some power to individuals on both sides of every labor market transaction. It gives propertyless individuals the power to communicate that the goals, conditions, or pay of any class of jobs are unacceptable. Dissenters and the disadvantaged need this power because they know things about their situations that market regulators might not know; they see their situation in a way that the ruling coalition might fail to give sufficient consideration. A voluntary-participation economy gives every individual small but direct influence over social cooperation. It makes it easier for disadvantaged people to organize and increases their influence even if they fail to organize.

The enormous practical problem for egalitarians who are committed to mandatory participation is that a work obligation sides with the powerful by default in any dispute—whether the powerful group is a democratic majority or a property owning class. This default distribution of power continually works against efforts to help the disadvantaged. The power to say no gives dissenters and the disadvantaged the most effective and least destructive way to voice their discontent. One lone dropout is one voice for a better deal. A large number of dropouts is a powerful statement that something about the system is not working for everyone and a powerful incentive for the government and industry to find out how to make it in the interest of the dropouts to join up. If others don't want to change, dissenters can use the resources at their disposal to combine in ways that are not endorsed by the rest of society. The power to refuse won't obviate the need for all labor market regulation, but gives workers a form of control of their lives than they cannot enjoy without it.

As I understand it, even in the context of a mandatory-participation economy, liberal-egalitarianism provides three relevant checks to protect the vulnerable from insensitive or abusive authority. First, the authority is subject to democratic oversight. Unanimous agreement is neither likely to exist as a collection of beliefs nor free from manipulation as a decision rule, but any less-than-unanimous decision-making rule involves one group forcing its decisions on another group. Democracy is centrally important to good government, but majoritarianism can't always be counted on to protect dissenters and the disadvantaged. Dissenters (by definition) and the disadvantaged (very likely) have little influence in the political process. The majority might lack sufficient empathy for or knowledge of disadvantaged and dissenting individuals, and therefore, they might fail to choose goals, methods, and terms of the social project that are truly good, just, or fair to everyone.

Second, dissenters can use collective action to voice complaints. This check is extremely valuable, but does not disperse power down to the individual level. It is not necessarily accessible to the least advantaged people even if it is accessible to people with less-than-average advantages. There may be conflicts within the less advantaged group, and the agreement of some does not imply the agreement of all.

Third, liberal-egalitarian principles ask the majority to use empathy aided by devices such as the original position.[19] This check can be largely empty, if it does not involve the responsibility to cede power to them. Most people do not think of themselves as unjust. I don't believe many Russian Stalinists or czarist aristocrats thought of themselves as unjust in the burdensome duties they forced onto the vulnerable people in their societies. People in power are hardly constrained by a rule saying that they may force dissenters to serve their interests only if they feel justified.

Perhaps devices such as the original position ought to tell us the following: if we entered society expecting to be the least advantaged individual, receiving less than our fair share would not be our greatest fear. More likely our greatest fear would be that others would take power over our lives; We would want—more than anything else—the power to refuse the commands of the more advantaged. Of course, we should all care about each other and most especially the needy, but one of the most valuable things we can do for the needy is to stop forcing them to do things for us. A voluntary-participation economy can make use of the three checks to protect the vulnerable available under liberal-egalitarianism and an additional check that is potentially far more valuable: each individual has the power to choose not to participate.

Mandatory participation supporters might argue that whatever the advantages of voluntary participation, it allows people to avoid duties, leaving *x* unsatisfied. Allowing individuals to decide whether to participate seems to invite them to treat the fulfillment of a duty as an opportunity for selfishness. If genuine duties exist, they might argue, a good government must enforce them. But this does not necessarily follow. If we are to consider the possibility that dissenting individuals will use the power available to them selfishly, we must also consider the possibility that the ruling majority (or whoever has the power to make the rules) will use their power selfishly. We cannot assume that the social project has any greater moral weight than that it benefits the people who successfully influence its decisions.

Returning to the example from chapter 2, the recognition of moral duties did not convince Garrison Frazier to support forced service. General Sherman asked how best to enlist freedmen in the military. Although the outcome of the war was still uncertain, and a northern victory was essential to securing a permanent end to slavery, Frazier answered, "I think, sir, that all compulsory operations should be put a stop to. The ministers would talk to them, and the young men would enlist."[20] Frazier clearly recognizes that there is a moral duty, but he has more confidence in individuals' ability to live up to their duties voluntarily than in the majority's ability to impose them justly.

If either side is capable of error, there are four reasons why a voluntary-participation economy might obtain as good or better compliance with *x*, *y*, and *z*. First, even if mandatory participation could assure compliance with *x*, the government authority might force less favored people to do things that aren't duties but are just as much or more demanding. Considering the great number of frivolous goods and services produced in modern economies, a blanket responsibility to work must force people to do things that aren't actually duties.

Second, mandatory participation has its own free-rider problem. The government might give favored people credit for doing things that aren't duties, while forcing less favored people to do the more demanding, actual duties. For example, one person might be allowed to fulfill a duty to "work" by being a board member of a tobacco company or a university professor even if these jobs require very little effort and have questionable social value. Another person might only be able to fulfill their duty to "work" by performing one of many unpleasant, demanding jobs in manual labor.

Third, force isn't the only way to get people to do things. Other methods exist, such as positive rewards. A person living at the minimum necessary to secure independence may still have far less than participants in the social project. If everyone has a price, and rewards are sufficient, free people will do *x* out of their own self-interest.[21] The act of refusal communicates an objection to the terms of cooperation, indicating that the rewards for participation are not enough to be worth the effort. Individuals might selfishly demand too much, but people who control resources might also selfishly offer too little. If the social project produced nothing but public goods, it would generate no private goods with which to give private rewards for contribution and it would be unreasonable for someone with a duty to contribute to insist on a private reward. But that's not the way our economy works. Most of it is devoted to the production of private goods. If the social project is mutually beneficial, and devoted largely to the production of private goods, it must be possible to give people private rewards for contributions that are much greater than the level needed to secure personal independence. Mandatory participation might be motivated less by the fear that individuals will refuse participation than by unwillingness to pay them enough to elicit voluntary participation. If so, it might reflect the ruling coalition's failure to comply with *z*.

Fourth, comparing the worst-case scenarios of the two institutional arrangements greatly favors voluntary participation. In a voluntary-participation economy, no one is forced to do anything actively, and so there seems to be little possibility of violating *y*, but there are risks to *x* and *z*. Dissenters might not do their duties (violating *x*) or they will demand overgenerous rewards for doing them (violating *z*). However, presumably everyone receives similar rewards for similar duties, implying that overgenerousness won't cause a horizontal distributional problem: they will be no more highly rewarded than anyone else doing similar work. If the demand for overgenerous reward causes a distribution problem, it will be a vertical distribution problem. That is, the error will be of over-rewarding the less advantaged relative to the more advantaged—the type of problem that ought not to be a major concern for egalitarians.

Voluntary participation does not eliminate the risk that the ruling coalition will be unjust to dissenters. They might create a joint project that is unfair to dissenters in its goals, methods, or terms. However, if dissenters decide it is not worth participating in the project because of these problems, at least they can live at a decent minimum and they can interact with whomever they wish. If they choose to participate, the system must be—in their individual judgment—sufficiently fair and desirable to warrant participation. Only a voluntary-participation economy ensures this basic level of fairness for all participants.

A mandatory-participation economy protects more diligently against the risk that dissenters will be unfair to the ruling majority than against other possible injustices. It is unclear why—of all the ways in which society could be unjust—this one deserves the most attention. By focusing on this risk, a mandatory participation economy risks forcing its least-rewarded members to live in poverty, to fear destitution, to perform actions they have no duty to perform, to suffer because side constraints about fairness and justice are violated, or to make up for the free riding of more highly rewarded people who are given credit for doing things that are not actual duties. In short, voluntary participation protects the disadvantaged from the powerful; mandatory participation protects the powerful from the disadvantaged. If so, egalitarians should be strongly in favor of voluntary participation.

The power to force people to do things is probably the most dangerous power one group can hold over another. The worst forms of oppression in history could not have coexisted with ECSO freedom. Ancient emperors, medieval lords, early modern slave owners, and modern dictators took power, killed people, forced others to do things, or made them live in horrible conditions. These kinds of injustice are far more striking than the prospect of someone sitting out of a just project. Even the injustice of taking more than one's fair share is not very striking compared to forced labor. Liberal-egalitarians have sought to manage forced labor more equitably and to harness it for the common good, when they should seek to eliminate it.

To conclude, even if people have an obligation to contribute to a just system of social cooperation, giving individuals the power to say no to working conditions they find unacceptable might be a better method to create a just system of social cooperation than giving a democratic majority the powers both to determine the conditions of fair cooperation and to enforce participation. Under mandatory participation, the government can give individuals choices of what work to do, but it cannot give them a check over the list of available jobs or working conditions. The ruling coalition must be prepared to speak for justice (rather than merely for majority opinion) on every issue that might give individuals a reasonable cause for objection.

Of course, the ruling coalition has to speak for justice in extreme cases such as the formation of criminal law, but if it is aware of its limitations, it should seek to avoid speaking for justice when it is not necessary. Speaking for justice in the realm of the entire economy is an enormous moral and practical responsibility that the ruling coalition would not need to take on if they were willing to say (as the prologue suggests), *our system of social cooperation is as fair and mutually beneficial as we know how to make it, but it is up to you to decide whether it is fair and beneficial enough to earn your participation.*

3. The Value of Independence Outside the Market

Although this chapter so far has focused on the labor market, the power to say no is also important for nonmarket interaction and as a safeguard for most other freedoms. For example, independence can protect the religious freedom of a homeless person who may be forced to choose between going hungry and sitting through a religious speech at a soup kitchen. It can protect the freedom of speech of a person who is afraid of losing her job for making controversial remarks. Importantly, it can help fight problems related to dependency in marriage and to mental and physical health.

According to Carole Pateman, feminists have argued for centuries that mainstream political theory has treated personal interaction differently than public interaction, as if the family was a separate sphere where the rules of justice do not apply.[22] I have hopefully avoided that pitfall here, arguing that no contract can override an individual's status as a free person. Marriage, like employment, is supposed to be a mutually beneficial arrangement in which two people decide to cooperate toward goals that are good for both of them. We like to think of marriage as a perfectly cooperative arrangement in which people fully put their interests together, but it is an imperfect institution, which, like employment, involves potential conflicts of interest. It involves toil, effort, sacrifice, and distribution of benefits. If one partner is financially dependent on the other, the financially powerful partner can use that power to make marriage an unequal partnership.[23]

People can escape propertylessness not only by getting a job but also by marrying someone who is willing and able to support them. As long as people are able and free enough from care responsibilities to hold jobs, they are not any more dependent on marriage than employment. However, many couples still follow the convention in which men specialize in making money and women specialize in caring for children.[24] Such specialization can cause women to develop financial dependence on men. Divorce laws protect women to some extent but often not enough, and women are sometimes unable to hold their former husbands to their responsibilities.[25] Women who do leave their husbands often face poverty and dependence on what can be a tyrannical conditional system of income support for single mothers.[26] Cases in which women suffered cruelty of husbands for years because of financial dependence are not unusual. This problem follows largely from an asymmetry in the two parties' ability to withdraw from the relationship;[27] women might want to be cruel to men, but men tend to have much more power to walk away than women,[28] especially women with children. We can imagine cases without asymmetry in the ability to withdraw (such as in marriage without the possibility of divorce) in which other asymmetrical powers (such as physical strength, control of property, or legal rights[29]) causes one party to have power in the marriage. However, the problem here still involves the lack of the power to say no, even if that power is not the one that is asymmetrical. The protection of ECSO freedom, by providing women with the resources they need to maintain their independence (in case they ever need it) would make them much more able to walk away from such a situation.

Anyone who is unfree to refuse is vulnerable to unfair or abusive treatment in market and nonmarket relationships. The protection of ECSO freedom helps individuals protect themselves from unfairness in many areas because it gives them the power to walk away from any unjust arrangement. This alone will not make the sexes equal, but it will create a baseline protection against the worst abuses.

Conditional benefits would seem to be ideal for people who are unable to work because of a mental or physical disability. Hopefully, a conditional welfare system would have more money available to meet the needs of people with disabilities. However, it does not always work out as well in practice largely because of the difficulty in determining who can work and what kind of support is best for those who cannot. Consider Alison who is diagnosable with schizophrenia but fears doctors and has not sought treatment. She has been unable to hold a job for the last two years and has lived on the streets for 18 months. She probably will continue being homeless until her situation deteriorates to the point at which someone forces her into the mental health system. Unconditional access to the resources she needs to maintain a home and a decent diet will not cure her mental disability, but it would be a much more humane way to treat a person who fears the mental health system.

Denis has a developmental mental disability that gives him lower intelligence than other people. His intelligence level is not quite low enough to qualify for government benefits, but it is low enough so that he can't qualify for anything but minimum-wage work. He is 43 years old and has been a dishwasher in a restaurant for 24 years. Perhaps his job gives him a sense of satisfaction or contribution. Perhaps it is a source of stress and inspires feelings of inadequacy. In either case it seems inhumane to take advantage of his condition to force him to do low paid, unpleasant labor that the rest of us benefit from.

I could give other examples of people with mental or physical attributes that make it difficult for them to thrive either in the paid labor market or on public assistance, but the point is simply that only a system of unconditional support can ensure that no one lacks for the basic needs because of some physical or mental disability.

4. Conclusion

Most of us are aware that economic destitution can lead people to do things that they would not normally do: to prostitute themselves, to sell their internal organs, to accept cruelty from a marriage partner or an employer, to beg, to eat out of a garbage can, to send their children to work in sweatshops, to sell themselves into servitude, and to do many other degrading things. Some people will do these things even if they are not forced by desperation, but almost anyone will do some of these things if they are desperate enough. We can understand from this observation that we need to treat the symptom, for example, by regulating labor markets and providing unemployment insurance, but treating the symptom is not enough, we need to treat the cause. We need to recognize that propertylessness is a state of unfreedom, and abuse and unfairness are some of its consequences. Propertylessness is not the only source of vulnerability in the labor market, but it is not enough to try to be more humane while we intentionally use propertylessness as a work incentive.

CHAPTER 7

What Good Is a Theory of Freedom That Allows Forced Labor? Independence and Modern Theories of Freedom

Take this job and shove it. I ain't workin' here no more.

—*David Allen Coe*[1]

The observation that propertylessness effectively forces individuals to accept employment is not new. What is most new in this book is the central role this observation takes in a theory of status freedom. This chapter compares the theory of status freedom outlined in this book with the modern literature on freedom. It argues that recent literature on freedom has paid insufficient attention to status freedom[2] and that a concern for status freedom as ECSO freedom or independence would make theories of freedom more plausible. The following chapter (chapter 8) discusses independence in the context of modern liberal-egalitarian theories of justice.

Section 1 briefly recounts similar observations about the effective unfreedom of workers that have been made in modern academic literature. Section 2 discusses Nozick's right-libertarian account of freedom. Section 3 compares Berlin's negative freedom to Raz's theory of status freedom as autonomy, arguing that ECSO freedom combines the most important parts of both conceptions of freedom. Section 4 considers the relationship between independence and Pettit's republican non-domination, arguing that there is some overlap and that independence better captures what it means to be a free person. Section 5 discusses the relationship between indepentarianism and sufficientarianism. Section 6 compares the indepentarian theory of ECSO freedom to real libertarianism and left-libertarianism.

1. Effective Freedom in the History of Political Thought

I will call the connection between free access to resources and freedom from forced labor the problem of effective (un)freedom. It involves at least two observations: that people who have no access to the resources they need to survive are unfree to refuse service to those who control resources and that this situation is the result of coercive interference. Political theorists have made one or both of these observations for centuries at least,[3] and our distant ancestors—who lived before the institution of private landownership was instituted—understood it well.

Ethnographic studies of hunter-gatherer bands in all climates and terrains show strong respect for individual independence. Hunter-gatherer bands typically had no leaders, no fixed rules, no forced service, and direct access to resources. If an individual managed to kill a large game and wanted to camp with the band, they had to share, but they had no responsibility to go out and hunt if they didn't want to. Band members had no responsibility to remain with the band or to provide for it. If they wanted to go forage for themselves, join another band, or start one of their own, other hunter-gatherers would respect their freedom to do so. Some anthropologists claim that hunter-gatherers could go through their entire adult lives without ever hearing an order, even during combat with other bands. Yet, they were able to maintain caring, mutually supportive communities on a volunteer basis.[4] The simplest known farming communities, loosely organized as autonomous villages, also assured individuals direct and unconditional access to the land.[5] One of the most prominent theories of state formation is circumscription theory in which states assert control over individuals only once they assert control over the land, making individuals unable to make their living on their own.[6]

I have been talking about metaphorical debt in which a human being with needs effectively owes her labor to someone from the group that dominates the resources capable of meeting her needs, but David Graeber describes how governments from ancient times to the twentieth century have used literal debt to get indigenous people off the land and into wage work. They simply declare that the indigenous people owe taxes that can be paid only in money obtained usually by accepting wage work and sometimes by relinquishing one's claim to take subsistence from the land.[7]

In 1690, John Locke nearly recognized the possibility that one person's control of resources can make another person less free when he wrote that appropriation is valid "at least where there is enough, and as good left in common for others."[8] However, he seemed to believe that access to common resources can be sufficiently replaced by employment opportunities, initiating a long line of thought asking people to ignore the loss of freedom created by effectively forced labor. That line continues to this day in the political theory of both Left and Right.

Jean-Jacques Rousseau, like most other state-of-nature theorists, made many striking errors in his descriptions of how our distant ancestors lived, but what is perhaps more striking about Rousseau is what he got right. He mistakenly believed that our foraging ancestors actually lived on their own rather than in groups, but he correctly surmised that they were able to forage on their own, and he correctly recognized the importance of the loss of the ability to support oneself. He wrote, in 1754, "It is impossible to make any man a slave, unless he be first reduced to a situation in which he cannot do without the help of others."[9] In 1776, Adam Smith recognized that the need for a job disadvantages workers in bargaining for wages, but he did not connect this observation to indirect force.[10]

Thomas Paine made one of the strongest and most famous early statements of the connection between property and poverty in his 1797 pamphlet "Agrarian Justice." He argues that poverty is forced onto individuals by the creation of property rights in land for some without compensation to the propertyless, writing, "The life of an Indian is a continual holiday, compared with the poor of Europe; and, on the other hand it appears to be abject when compared to the rich." Paine compared the denial of access to land with the denial of air to breathe. He argues for compensation sufficient to allow individuals to buy a small amount of land and livestock.[11] Thomas Jefferson largely concurred with Paine's analysis in a letter written that same year.[12]

The problem of effective unfreedom was widely discussed in the nineteenth century, sometimes under the name of "wage slavery," by socialists, communists, anarchists, early trade unionists, and ironically, proponents of chattel slavery.[13] Marx and Engels description of the proletarian condition clearly recognizes that workers are denied direct access to the means of production and thereby forced to sell their labor to members of the ownership class.[14] They recognized that this condition did not exist in human societies before the landownership was first instituted.

Late nineteenth-century predecessors of left-libertarianism, such as Herbert Spencer and Henry George, made much of the observation of effective unfreedom. Spencer made a particularly apt description, writing,

> [I]t is manifest that no one, or part of them, may use the earth in such a way as to prevent the rest from similarly using it; seeing that to do this is to assume greater freedom than the rest.... Supposing the entire habitable globe to be so enclosed, it follows that if the landowners have a valid right to its surface, all who are not landowners, have no right at all to its surface. Hence, such can exist on the earth by sufferance only. They are all trespassers. Save by the permission of the lords of the soil, they can have no room for the soles of their feet. Nay, should the others think fit to deny them a resting-place, these landless men might equitably be expelled from the earth altogether. If, then, the assumption that land can be held as property, involves that the whole globe may become the private domain of a part of its inhabitants; and if, by consequence, the rest of its inhabitants can then exercise their faculties—can then exist even—only by consent of the landowners; it is manifest, that an exclusive possession of the soil necessitates an infringement of the law of equal freedom.... Until we can demonstrate that men born after a certain date are doomed to slavery, we must consider that no such allotment is permissible.[15]

Spencer ignored this observation in later writing, but George made it the centerpiece of his critique of modern society, calling for land rent to be paid in compensation to the propertyless.[16]

Robert Hale, an early twentieth-century legal theorist, clearly connected both the observations of effective unfreedom. According to him, if the law designates other people as owners of anything with which an individual might secure her own diet, those laws coerce her to offer whatever services she can to someone with property.[17]

Many contemporary political theorists have made one or both of the observations of effective unfreedom. Jeremy Waldron argues that the poor and propertyless are not merely needy, but unfree in the most liberal, negative sense, arguing that they are capable of building their own shelter, but they are barred from doing so by property law, but he does not connect this kind of unfreedom with effectively forced employment.[18] Amartya Sen focuses much of his attention to the problem that people can be so desperate that they are effectively forced to do things they otherwise would not, but he does not discuss the possibility of freeing individuals from effectively forced labor, preferring instead to focus on how to secure—through trade or home production—the functionings necessary to secure a decent life.[19]

Many modern political theorists, including Brian Barry, G. A. Cohen, Serena Olsaretti, Michael Otsuka, Fabienne Peter, Andrew Levine, Hillel Steiner, Almaz Zelleke, and others, have made observations supporting either one or both observations of effective unfreedom.[20] Levine and Peter both stress that individuals in a market economy choose among the set of available jobs without a real option to refuse the entire set.[21] Noam Chomsky connects this kind of observation with extreme unfreedom, writing, "As long as individuals are compelled to rent themselves on the market to those who are willing to hire them, as long as their role in production is simply that of ancillary tools, then there are striking elements of coercion and oppression that make talk of democracy very limited."[22] Left-libertarians make many diverse connections between freedom and access to natural resources.[23]

With the large number of political theorists who have recognized this problem, it is surprising that the issue is not more central to the modern debate about freedom. Some property rights advocates feel free to ignore the issue entirely. Tibor Machan, for example, writes as if it were natural for one group of people to subordinate themselves to another: "The best solution to lacking what one needs is to go to work and produce what will alleviate it. If one hasn't got a job, one is supposed to find one in the market place."[24] Extreme property rights advocates are not the only ones who ignore these issues. The rest of this chapter discusses several prominent contemporary political theories to show how they could be strengthened by attention to independence.

2. Freedom as Formal but Ineffective Self-Ownership

Many property rights advocates, including most prominently Robert Nozick, promote liberty as formal (or nominal) self-ownership with little concern for effective self-ownership of any kind. This section first shows how nominal self-ownership is rendered ineffective in natural property rights theory, and then discusses whether nominal self-ownership plus some other condition (other than independence) can make it a reasonable conception of status freedom.

A. Ineffective Self-Ownership in Natural Property Rights Theory

Nozick connects freedom not only with self-ownership but also with the ownership of property, if one happens to own property. To be free is to be free from coercion that in any way interferes with the exercise of one's property rights or one's formal self-ownership rights. Nozick's ideal government recognizes property rights to external assets via an entitlement theory of a natural private property rights, existing prior to, regardless of, and/or with greater moral authority than government. Three principles supposedly exhaust justice in holdings of property: original acquisition (Lockean appropriation), transfer (voluntary gift or trade), and rectification (left unspecified). The state should make the fewest laws formally restraining what individuals can do within the set of entitlements they hold in accordance with these principles, but they should not question the effect that entitlements have on the freedom of the unentitled. He claims that the legitimate concern of social justice is not with the end-state pattern in the distribution of property but with whether the actions by which the distribution came about were just. He uses this claim to argue that redistribution of holdings attained according to his principles of entitlement is impermissible.[25]

Onora O'Neill criticizes Nozick for not deriving his entitlement theory soundly from the premise of individual liberty he purports to defend.[26] This section argues that his system of entitlements effectively denies meaningful self-ownership to individuals, and therefore, he fails to derive entitlements from individual liberty; he puts entitlement rights *above* the individual freedom his rhetoric celebrates.

The closest Nozick comes to considering the unfreedom of the propertyless is in his effort to fill out the principle of appropriation with a Lockean proviso. He discusses how one person's appropriation interferes with another person's liberty to use collective resources for subsistence. He concedes that appropriation interferes with this liberty, but argues that compensation is due only to those to whom "the process of civilization was a *net loss*."[27] He cites a number of benefits of the market economy[28] and asserts that they are enough so that no compensation is due.[29] Nozick does not delve into the question of what to do if property rights do not satisfy the proviso. Even on the surface, the assertion that the proviso is fulfilled is not obviously true. Are we sure that all people in the entire global economy (even the homeless in New York and the sweatshop workers in Indonesia) lead happier, more fulfilling lives than all the remaining hunter-gathers in Borneo or Brazil? This is a strange assumption in a nation in which homeless people die of exposure every winter because they are prevented from building shelters and lighting fires, because doing so is supposedly a violation of other people's property rights. Are we sure that this assertion is true in all possible market economies? Did every Victorian industrial worker lead a better life than the virtually toil-free

Polynesians of the same era? Anthropological evidence comparing the lives of hunter-gatherers and subsistence farmers to people in modern industrial societies clearly contradicts Nozick's claim. We can probably say that the *average* person is better-off in modern society, but many in the bottom tier of modern society, in both industrialized and industrializing countries, are clearly worse-off than the hunter-gatherers who survived into modern times.[30]

Nozick's end-state, standard-of-living specification of the proviso also represents a significant contradiction in his theory. Although he asserts that justice does not depend on end-state distribution of property,[31] and he states that his theory does not rely on end-state principles,[32] he justifies the interference involved with appropriation on the basis that it improves the end-state distribution of property.

More important than the self-contradiction or the questionable empirical claim, Nozick's end-state standard-of-living specification of the proviso is out of place in an argument that is supposed to be based on freedom from interference. The question of whether the propertyless are free from interference cannot be reduced to an empirical question of whether the market economy increases the standard of living of workers over what they could each produce individually with access to common property. He states that individuals have rights that no one else may violate; neither individuals nor the state may use coercion to force some citizens to aid others or even for their own good.[33] I will show that Nozick's theory of appropriation sanctions the use of coercion to violate the right (which he admits exists): the right to be free from interference while one uses natural resources. This coercion forces one person to aid another. And Nozick attempts to justify it by saying that it is for their own good. Examine Nozickian appropriation in four steps:

Step 1: State of nature (everyone has the liberty to take subsistence from the land).
Step 2: Appropriation divides people into propertied and propertyless (only the propertied have the right to take subsistence or anything else from land).
Step 3: Destitution forces the propertyless to perform services for the propertied (i.e., they seek employment).
Step 4: The propertyless receive payment for their services (supposedly securing their subsistence and a higher standard of living than in step 1).

As I've said, in contradiction of all Nozick says about favoring process over end state, he compares the desirability of the end state in step 4 to the desirability of the initial state in step 1, declares it better for everyone and that the goodness of the outcome in step 4 justifies the coercive process that brought society from step 1 to step 4. This process involves two incidents of coercion, one direct and one indirect. In step 2, property is appropriated but the propertyless have not yet taken jobs. Through coercion, the propertyless have lost the liberty to use natural resources to secure their subsistence. Appropriators use direct force to gain control of resources. In step 3, the propertyless perform services for the propertied because they have no other means of survival. This action is the reverse of what one would expect from Nozick's appealing idea of a principle of rectification. Because the propertyless lost liberties in step 2, any reasonable specification of the rectification principle would ensure that the direction of obligation runs from the propertied to the propertyless. Instead, the legal system directs the obligation in the reverse order. The propertyless must provide services for the propertied as if they were born in debt to the people who control the earth's resources. Thus, the second, indirect coercion gives the propertied control of the labor services of the propertyless, who are legally prohibited from working for themselves. They must work for the propertyless. Finally, in step 4, the payment the propertyless receive for their labor somehow doubles as rectification for all incidents of interference that happened along the way.

From a similar observation Cohen asks, "How is libertarian capitalism libertarian if it erodes the liberty of a large class of people?"[34] This process is the same as one typically decried by right-libertarians. For example:

Step 1: Bob has a dollar.
Step 2: Government takes the dollar to build an opera house.
Step 3: Bob buys a ticket to the opera.
Step 4: Bob enjoys opera and is happier than he was at the start.

From the entitlement theory of justice, the desirability of the end-state distribution in step 4 relative to step 1 is no justification at all for the coercive steps that were required to get there. There is clearly an inconsistent application of coercion in Nozick's theory of entitlement. If the assertion that Bob's enjoyment of opera is not a justification for taking away his liberty to spend a dollar as he wishes so that the government can use that dollar to provide him with an opera, the assertion that industrial workers have a higher standard of living than people in a "state of nature" is not a justification for taking away the liberties they have in the state of nature.[35]

The relevant question is not about standards of living but an individual's status as a free person. Nozick compensates individuals for their lost liberties only by providing the opportunity to become the forced servants of the property-owning class. If a trader goes to a continent where people live in a state of nature, captures a person, brings her to America, and makes her a slave, no after-work, post-trade, and end-state standard of living will make the slave a free person, or make her service a free choice, or justify the trader's actions. Loss of freedom can only be fully compensated by the restoration of freedom.

People with access to a sufficient amount of resources have status freedom in the sense of ECSO freedom. They might not be free from work as toil, but they are free from work as labor in the sense of accepting a subordinate position to employers[36] who control access to property. Human beings ought to be free; no end-state principle, no pattern of distribution, and no post-trade standard of living can justify taking their freedom away. Slaves with luxuries are still slaves even if they have more luxuries than when they were free. With the possible exception of strong duties,[37] the only thing that can justify one person being a servant to another is that she freely chooses to do so while maintaining her status as an independent, free person.

Nozick is right to criticize end-state principles, but to do so he must subject his principle of appropriation to the same standard. He must look at *the pre-trade starting point of workers* in terms of ECSO freedom (their position in step 2), not to their place in the end-state distribution in terms of standard of living (their position in step 4). At step 2, after the appropriator has taken resources and before necessity has forced the propertyless to become servants of the people who control property, the propertyless are clearly worse-off. They have lost something and gained nothing. Furthermore, they have lost something essential to their status as free individuals—independent access to the resources needed for survival. As low as the standard of living of a person in a "state of nature" might be (step 1), the pre-trade starting point of a propertyless industrial worker is lower (step 2). Under the morally relevant comparison (step 1 to step 2), there is no question that unilateral appropriation harms the propertyless: they have lost access to resources, they are forced to subordinate themselves to others, and their destitute starting point adversely affects what they are able to attain in steps 3 and 4. If appropriators are to take property without denying others' independence, the appropriators are obliged to pay compensation sufficient to return them to that status. Any defender of liberty worthy of the name cannot put individuals in the position where they have no choice but to subordinate themselves to others.

B. Nominal Self-Ownership and Nominal Self-Ownership Plus Something

Propertyless workers retain nominal self-ownership throughout the discussion in subsection A above. Here I want to show that nominal self-ownership alone does not deliver a form of freedom that even its strongest advocates could accept as meaningful. If self-ownership is meaningful, it must be meaningful in combination with something else, but candidates for that something else are not readily apparent.

Suppose you visit two neighboring islands. Mr. Howell shows you around, and says, "On that island, slavery is allowed. There is Eunice Howell and her slave Mary Ann, who does any work Eunice Howell commands. She eats only what Eunice Howell gives her. She sleeps in a cage at night. Eunice Howell whips her if she disobeys, and if she is very disobedient, Eunice Howell throws her into a hole until she is so hungry that she begs forgiveness. Mary Ann has no self-ownership. It's barbaric and we don't do that sort of thing on this Island. Now meet my free hired servant Gilligan." You notice that Gilligan does any work Mr. Howell commands. He eats only what Mr. Howell gives him. He sleeps in a cage at night. Mr. Howell whips him if he disobeys, and if he is very disobedient, Mr. Howell puts him in a hole until he is so hungry that he begs forgiveness. You ask, "In what way is Gilligan free?"

Mr. Howell replies, "He has full, nominal self-ownership. He merely lacks property. The hole is the only piece of public property on this side of the island. If he doesn't like being in the hole or drowning in the ocean, he must agree to my terms as property owner. All of our interactions are mutual agreements between people with full nominal self-ownership—and he's completely free of taxation!"

Mary Ann, the slave, has no legal right to refuse Eunice Howell's orders, and can be punished for doing so. Gilligan, the ostensibly free man, has the legal right to refuse Mr. Howell's orders but only as a matter of legal formality. If he does in fact refuse he faces the same thoroughly bad situation as the chattel slave Mary Ann. The only difference is that, in Gilligan's case, the law does not define that situation as "punishment." It defines it merely as a lack of access to property. The identity of Gilligan and Mary Ann's situations demonstrates that self-ownership alone is valueless. It cannot assure that a person is in any meaningful way different from a chattel slave.

Mr. Howell cannot meaningfully defend the power he holds over Gilligan by saying that any redistribution of property toward Gilligan interferes with Mr. Howell's freedom. Redistribution of landownership to Gilligan will interfere with some things Mr. Howell might want to do, but it does so no more than redistribution of person-ownership to Mary Ann interferes with some things Eunice Howell might want to do. The enforcement of Eunice Howell's property rights in Mary Ann involves a more significant interference with Mary Ann. The enforcement of Mr. Howell's property rights in land involves a more significant interference with Gilligan. Choosing to defend property rights denying Gilligan's ECSO freedom not only gives the priority to Mr. Howell's secondary liberties over Gilligan's core liberties but also privileges Mr. Howell at the expense of equal freedom from interference.

Similarly, Mr. Howell cannot somehow show that Gilligan is a free person by defending the history of Mr. Howell's property rights under entitlement theory. Nothing in the history of Mr. Howell's entitlement changes the fact that Gilligan's position is identical to the position of a chattel slave. Here, I'm making an argument that patterns preserve liberty,[38] and I'm trying to show the significance of the extent to which the pattern of property ownership affects liberty. If the pattern of ownership can effectively make a nominally self-owning person into a slave, any loss of liberty in that direction must be recognized as a serious threat to freedom.

We've seen that self-ownership is meaningless in some situations. What can we combine with self-ownership in an attempt to make it meaningful? The first candidate might be reasonable pay and working conditions. Suppose the island's government passes a Fair Labor Standards Act prescribing humane treatment for Gilligan. The act prescribes how many hours per week people can work, how difficult or unpleasant the work may be, how much they must be fed, and so on. These laws improve his life, but these laws do not make him free. Freedom is about choice. Humane treatment is valuable, but it is not freedom. The humane treatment of chattel slaves or effective slaves does not make them free persons. Gilligan's service is still the result of force.

The second candidate for a principle to augment self-ownership is a wide range of choices of employers. Suppose that Eunice Howell dies and leaves her island to her ten identical children, such that each one owns a pie-shaped slice of the island abutting Mary Ann's punishment hole. Mrs. Howell also leaves Mary Ann to all ten of her children with the stipulation that Mary Ann can choose which of her children to work for. It just so happens that none of Eunice Howell's children are willing to treat Mary Ann any better than the one Eunice Howell did in the original example. Mary Ann is still a chattel slave. Clearly, a choice of masters does not make a slave into a free person.

Suppose Mr. Howell dies at the same time and leaves his island to his ten identical children, such that each one owns a pie-shaped slice of the island abutting the hole where Gilligan is allowed to be if he refuses to work. Gilligan can now choose to work for any one or any combination of the new Mr. Howells, but he must work for one of them or go back to the hole. It just so happens that none of them are willing to treat him any better than the one Mr. Howell did in the original example. Once again, Gilligan's situation is identical to that of a chattel slave. Clearly, a choice of masters does not make an effective slave into a free person.

Gilligan's interaction with the others *as a whole* is forced even if he is not forced to accept any one of them. If we relax the assumptions of the example slightly, competition between employers for his labor might increase wages to the point at which he would accept the offer if he were free to refuse it. But he is still not free of the Howells. He must pursue their goals and their terms, *whether or not* those terms and goals are acceptable to him. None of the new Mr. Howells single-handedly causes Gilligan's situation, but his situation is the result of the interference of laws enforcing such broad property rights and their actions as a group. The Howells might not be aware of Gilligan's predicament or its cause. Nevertheless, as a group, their domination of resources makes him unfree to refuse participation in their projects for their goals on their terms.

Of course, propertyless people in the industrialized world are not forced into holes, but they can be forced to live on the street, to beg for food, and to eat out of garbage cans. Although the life of a homeless person is not as bad as a slave tied to the whipping post, it is in the range that is thoroughly bad in an absolute sense, and therefore, people who enter the labor market because they have no access to resources otherwise do not enter the labor market as free individuals. The choice of a propertyless person to accept employment is not a voluntary agreement of a free person. The wages and working conditions they accept and the goals they agree to pursue do not reflect the voluntary choices of free individuals. These are the ways in which ECSO freedom is more meaningful than self-ownership.

3. Autonomy and Effective Basic Autonomy

Autonomy, as Joseph Raz defines it, is a status freedom concept, but it is broader than ECSO freedom, which can be understood as basic (but effective) autonomy. According to Raz, autonomy is self-mastery: "The autonomous person is (part) author of his own life."[39] He or she pursues self-chosen goals and relationships, as opposed to making coerced choices or lacking the internal ability to make choices. The theory of autonomy is not only the absence of heteronomy (rule by others) but also some degree of self-mastery (the ability to make meaningful, well-informed choices).[40] Raz writes,

> Autonomy is opposed to a life of coerced choices. It contrasts with a life of no choices, or of drifting through life without ever exercising one's capacity to choose. Evidently the autonomous life calls for a certain degree of self-awareness.[41]

The part of autonomy involving the absence of rule by others is not only consistent with ECSO freedom but also seems to be nearly equivalent to control self-ownership. I do not know the extent to which Raz is concerned with making autonomy effective in the sense this book describes, but of course, all the above arguments for effectiveness apply.

Raz's autonomy can be thought of as "full autonomy" and ECSO freedom as "non-heteronomy" or "effective basic autonomy." It is in this sense in which the label "ECSO freedom" coincides with its phonetic pronunciation "exo-freedom"—external freedom. A fully autonomous person has both internal freedom (a mind capable of making meaningful choices) and external freedom (the absence of rule by others). A person with ECSO freedom may not have the maximum level of functioning, but at least she has external freedom. ECSO freedom, I believe, is a prerequisite for full autonomy.

I need to explain why basic autonomy is more expressive of what it means to be a free person than full autonomy. One simple reason is that ECSO freedom can be built on a negative freedom base, as chapter 2 explains. A more complex reason has to do with Berlin's skepticism of freedom as self-mastery, which he labels "positive freedom." He argues from the standpoint of value pluralism, in which there are many different competing values in life that cannot be judged against one ultimate unifying value. The value of human life comes from the capacity to make choices between these competing values. If our ends did not conflict, "the necessity and agony of choice would disappear, and with it the central importance of the freedom to choose."[42] Self-mastery, in this sense, may be a value, but it is not freedom. In the words of his biographer, John Gray,

> In the positive view…freedom consists not in choice but in obedience to rational will. Whereas choice presupposes genuine rivalry among conflicting goods, rational will points to one and only one course of action, one form of life, for the individual.[43]

People who hold the "positive" view, according to Berlin, can be led to manipulate the definition to make freedom mean whatever they wish. His ultimate fear is that the promotion of self-mastery can lead to totalitarian oppression, but even in a well-functioning democracy, value pluralism provides a reason to be skeptical about theories of self-mastery. Under value pluralism, one adult has little basis to accuse another adult of lacking self-mastery. Healthy value-pluralistic skepticism about any group's preferred understanding of self-mastery is reflected in laws limiting the confinement of individuals with a diagnosis of mental illness or disability to cases in which the individual is a demonstrated danger to themselves or others. If we have good reason to be skeptical of any too-strongly promoted or too-specifically defined notion of self-mastery, we have reason to make basic autonomy our central focus.

However, Raz's autonomy does not necessarily conflict with Berlin's value pluralism; autonomous people in his terms fashion their own destiny through successive decisions. Berlin's skepticism is no reason to throw out every aspect of autonomy or status freedom in favor of a conception of freedom purely as scalar, negative freedom. I have argued above that the most important goal in securing freedom is not to ensure the *widest* area of noninterference, but the *most important* area of noninterference, and some notion of autonomy can help understand what choices are the most important.

Berlin's concern implies that there ought to be limits on the state's ability to promote full autonomy. It doesn't mean that the state can do nothing to promote greater self-direction and self-awareness, simply that such promotion should not involve coercing adult individuals for their own good. It might permit noncoercive methods such as education that promote greater powers of self-direction without threatening independence.

4. The Pros and Cons of Freedom as Non-Domination

Civic republicanism or simply republicanism promotes another prominent theory of status freedom that has obvious similarities to ECSO freedom.[44] This section discusses what is good about republican freedom and why I believe it does not identify what it means to have status freedom as well as ECSO freedom.

Quentin Skinner defines republican freedom as "libertas" (which he traces back as far as Livy): the ability "to stand upright by means of one's own strength without depending on the will of anyone else."[45]

This definition obviously involves independence. Many early republicans believed freedom was something only landowners could have. Philip Pettit, probably the most influential modern republican, defines republican freedom as "non-domination." [46] According to *The Stanford Encyclopedia of Philosophy* (quoting Pettit), "The paramount republican value is political liberty, understood as non-domination or independence from arbitrary power...[meaning] a person or group enjoys freedom to the extent that no other person or group has 'the capacity to interfere in their affairs on an arbitrary basis'"[47] Pettit's focus on arbitrary interference makes his definition narrower than libertas seems to imply.

Under republicanism, interference is not a threat to freedom if it is consistent with the rule of law and results from a democratic procedure in which all are free to participate and the concerns of all are taken into account. Dictatorial rule always makes individuals unfree even if the dictator doesn't actually interfere with anyone. A democratic polity must protect individuals from dictatorial government and from domination in the private sphere.[48] Pettit offers a very clear explanation of non-domination in the appendix to Chapter two of his book, *Republicanism*.

> All conceptions of power, roughly speaking, make different choices at the choice points—the points marked by "OR"—in the following schema.
>
> 1. Power is possessed by an agent (person/group/agency) OR by a system
> 2. so far as that entity exercises OR is able (actually or virtually) to exercise
> 3. intentional OR non-intentional influence,
> 4. negative OR positive,
> 5. in advancing any kind of result whatever OR, more specifically, in helping to construct certain forms of agency OR shape the choices of certain groups.[49]

Then he defines dominating power—the power that free people are not subject to—in terms of those five statements.

> Power of this general kind exists when there is:
>
> 1. an agent, person, or corporate group
> 2. that is able (or actually able) to exercise
> 3. intentional influence
> 4. of a negative, damaging kind
> 5. in helping to shape what some other person or persons do.[50]

In other words, one person is dominated by another (and therefore unfree) when another person or organized body is able to assert intentional influence (or arbitrary interference) that shapes another person's range of choices in a negative way. For example, an employer dominates her employees if she has the power to fire them for engaging in political activities in their off-hours. It doesn't matter whether she ever exercises that power; as long as she has it, the workers are unfree.

Several prominent republicans, including Pettit, Frank Lovett, and Daniel Raventos and David Casassas, argue that independence (defined similarly as it is defined here) is important to protecting individuals from domination in the private sphere and that basic income is a good way to secure independence.[51] Thus, republicanism and indepentarianism have similar policy implications, but indepentarianism comes from greater skepticism about power—including nonarbitrary, systemic, and unintentional power.

Philip Pettit dwells primarily on the difference between freedom as non-domination and freedom as noninterference at the second choice point (potential not merely actual interference), but the differences between non-domination and ECSO freedom appear at the first and third choice points. Freedom from potential arbitrary interference is a significant threat to freedom that is too easily overlooked by people who have lived in republics all their lives. However, because domination requires agent-centered, intentional influence, someone can enjoy freedom as non-domination and yet lack effective control over her own destiny. According to Pettit, "[N]on-domination is itself a form of power. It represents a control that a person enjoys in relation to their own destiny."[52] Non-domination may be a power *in relation* to their own destiny, but it does not ensure the power to have *control over* their own destiny. Actual power over their own destiny requires that people are also free from unintentional and systemic factors that could potentially have an enormous effect on them. ECSO freedom identifies people as unfree whenever they cannot control their interactions with others. People who cannot control their interactions are only unfree in terms of domination if that lack of control either follows from or leads to the intentional, arbitrary influence of some agent.

I want to show that the actions of other people (acting within a system) can effectively exert force on an individual without anyone intending to use force over that individual. It is conceivable that people could completely lack control over their own destiny purely because of unintentional systemic factors. By ignoring systemic unfreedom, non-domination misses some of the most important sources of unfreedom in the world today.

For example, Waldron describes the homeless as being unfree in some of the most basic ways, without a place to sleep, eat, urinate, and without any place to exercise civil liberties.[53] They have to sleep on the street, eat what they can find in a garbage can, urinate in the gutter, and so forth. They must accept the given rules of participation in an economic system if they want to avoid this life, and that is enough to say that they are unfree in terms of ECSO freedom. But it is not enough to say that they are unfree in the sense of domination. One must go a step further to find out whether their desperate situation either follows from or makes them vulnerable to the intentional, arbitrary influence of some particular agent. Waldron also argues convincingly that no one intentionally put the homeless in their position; homelessness is an unintentional side effect of the property rights regime.[54] A policeman might have arbitrary power over a homeless person. A soup kitchen might be able to force homeless people to listen to a sermon, but this is not what makes the homeless unfree. Homeless people might be able to simply walk away from any particular agent who tries to establish dominating power over them, but they are still unfree to control their life in relation to the property system.

For a second example, consider the systemic nature of Karl Marx's theory of exploitation. In his theory, material deprivation (or propertylessness) can force an entire class of people to seek employment from another class of people.[55] Systemic factors force employers to pay wages just enough to reproduce labor and to extract whatever value they can from the workforce. No one firm can arbitrarily choose the wage rate or working conditions. Yet, individuals must work long hours, at low pay, and in poor working conditions. The central problems of that situation are systemic and unintentional, not agent-centered and intentional. Marx discussed a situation in which systemic unemployment gave particular firms dominating power over their employees. In addition to the poor pay and working conditions, employees also *might* have to accept the arbitrary power of employers over many of their individual actions.

Two questions are important. First, is this additional, arbitrary factor the only one that makes the situation wrong? Under ECSO freedom the forced acceptance of low pay, long hours, and poor working is bad enough to make workers unfree no matter how this situation came about. Under non-domination the forced acceptance of these factors alone does not make workers unfree unless these factors are the result of the arbitrary power of some identifiable agent within that system.

Second, are low pay, long hours, and poor working conditions *always* accompanied by dominating power? No, it is at least possible to have a low-wage "equilibrium," in which there are many job openings and many employers to choose from. Workers can readily find a job; the market simply dictates that whatever job they find will have similarly low wages, long hours, and poor working conditions. There are so many low-wage employers offering the very same conditions that no one firm has much discretionary power over its workers. Employers are compelled by impersonal market forces to pay the market wage for a given amount of effort. Workers are compelled by market forces and the fear of homelessness to accept an offer from some firm but not one particular offer from one particular firm. If one firm owner tries to impose arbitrary conditions on workers—beyond that which is dictated by the market—workers will simply leave for one of the many other firms paying the market wage. Workers could face a lifetime at the bottom of a social hierarchy and at the edge of material deprivation without any one person or agent exercising intentional arbitrary power over them. A worker in this position does not experience arbitrary, intentional domination, but they do experience unfreedom. This is an unfreedom that ECSO freedom captures and freedom as non-domination does not.

When I look around, I do not see (personal, intentional, and agent-oriented) domination as the central problem. Low-wage jobs in the United States today are often characterized by high turnover and very little control over or concern for the lives of employees. There are some villains, but for the most part there are normal, even good people interacting in a dysfunctional system that gives people at the bottom very little control over their own life without necessarily giving dominating power over them to anyone else in particular. If such a situation would be a serious threat to status freedom, Pettit's republican conception of freedom is too narrow to capture what it means to be a free person.

One might argue that a well-functioning democracy that genuinely took the concerns of everyone into account would not allow homelessness, long hours, low pay, or poor working conditions to exist, but such an argument includes too much substantive theory about what laws should be into a theory that is supposed to be primarily about how laws are made. We have to accept the possibility that a well-functioning democracy in which all people, including the disadvantaged, fully participate would make a well-considered decision to allow propertylessness and destitution to exist or use them as threats to motivate workers. Even if a democracy gives equal voice to everyone, a majority of people might nevertheless require long hours of mandatory service, pursue goals that dissenters find objectionable, and create conditions that weigh heavily on the disadvantaged. Therefore, I conclude that although the republican concern with arbitrary and potential force is important, the republican conception of freedom has to be broadened to include possible threats to freedom coming from systemic factors and nonarbitrary factors. That is, it needs to incorporate some concern for ECSO freedom.

5. Indepentarianism and Sufficientarianism

Sufficientarianism is a theory of distributive justice giving a strong priority to sufficiency—to ensuring that everyone has enough in an absolute sense. The basic idea of sufficiency is that meeting basic needs matters more (all else equal) than many other things such as improving average income or overall inequality.[56] Some sufficientarians argue that other distributional concerns do not matter at all in comparison to the concern for sufficiency. I am critical of this idea, simply because giving lexical priority to any good thing usually leads to implausible results when compared to an extremely large amount of some other good thing.[57] Not all versions of sufficientarianism are vulnerable to this criticism.[58]

The concern with absolute basic needs implies a connection between sufficientarianism and indepentarianism. Although sufficientarianism is not usually thought of as a theory of freedom, the theory of ECSO freedom provides *a freedom-based argument for sufficiency.* In fact, that might have been an apt title for this book, the argument being one needs sufficiency (in everything else) to have enough freedom necessarily to qualify as a free person. However, a freedom-based view of sufficiency makes the arguments in this book different in important ways than those usually connected with sufficiency. Sufficientarianism is usually combined with utilitarian or prioritarian concerns once sufficiency is reached, the property theory I intend to outline in my second book is closer to left-libertarianism or civic republicanism.

The relationship between the concepts of sufficiency and independence is complex. On the one hand, the theory of independence adds one item to the list of basic needs required for sufficiency: the freedom from forced labor. On the other hand, the argument for ECSO freedom as independence implies that a person has to reach sufficiency in all their other basic needs to have independence. Thus, independence is a slightly more expansive term than sufficiency, usually defined, but if the arguments in this book about the importance of freedom from forced labor are correct, the concept of sufficiency is worth expanding.

Many sufficientarians have not been clear whether they expect sufficiency to be achieved before or after trade. Is it enough that everyone with a job reaches sufficiency or must everyone entering the labor-market reach sufficiency? The view Axel Gosseries calls "responsibility-insensitive sufficientarianism" implies that access to basic needs should be unconditional. One of the appealing arguments for sufficientarianism is that it defines a limit to which a good society will hold people responsible for their actions.[59] It seems reasonable to say, "You blew all your opportunities on frivolous, lazy, or risky behavior; you will no longer be rich or even as well off as most people," but it seems overly harsh to say to the same person, "and we will also deny you all access to food, shelter, and healthcare." Indepentarianism shares these ideas and adds that the concern for freedom from effectively forced labor is a basic need.

6. Indepentarianism and Left-Libertarianism

Left-libertarians begin with the recognition that all people have an equal right to self-ownership and, because natural resources are gifts of nature, an equal right to natural resources. Left-libertarian freedom is the freedom from interference within the confines of those basic rights. From the equal right to natural resources, left-libertarians derive support for equal ownership of natural resources or the ownership of an equal share of the value of natural resources. Most left-libertarians support the equalization of resource rents (or sometimes all rents), delivering each individual an equal share of the market value of natural resources in the form of a basic income and/or government services.[60]

As the introductory chapter mentions, the concern with equal access to natural resources and the support for unconditional benefits makes indepentarianism similar to left-libertarianism. However, indepentarianism does not rely on any natural property rights theory; relying instead on the equal absence of property rights and on an equal right to freedom from interference including interference with the uses one might make of natural resources. The equal absence of ownership might be similar to an equal claim of ownership, but it leads to a slightly different property theory. I have not fully laid out indepentarian property theory in this book, and so a thorough discussion of those differences will have to wait.[61] However, I will discuss the differences stemming from indepentarianism's use of a status conception of freedom. As far as I can tell, all well-known versions of left-libertarianism rely entirely on scalar conceptions of freedom.

Unlike an indepentarian version, the size of a left-libertarian basic income has no necessary relationship with human needs. The revenue available for basic income under left-libertarianism is tied to the empirical value of rents. Whether it is more or less than enough to meet people's basic needs, it satisfies the left-libertarian conception of justice as long as it equalizes the market value of natural resources. Yet, many left-libertarians take pains to argue that rents make up a significant percentage of any nation's income, and that rent-based redistribution will be significant. Why bother, if the amount of the rents to be equalized makes no difference to the theory? I believe that the desire to show the significance of rent equalization reveals an unstated concern for sufficiency or status freedom and that left-libertarian theory would be improved if this concern was developed into an explicit principle of left-libertarian justice.

Indepentarianism is not empirically limited by the value of rents, because it cashes out everyone's equal non-ownership of resources in a different way. The freedom people can derive from resources is not the ability to get an equal share of stuff but the ability to meet their needs and secure their independence. The ethical problem with any group's domination of resources is that they interfere with other people as they try to use resources to meet their needs and secure their independence. Therefore, indepentarian theory requires them to find some way to compensate everyone else sufficiently and unconditionally. If rent equalization provides at least enough resource revenue to do that, left-libertarianism and indepentarianism might lead to the same distributive outcome. But if rent equalization does not secure people's basic needs, indepentarianism requires the group that dominates resources to find some other way to sufficiently compensate the propertyless. They might have to give the propertyless a disproportionately large share of resource rents, or they might have to share revenue from the value added to resources or from some other source.

7. Indepentarianism and Real Libertarianism

Real libertarianism is an offshoot of left-libertarianism that justifies basic income on a scalar conception of liberty that Philippe Van Parijs calls "real freedom:" the freedom "to do whatever one might want to do."[62] His argument for unconditional basic income is one of the most thorough and influential in modern political theory. Van Parijs argues that the more access people have to external assets, the freer they are to do what they might want to do. The government should support all individuals' access to external assets as much as it can without interfering with individual self-ownership. Referring to economic theories of market imperfection, Van Parijs extends the left-libertarian argument for resource-rent equalization to job rents as well and endorses an income tax. Inspired by Rawlsian and Dworkinian arguments as well as left-libertarian ones, Van Parijs endorses the highest sustainable unconditional basic income as a way to give the least advantaged individual maximum real freedom. Like the left-libertarian version, real libertarianism ties the level of basic income to an empirical issue about available revenue rather than a conception of human need. Van Parijs's motivation for bringing in job rents seems to be to show that the basic income level will be large. As with left-libertarianism, I think this effort indicates an unstated concern with sufficiency or status freedom, and that the theory would be stronger if that concern was made explicit.

As long as the highest sustainable level of basic income is at least enough to meet individuals' basic needs, real libertarianism and indepentarianism might again lead to similar distributional outcomes. However, the theories are motivated by very different reasons and lead to very different outcomes if the highest sustainable level of income is not enough to meet people's basic needs. Real libertarianism's motivation for a basic income is that all people should have equal access to as many external assets as we can get them unconditionally. They don't have to work for that level of external assets, but whether having those assets frees them from effectively forced labor is inconsequential. These assets might be enough to meet their basic needs, but whether they do or not is also inconsequential for the theory. These are very different philosophical goals even if they lead to similar policy implications.

Those policy implications diverge if the highest sustainable basic income is not enough to meet individuals' basic needs. In those circumstances, real libertarianism implies that an unconditional basic income should meet as many of people's needs as it can each year. Thus, it should be at the highest sustainable level for everyone regardless of whether that amount is enough to meet basic needs. And real libertarianism implies the responsibility ends there. In circumstances in which society cannot secure everyone's independence throughout their lives, indepentarianism implies that society should secure their independence for the maximum number of possible years. That is, the basic income should be set at a level necessary to meet individual basic needs for the maximum number of years, presumably requiring the minimum necessary number of years of service in early adulthood and allowing individuals to gain independence as soon as possible. And the responsibility does not end there. Chapter 9 discusses further responsibilities of a society that determines independence to be unsustainable. It argues that society has a responsibility to make sure that the years of service are equally onerous for everyone and a responsibility to get out of whatever situation makes independence unsustainable as soon as possible.

CHAPTER 8

If You're an Egalitarian, Why Do You Want to Be the Boss of the Poor? Independence and Liberal-Egalitarian Theories of Justice

The liberty of man in society is to be under no other legislative power but that established by consent.

—*John Locke*[1]

The history of... consent theory of the last three centuries largely consists of attempts by theorists to suppress the radical and subversive implications of their own arguments.

—*Carole Pateman*[2]

By far the largest school of thought in contemporary political theory is liberal-egalitarianism. Recently, many egalitarians have been very concerned with improving the living standards of people at the bottom but often in the context of a mandatory-participation economy. This section examines three egalitarian theorists, Elizabeth Anderson, Stuart White, and John Rawls.[3] Anderson and White both specifically endorse mandatory participation. Rawls is less clear. Although some of his writings provide good arguments for voluntary participation, he seems to come down on the side of mandatory participation all things considered. This chapter examines arguments for and against voluntary participation in these three authors, and argues that a mandatory-participation economy does not live up to liberal-egalitarian ideals.

Egalitarians tend to view the economy or society as a social project, as if we were all working together toward joint ends. White, for example, discusses an individual's job as a "productive contribution" to "the social product," as if the economy were one big factory pumping out product for society.[4] Rawls describes his ideal of society as a "fair system of cooperation" and a "mutually advantageous cooperative venture,"[5] and his original position envisions people planning a project that will make them all better-off than working by their own efforts. The natural resources and individual efforts are devoted to the social project. To the extent that it is a joint project, it is a thin project designed to create basic goods to help individuals further their own goals as they see fit. Still, not all theories of justice view society in this way. This chapter does not take issue with that way of looking at the economy or with most aspects of liberal-egalitarianism; it merely argues that an organized social democracy has as much responsibility as a disorganized ownership class to avoid dominating resources in a way that limits personal independence.

The three theories are not completely clear how the obligation to contribute to the social project is to be enforced, but they indicate that people who refuse to participate in the joint project would not have access to property or public funds.[6] I take this to mean that dissenters would be left propertyless, meaning that they could be subject to destitution and homelessness. They might be able to avoid homelessness by receiving gifts from property owners, but of course, this opportunity makes them subject to the arbitrary will of property owners, such that otherwise equally situated dissenters are likely to face different levels of poverty. I am not completely confident in my interpretation of how mandatory participation is to be enforced, but the point of this chapter is to argue that liberal-egalitarianism would be stronger if it included respect for personal independence not to criticize any particular method of enforcement or against any particular theorist. Other enforcement options exist, such as corporal punishment, social pressure, and jailing people who refused to participate.[7] Stating the alternative to participation as homelessness might sound harsh, but under liberal-egalitarianism, access to food and shelter would always be available by meeting the conditions imposed by the government. I am sure most liberal-egalitarian proponents of mandatory participation believe that access to goods through participation would be so generous that few if any people would actually be homeless.

There are two obvious arguments for an egalitarian work obligation. First, the redistributive measures and choices of occupation in the system guarantee freedom in the most important sense, making the freedom to object to a work obligation unnecessary. Second, the refusal of participation unjustly imposes costs on those who do participate. This chapter addresses only the first of these arguments, comparing the view of freedom within a contributory obligation scheme to ECSO freedom, which entails the power to reject active participation in any joint project. The first three sections discuss Anderson, White, and Rawls in turn. The fourth section makes more general responses.

1. Elizabeth Anderson

Anderson's "democratic equality" includes a conception of status freedom, linked very closely with equality and defined as "freedom from oppression."[8]

> Equals are not dominated by others; they do not live at the mercy of others' wills. This means that they govern their lives by their own wills, which is freedom.... Once all citizens enjoy a decent set of freedoms, sufficient for functioning as an equal in society, income inequalities beyond that point do not seem so troubling in themselves.[9]

Anderson specifically sides with Waldron's assessment of homelessness as a threat to freedom, "Homelessness—that is, having only public dwelling—is a condition of profound unfreedom."[10] But, I will show, she fails to fully operationalize people's ability to "govern their own lives by their own wills."

Rejecting luck-egalitarianism, Anderson states emphatically that all people should not have to pass judgment to gain access to the functionings they need to secure freedom from oppression:

> Under democratic equality, citizens refrain from making intrusive, moralizing judgments about how people ought to have used the opportunities open to them or about how capable they were of exercising personal responsibility. It need not make such judgments, because it does not condition citizen's enjoyment of their capabilities on whether they use them responsibly. The sole exception to this principle concerns criminal conduct.[11]

Actually, she has a second, unstated exception. Although she says that everyone will have *access* to these functionings, she allows that some people could "choose" to function at a lower level.[12] She bases her justification for redistribution on mutual obligation, and therefore, she is willing to make redistribution conditional on fulfillment of a work obligation. She considers those who do not fulfill this socially imposed obligation to be "choosing" to function at a lower level, even though the police will have to stop them from using resources to meet their own needs.

By allowing people to "choose" to function at a lower level, Anderson puts them in the position in which she must make intrusive, moralizing judgments, not between those who work and do not work, but between those who should and should not be held to work conditioned benefits. In her system, some forms of nonmarket contributions (such as care work) fulfill the contributory obligation. Some forms of disability exempt people from the work obligation. So does involuntary unemployment. And presumably people with a legitimate grievance against their employer would not have to work until suitable work can be found. Anderson cannot separate those who should and should not be held to a work requirement without making "intrusive, moralizing judgments." There are thousands of different kinds and levels of disability, thousands of potentially legitimate nonmarket contributions, thousands of potentially legitimate grievances, and every unemployed person is unemployed in their own way. Her authorities will have to decide questions like the following. Are you disabled enough that you *ought not* be held to the work requirement? Are your nonmarket contributions sufficient that you *deserve* a work exemption? Do you have a *morally legitimate* grievance against your employer? Have you looked hard enough for a job that you have an *ethical* claim to be involuntarily unemployed? These *are* intrusive, moralizing judgments.

Although the intrusive, moralizing judgment of the luck-egalitarian theory she criticizes may not involve these distinctions, most, if not all, of the intrusive, moralizing judgments made by modern welfare states involve separating those who should or should not be held to a work requirement. By endorsing the deserving-underserving poor dichotomy, Anderson has endorsed the enormous system of intrusive, moralizing judgments that exists in welfare states today. Anderson can't have it both ways; there is no way to separate the sheep from the goats without moralizing. Her system is inherently judgmental, and she needs to take on the difficult job of defending why she thinks intrusive, moralizing judgments are a good idea in the circumstances where she uses them but not a good idea in the circumstances in which the authors she criticizes use them.

Anderson's inconsistency on moralizing judgments is not the central problem with "democratic equality." The deeper problem is that it makes freedom conditional. Anderson writes,

> Only the commission of a crime can justify taking away a person's basic liberties and status as an equal in civil society. Even convicted criminals, however, retain their status as equal human beings, and so are still entitled to basic human functionings such as adequate nutrition, shelter, and medical care.[13]

Yet, she is willing to deny these functionings (or many of them) to those who refuse to work, even though her own words imply it is a worse punishment than imprisonment. Anderson's characterization of the propertylessness that will exist under democratic egalitarianism as a mere "choice" ignores the issue of whether using homelessness (or some other form of deprivation) to force workers to participate against their will makes them unfree.

Anderson offers two protections to ensure that the work obligation will not be oppressive: it must be determined democratically, and it has to give weight to the concerns of the disadvantaged. Who will appoint the judges to determine when society reaches that standard? It would have to be the same ruling coalition that makes the policy. The weak and the vulnerable are at the mercy of the majority without any independent control over the terms they will work under and the goals they will pursue. She apparently believes that as long as the range of options is democratically approved, it will be fair enough that no one could reasonably object even to the worst options on the list. She has more faith in the democratic process than I do. Under democratic equality the options available to the disadvantaged will be as good, fair, and reasonable as the majority want them to be with no assurance that those options will be as good, fair, and reasonable as the people who actually have to take those options think they should be. Having one vote out of millions on the list of activities you are allowed to perform and the rewards you will receive has some value, but it is not the freedom to "govern their own lives by their own wills." Her proposal does not live up to the ideal she expresses. Forced labor is unfreedom, no matter who applies the force (a feudal hierarchy, a capitalist aristocracy, a socialist dictatorship, or a democratic egalitarian governing coalition with the best intentions in mind). Respect for personal independence allows disadvantaged individuals to decide whether the ruling majority has given adequate concern to the disadvantaged and provided a sufficient range of job opportunities. This institution provides a more robust and secure freedom from oppression.

2. Stuart White

Stuart White proposes "justice as fair reciprocity" in which,

> (i) Citizens are properly possessed of various social rights; (ii) these rights are instrumental to an ultimate goal that is radically egalitarian; and (iii) where these rights work to secure citizens a sufficiently generous share of the social product, and sufficiently good opportunities for productive contribution, citizens have definite, potentially enforceable obligations to make a productive contribution to the community in return.[14]

White describes a society of reciprocal obligations. Society is obliged to find a way to eliminate "the proletarian condition," meaning that workers are as free as everyone else and share sufficiently in the social product.[15] Once society meets this condition, all people are obliged to work together for a joint project. Society, in turn, is obliged to ensure that everyone has a good choice of fulfilling, well-paid occupations.[16] White's definition of the proletarian condition does not include what I would consider to be its essence: that workers have *nothing to sell but their labor*,[17] which I interpret to mean that they have *no choice but to sell their labor*. Under my interpretation, White's plan fails to eliminate the proletarian condition, because (although workers are promised better wages and working conditions) they are explicitly held to the obligation to sell their labor. Perhaps, White interprets the phrase to mean, *nothing else to sell along with their labor*. To White, it is acceptable to put workers in the position in which they *must* sell their labor but only as long as they receive a fair share of the profits from social capital in return.

Freedom is not the central motivation behind justice as fair reciprocity, but it seems to be the constraint behind the requirement that society gives individuals a wide choice of challenging work. This strategy faces a problem as discussed in chapter 2: the worker has only as much choice over the terms and goals of her work as the ruling coalition allows. I am not convinced that this is sufficient freedom. Take an example from *The Sound of Music*. Suppose the newly united German-speaking state asks Mr. von Trapp to perform his obligation to social cooperation by being the captain of a warship. Mr. von Trapp feels the need to flee the country to avoid it. Certainly, he was made unfree. But could the Nazis have freed him by saying, "OK, you don't want to be the captain of a ship, would you like to be first mate? Second mate? Seaman? Cook? Infantry commander? Armaments supplier? Person who cleans the toilets at headquarters?..." There is no *number* of choices of occupations, such that, once the Nazis offer him that number, Mr. von Trapp becomes free even though he is obliged to contribute to the Nazi project. If the goals of the joint project make any of these options personally unfulfilling to Mr. von Trapp, no number of choices of how to participate in the Nazi project make a non-Nazi dissenter free. Similarly, it does not matter whether there is wide social agreement in greater Germany that these occupations are fulfilling, worthwhile, well paid, and for a just goal. It does not matter whether Mr. von Trapp receives a large, generous share of the social product including returns to capital. If he objects to the goal of the joint project, no amount of choices—no matter how equal they are, how willingly others accept them, or how many people believe they are reasonable—will make him free.

White could respond that society has no right to force an individual to participate in an *unjust* social project like the Nazi project; they can only force individuals to participate in a *just* social project. Consider another example. Mr. von Trapp is now a Nazi living in a democratic liberal-egalitarian country. He objects to the project because it is egalitarian, democratic, insufficiently warlike, and fair to nonwhite racial groups. He doesn't commit Nazi crimes. He merely wants to sit out of the social project. If society forces him to participate, do they make him unfree? What made Mr. von Trapp unfree in the first example? Was it the force the Nazis exerted on Mr. von Trapp or the wrongness of the Nazi project? Wrongness is a constituent part of injustice, but choice and the absence of force are the constituent parts of freedom. If freedom is a morally neutral term, forced participation in the Nazi project makes Mr. von Trapp unfree in the same way as forced participation in a non-Nazi project makes the Nazi unfree.

In the Reformation era, both Catholic and Protestant governments commonly persecuted members of the opposing group. Each objected to the other's persecution not on the grounds of freedom of religion (a concept that few endorsed at the time), but on the grounds that the state was persecuting the *wrong* religion. One can endorse a mandatory obligation despite its effect on individual freedom, but one should recognize its effect on freedom.

Egalitarians such as Anderson and White could respond that they ask for a contribution only to a thin ideology, not to a strictly ideological state in the sense of a theocratic, Fascist, or even anti-Fascist state. It is true that a liberal-egalitarian ideology is thinner than many others, but a lifetime, fulltime obligation to participate in an economy that produces far more luxuries than necessities is certainly not the thinnest possible ideology.

Freedom may be morally neutral, but its presence or absence affects justice. Respect for people's status as free individuals is part of what makes a social project just. The claim that we don't force people to participate in our project must be one of the reasons we can say our project is just. A society that protects individuals from making a forced contribution must be closer to the first-best ideal of a free society, and it must better protect the vulnerable against the tyranny of the majority.

3. John Rawls

Rawls proposes a theory in which the hypothetical agreement of all participants is the central justification for social cooperation. He envisions the economy (and society in general) as one large, social project, "a cooperative venture for mutual advantage" in which "there is an identity in interests, since social cooperation makes possible a better life for all than any would have if each were to try to live solely by his own efforts."[18] Therefore, society is an effort by people to come together to produce an outcome that is a mutual benefit as they see it themselves; if it achieves that goal everyone has an interest in its success—thus an "identity of interests." There are no prior entitlements in Rawls's theory of justice. Nothing like Lockean appropriation, Nozickian entitlement, or left-libertarian equal entitlement justifies ownership. All resources are devoted to the social project, which is justified by his theory of justice, the main points of which are so well-known that I will recount them very briefly.

The basic structure of society is just if it is consistent with what people would agree to in a just original position, behind a veil of ignorance that prevents people from knowing who they will be when the structure is put into place. Not knowing who they will be, each person assumes they will be the least advantaged person when the veil is lifted, and therefore, they agree to give lexical priority first to liberty, then to equal opportunity, and third to "the difference principle." The third ranking principle receives most of the attention both in Rawls's writings and in other author's responses to his theory of justice, largely because it has the greatest effect on distribution. According to the difference principle, social and economic inequalities are to be to the greatest benefit of the least advantaged members of society. This benefit is understood in terms of primary goods—a list of things all people need to pursue a wide range of personal goals. Higher pay and other forms of reward for those better-off than the least advantaged are justified only if they provide an incentive to increase social output in a way that benefits the least advantaged members of society (or perhaps the least advantaged contributors to the social project). The difference principle is an important expansion of a basic idea from social contract theory. Not only must all people be better-off in society than they could be living by their own efforts, but the least advantaged among them must also be better-off than the least advantaged person under any other social structure. Therefore, Rawlsianism would seem to be the most egalitarian feasible economic system.[19]

Although hypothetical agreement is centrally important to Rawlsian theory, in practice, the theory does not stress literal agreement. It is enough for democratic decision makers to imagine what that agreement would be. The requirement that people do not know who they are in the original position requires the agreement to be hypothetical. Society strives to build agreement in the long run by creating a structure that will be endorsed by an overlapping consensus. That is, people of different beliefs agree that the social project works for them and is consistent with their beliefs about justice. Rawls uses a Rousseau-style ideal theory ("taking men as they are and laws as they might be"[20]) in which one imagines what laws would be appropriate if an overlapping consensus were in place. Rules would still require enforcement, because people have all the weaknesses of people as they are. However, because all people believe the basic structure is just, they agree that the enforcement is just. Although Rawls recognizes the problem of reasonable disagreement on political issues,[21] ideal theory agreement provides a guide to policy in less ideal circumstance. Therefore, although hypothetical agreement is central to the justification of the project, day-to-day, individual agreement is assumed rather than assured (By day-to-day, I mean decisions that are not part of the basic structure.)

Many political theorists have made connections between Rawlsian theory and an unconditional basic income, most particularly Van Parijs and Simon Birnbaum,[22] and *A Theory of Justice* considers a negative income tax (a form of basic income guarantee) as a policy that might help secure the social minimum required by the basic structure.[23] However, Rawls's early writings are not clear on whether individuals have a work requirement, and his later writings seem to take a clear stand against the power to refuse participation. Subsection A discusses Rawlsian arguments that can be used to support voluntary participation and/or unconditional income. Subsection B discusses Rawlsian arguments in favor of mandatory participation.

A. Rawlsian Arguments in Favor of Independence and Unconditional Income

There are several very Rawlsian reasons to recognize independence, most obviously that it would make the least advantaged people better-off. Imagine two societies trying to implement Rawlsian ideals. They are alike in every way expect one forces the disadvantaged to work; the other does not. Assuming being subject to force makes people worse-off, disadvantaged people would be better-off in the second society. Therefore, people in the original position should work that into the difference principle. An unconditional income would also go well with Rawls's idea of a property-owning democracy. According to Leif Wenar account, a property-owning democracy does not merely redistribute income through a traditional welfare state; the government "takes steps to encourage widespread ownership of productive assets . . . to enable all citizens, even the least advantaged, to manage their own affairs within a context of significant social and economic equality."[24] In addition, Rawls recognizes the connection between liberty and basic needs, writing,

> The first principle covering the equal basic rights and liberties may easily be preceded by a lexically prior principle requiring that citizens' basic needs be met, at least insofar as their being met is necessary for citizens to understand and to be able fruitfully to exercise those rights and liberties. Certainly any such principle must be assumed in applying the first principle. But I do not pursue these and other matters here.[25]

Another reason to support independence comes from the reasoning behind the incentive pay authorized by the difference principle. The Rawlsian ideal behind the veil of ignorance is complete equality. All will contribute to a project that benefits everyone, and so all who contribute equal effort should receive the same even though some have talents that produce more than others. But if we paid everyone equally, the talented would not use their talents to the fullest, taking easier, less productive jobs than they otherwise would. We could just force the talented to take the more difficult jobs, but we don't because we want to avoid what Ronald Dworkin called "the slavery of the talented."[26] Even if the basic structure of society is just, and it requires a contribution utilizing Roy's full talents, in day-to-day interactions we respect Roy's self-ownership enough to give him the right to choose his occupation from all those he is qualified for. Therefore, we give him incentive pay to take the more demanding job.

More than the slavery of the talented, I worry about a similar problem that Alexander Brown calls "the slavery of the not so talented."[27] The following example shows that mandatory participation applies a level of force to the least advantaged that is equivalent to or greater than that which could cause slavery of the talented. Suppose Gilligan is the least advantaged individual capable of contributing in a mandatory-participation economy that applies the difference principle. If he were any more disadvantaged, he would be disabled and not held to a work obligation. He is only eligible for the lowest level of job opportunities. Call that level 1. There are many jobs at that level (as required by the theory), but they are all at the lowest level of pay and working conditions. Roy (the talented person) would choose an easy level 5 job (as a professor) if all jobs paid the same. With incentive pay, he takes a level 10 job (as an inventor). Roy agrees that level

1 jobs are unattractive. Roy would need even more incentive to take a level 1 job than the large pay he accepts to do a level 10 job. Say Roy and Gilligan agree that they would prefer a basic income (call that level 0) than a level 1 job, if they could get a basic income. They also agree that they would prefer the level 5 job to basic income, if they could get that job.

With incentive pay, Roy and Gilligan both have this order of preference: 10 > 5 > 0 > 1 (inventor > professor > basic income > dishwasher). At equal pay, Roy and Gilligan both would have this order of preference: 5 > 10 > 0 > 1 (professor > inventor > basic income > dishwasher). Society makes basic income unavailable to force Gilligan to choose a level 1 job. The choice set available to him is (1). The choice set available to Roy is (10 > 5 > 1), because of his greater talent. If Roy is capable of performing the duties of all four of the options, his two most desired options are available. He barely misses option 0, and he hardly thinks of option 1 as being part of his choice set because those options are so much less attractive than options at level 5 and 10. We could make options in level 5 and 1 unavailable so that Roy may only choose options at level 10. If so, he would still have better options available than Gilligan. We don't do this because we respect his self-ownership. Instead, we give him incentive pay to choose 10 instead of 5. But, because we have a mandatory participation economy, and Gilligan is untalented, we will make options 0, 5, and 10 unavailable to him. The loss of option 0 is felt by Gilligan in a way it is not felt by Roy, because (as they both agree) the only option available to Gilligan (level 1) is even worse. Roy and Gilligan agree that having only level 1 options available is worse than having only level 10 options available. By making only level 1 jobs available to Gilligan, it seems we force him into a level 1 job just has much as we would have forced Roy into a level 10 job by making only those options available. Therefore, the same day-to-day respect for self-ownership that made us refuse to force Roy to take a level 10 job by making it the only option available, must make us refuse to force Gilligan to take a level 1 job by making it the only option available.

It seems incongruous for a theory that is supposed to be about the maximum advantages of the least advantaged to force the disadvantaged people to do things that are worse than the things it refuses to force the more advantaged person to do. By the assumption of the theory, everyone's contribution in some way benefits everyone else. So, by forcing the disadvantaged to work, we are essentially forcing the disadvantaged to aid the more advantaged when we could make the disadvantaged better-off by relieving them from the duty to aid the more advantaged. Therefore, the mandatory-participation version of Rawlsianism cannot be the most egalitarian feasible system.

These arguments connect with the effective unfreedom issue discussed in earlier chapters, and I think it makes a strong argument for basic income for anyone who will not accept a strict command economy. Liberal-egalitarians need to decide whether they agree that society forces individuals to do one of the jobs at level X if it denies them access to resources until they do one of the jobs at level X. If it is force (as argued in the earlier chapters), it violates Gilligan's self-ownership to present him with only the option of a level 1 job just as much as it would be to present Roy with the option of only the level 10 job. If denying access to resources until someone does X is not force, we do not force Gilligan to take a level 1 job by allowing him options only in this category, but then we also do not force Roy to take a level 10 job by allowing him options only in this category. If denying a person access to resources until they do X is not force, there would be no such thing as the slavery of the talented. If you would like to be a professor, but if society has determined that your talents will be better used as an insurance actuary or something in that category, it would be permissible for the government to so restrict your options.[28]

Therefore, the same respect for self-ownership that requires a Rawlsian economy to endorse incentive pay also seems to require it to endorse respect for independence. These reasons imply that Rawlsian theory is stronger if it respects independence and that much of Rawlsian theory supports at least some unconditional benefits.

B. Rawlsian Arguments against Unconditional Income

One reason to oppose unconditional benefits is embedded in the basic justification for a Rawlsian economy. In the original position, participants assume that everyone will contribute to the joint project. The Rawlsian government does not take from one person to give to another; it decides how to share the benefits of a joint effort. This appealing idea is lost if basic income amounts to taking the proceeds of a joint effort and gives it to those unwilling to contribute to that effort. Along these lines, Rawls establishes a "principle of fairness." While Rawls's principles of justice apply to the structure of society, the principle of fairness applies to individuals. This principle implies, "A person is required to do his part as defined by the rules of an institution,"[29] or "all are willing to work and to do their part in sharing the burdens of social life, provided of course the terms of cooperation are seen as fair."[30] This idea of agreement follows from Rawls's brand of ideal theory. Ideal theory assumes away 14 of the 17 reasons an individual might object to social participation listed in chapter 4. All reasons other than weakness of will, gaming the system, and laziness do not exist in ideal theory where by assumption everyone agrees that the terms of social cooperation are just. In ideal theory, everyone agrees that the terms, goals, and methods of the joint project are just; everyone agrees that they have a duty to contribute, but they recognize that they can be weak and selfish in day-to-day interactions. Therefore everyone agrees that the law may force everyone to make a contribution. Although Rawls recognizes the problem of reasonable disagreement, he doesn't connect this problem with an objection to the requirement to work under the principle of fairness.[31]

A Rawlsian might also be skeptical about unconditional benefits because the basic structure is justified by what we *would* agree to if we didn't know who we are. People must be anonymous in the original position. When I think of someone refusing to work, I think of dissenters or the disadvantaged refusing to accept unacceptable wages and working conditions. But these reasons are ruled out in Rawlsian ideal theory. Even the least advantaged person agrees that her wages and working conditions (and the goals and methods of the joint project) are just and consistent with the difference principle. So, they have no such reason to refuse. They have nothing to gain by refusing because they're already receiving the highest wages that a disadvantaged person can get in any feasible economic system.[32] A Rawlsian, therefore, might see people refusing to work as advantaged people seeking particular advantages—people who know that they are very skilled and that they can capture a larger share of wealth for themselves even though it comes at the expense of the least advantaged.

Rawls revised his list of primary goods in a way that seems to rule out unconditional benefits. He considers incorporating leisure time as a primary good, such that 24 hours minus a standard workday is the standard individual allotment of leisure, concluding,

> Those who are unwilling to work would have a standard working day of extra leisure, and this extra leisure itself would be stipulated as equivalent to the index of primary goods of the least advantaged. So those who surf all day off Malibu must find a way to support themselves and would not be entitled to public funds.[33]

I interpret this passage to mean that it is fair for those who do not work for the social product to sacrifice all income, because they are consuming more leisure than everyone else, and leisure is assumed to have the same value as the goods they sacrifice by not working. The phrase "find a way to support themselves" is difficult to interpret when all resources are devoted to the joint project. It could be that they have resources in accordance with the liberty principle and with property-owning democracy and that they can live off of these assets. But this passage seems to imply that the government will not do anything to make it possible for people to surf all day. It would certainly require a major clarification to show that the theory supports two minimums: the difference-principle minimum for contributors and the property-owning democracy/liberty-principle minimum for non-contributors. Therefore, I think that the most reasonable interpretation is that those who refuse to contribute will be propertyless and potentially homeless.

I'm not sure whether the Rawlsian-style arguments in favor of mandatory participation outweigh the Rawlsian-style arguments for voluntary participation. My primary concern here is not to figure out what Rawls or any other liberal-egalitarian really believed. Some Rawlsian arguments seem to support mandatory participation, others voluntary participation; and certainly coherent theories can be built combining many Rawlsian or liberal-egalitarian ideas with either one. My concern is whether mandatory-participation liberal-egalitarianism is a better theory than voluntary-participation liberal-egalitarianism. The responses below are written in that context.

4. Responses to Liberal-Egalitarian Mandatory Participation

This section argues that egalitarian theories, such as those by Anderson, Rawls, and White would be stronger and more plausible if they incorporated respect for personal independence. Section A argues that ideal theory should be defined in such a way that fundamental disagreement is possible and that the literal, unforced agreement of all participants is important in the ideal. Section B argues that the need for consent is even more important as the assumptions of ideal theory are relaxed. Section C considers the argument that mandatory participation generates feelings of social solidarity, arguing instead that a society that does not give to individuals until it gets something from them will cultivate the value that individuals should also not give until they get. Sections D and E argue that an exit option is important for Rawlsian disadvantaged individuals and not harmful for Rawlsian advantaged individuals. Section F concludes by arguing that it is distinctly inegalitarian for a powerful ruling coalition to force disadvantaged individuals to participate in its project.

A. The Missing Role of Consent in Liberal-Egalitarian Ideal Theory

When mandatory-participation liberal-egalitarians think of someone refusing to work, they seem to envision a selfish person shirking their duty to seek an unfair individual advantage. I see an oppressed person rejecting unacceptable wages and working conditions or unacceptable goals and methods of the joint project. Part of this difference is explained by differences in our definitions of ideal theory and part of it is explained by the emphasis we put on ideal theory.

I tentatively call my theory "justice as the pursuit of accord." Rawls calls his theory "justice as fairness"; White calls his "justice as fair reciprocity."[34] I envision the path to the ideal with the awareness that the approach will be asymptotic at best. Rawls and White envision the ideal and suggest ways to approximate it in practice. Too much focus on the ideal can be misleading as a guide to making steps forward in practical politics, if the conditions that justify policies in ideal theory are not likely to exist on the path toward it.

For example, Rawlsian ideal theory assumes wide public consensus that the social project is just and that everyone has a duty to contribute to it. *Because* everyone agrees that there are no reasonable objections to the social project, the government is justified in forcing the individuals to participate. We may force you, but only because you agree that we should force you. This condition exists *only* if we are in a Rawlsian ideal and not on the path to it. This justification is unusable anywhere short of universal agreement when there are people with reasonable objections to social participation. This kind of justification for a mandatory-participation economy works only once the overlapping consensus is finally reached. Until then, it can't justify any more than voluntary participation. Considering the difference between what is justified in ideal and nonideal situations and likelihood of living in nonideal situations, we have to consider nonideal theory. However, before I get to nonideal arguments, let me discuss the JPA version of ideal theory, which is hopefully less restrictive and more broadly applicable than Rawlsian ideal theory.

Sticking with Rousseau's vision of laws as good as they can be for people as they are, people as they are disagree not only about what the good life is but also about what is a just society. No matter how good the laws might be, the laws cannot make those basic disagreements go away. The best we can hope for is a set of laws that represent a compromise that both maximizes the number of people brought into agreement and minimizes the negative impact on those who have not signed on to the agreement. We must strive for universal agreement, always attempting to bring more people into accord, but we must remember that laws are made only by the ruling coalition. We cannot assume universal agreement to anything. This version of ideal theory incorporates a great deal of reasonable disagreement that Rawls, White and many others leave for nonideal situations. In the indepentarian version of the ideal, force cannot be justified by supposing that the person being forced agrees to be forced. Force can be justified by self-defense or necessity, and therefore, a lower level of force is justifiable. The ideal way for humans to interact is voluntarily. Force is a departure from the highest ideal (with laws *and* people as good as they can be); it will exist in the best society we can expect, but it represents an enormous sacrifice for people as they are.

In the JPA version of ideal theory, we cannot assume away any of the 17 reasons why an individual might object to participation. Even a well-ordered society will always have dissenters with reasonable objections to participation. The choice is whether to make them forced laborers or to encourage their willing participation. By relying on voluntary participation, JPA delivers a form of universal agreement that no mandatory-participation society can: every participant is a voluntary participant. There is universal agreement among all who participate that they would rather participate than not, even though they have another reasonable alternative to participation. The justification of an indepentarian structure is not an imaginary universal agreement; it is the willing participation of everyone who actually participates.[35] This must be a morally significant advantage.

Consider applying the JPA version of ideal theory to the Rawlsian original position. What would negotiators behind the veil of ignorance most want, if they expect to emerge as the least advantaged person not only receiving the lowest pay and most difficult working conditions but also having a different idea of what goals the social project should pursue and what methods it should use? With those expectations, I would most want independence, to be free from the daily humiliation of forced labor in a project that rewards me less than everyone else for contributing to a project that I believe in less than everyone else. Thus, even in ideal theory, devices like the original position ought to be telling us to respect independence. Therefore, the main indepentarian reason to oppose mandatory participation, even within a liberal-egalitarian social project, is the idea (discussed in chapter 5) that consent is a constituent part of justice—not merely allegiance to a hypothetical social contract, but real, day-to-day unforced consent.

Most egalitarian theories make mutual obligation rather than mutual consent the centerpiece of human interaction or at least of economic interaction. Mutual obligations exist, but mutual consent must be the far greater part of human interaction in a free society. Imagine two neighboring countries with liberal-egalitarian projects that are alike in every way except that one punishes nonparticipants with destitution and homelessness while the other uses only positive rewards to elicit participation. If the justness of human cooperation has anything at all to do with voluntary agreement of the humans who are cooperating, the voluntary-participation economy must be more just than the other.

Although the great majority of world output is dedicated to things that people have no natural duty to produce, Rawls, Anderson, and White all seem to assume an obligation to work a standard working day, presumably as part of a standard work year and a standard working life. If so, people are put under an obligation to produce the whole of our economic output; no part of it is left optional. It offers individuals freedom in their off-hours, but obligation drives their single-biggest lifetime activity. This is an incongruous standpoint for a theory that appeals to voluntarism as its justification. Voluntarism shouldn't be relegated purely to the hypothetical realm. There might be other principles that could override respect for voluntarism in some cases, but the moral superiority of voluntarism ceteris paribus seems undeniable from a liberal and/or an egalitarian perspective.

Several aspects of liberal-egalitarian theory indicate some sympathy with the idea that individual, day-to-day consent is an important consideration even in ideal theory. For example, Rawls writes, "Extorted promises are void.... Unjust social arrangements are themselves a kind of extortion, even violence, and consent to them does not bind."[36] Stuart White criticizes "desperate trades" at least in individual interaction.[37] To me, a prohibition against extorted promises and desperate trades is a prohibition against mandatory participation. Perhaps, the objection is not to extorted promises or desperate trades per se but only to unjust extorted promises. That is, it is wrong to force someone to participate in an unjust social arrangement but permissible to force them to participate in a just social arrangement. If so, one must believe that day-to-day consent has nothing to do with whether a social arrangement is just. If so, one's complaint is not with extortion. The problem with extorting people to accept an unjust social arrangement is entirely with the unjustness of the arrangement not with the extortion that brings people into the arrangement. If extortion is bad in itself, even extortion for a good cause is problematic and should be prohibited except in extraordinary circumstances when it is overridden by other values.

B. Consent as Protection against Political Vulnerability in Nonideal Theory

If we take people as they are, we also must be aware that laws are made by people who are fallible. We can still use ideal theory as a guide, but once we determine what we think is ideal, our next question must always be what if the ruling coalition makes a mistake. As long as we live in a nonideal world, ideal theory is valuable only if it can pass that test as well. We cannot rely on any justifications that apply only once the assumptions of ideal theory obtain. Ideal theory is a guide for what policies can be; its presumed existence can't be used to justify policies that would be unjust otherwise.

Once we move out of ideal theory and consider that the laws themselves might be wrong, the connection between the original position and the argument for independence gets stronger. Behind the veil of ignorance, I expect to be the least advantaged person with the lowest pay and least desirable working conditions. I also expect that the ruling coalition will be made up of fallible people who will make mistakes. I am subject to both market and political vulnerability. My pay might be lower and my working conditions worse not only than I want, but also worse than is morally justified. The social project will pursue goals and use methods that I object to, and it is possible that I am right and the ruling coalition is wrong. Expecting to emerge from behind the veil of ignorance into such a world, I can't imagine anything I would want more than independence. It's simply not enough to connect the original position with the ruling coalition's promise of equal opportunity and equal treatment.[38] We have to connect it to what is most useful to the disadvantaged and dissenting individuals who are subject to such great power. Rawlsian awareness of reasonable disagreement should lead to respect for individual's choice of whether they want to participate in any joint venture. If the ruling coalition denies all access to resources to people who refuse to serve the coalition's project no matter how strongly some disadvantaged people believe they would not have agreed to that in the original position, it simply does not take disadvantaged individuals' perspective sufficiently into account. It will make them feel like a forced laborer, which cannot be the best way (morally or practically) to bring them into accord with the social agreement.

The risks of ignoring nonideal theory are substantial. The ruling coalition is inherently a coalition of the powerful. Although not necessarily a representative of the most advantaged individuals, it cannot be composed of the least advantaged. If a coalition of the least talented or skilled individuals became the ruling coalition, they would cease to be the least advantaged, because controlling the government is a significant advantage. It is easy for a powerful coalition to imagine a range of opportunities and working conditions that the lower classes ought to find acceptable, and to imagine that the ruling coalition gives them due respect. Selfishness, a lack of understanding, or a lack of empathy could make the coalition's rules less than reasonable. We can, therefore, expect that the ruling coalition will make systematic errors in their treatment of dissenters and the disadvantaged. Given this tendency for systematic errors, we need to minimize the maximum potential injustice and look for institutions that will protect the vulnerable. Chapter 7 argued that the protection of personal independence is helpful in both ways.

We also need a constraint on the majority's behavior. A theory that tells them to attempt magnanimity is not an effective constraint. It is not a constraint to tell the ruling coalition that they must justify participation in the social project to their own satisfaction. Of course, they think the project is just; they created it. It *is* a constraint to tell them that they have to justify participation sufficiently to elicit voluntary participation.

C. Mandatory Participation as a Poor Strategy to Cultivate Social Solidarity

A supporter of mandatory participation might respond that society needs to cultivate an ethic of contribution and an ethic of solidarity. We all stand together. Everyone contributes. Everyone benefits. Inviting people not to contribute until they selfishly feel like they're paid enough to make it worth their while relative to relaxing and collecting a basic income seems to conflict with the idea of solidarity that justifies the payment of taxes that benefit the poor. If everyone does their bit, we can feel justified in asking those who contribute more to share some of what they produce with those who contribute less. White states this kind of argument for a contributory obligation, writing, "Fair reciprocity, even in its non-ideal form, . . . does not call on citizens to solidarize with others regardless of their willingness to do their bit by way of productive contribution to the community. In this way, it affirms the dignity, by honouring the effort, of hard-working, tax-paying citizens." And, "I would question whether in any even modestly sized community 'trust and solidarity' can be built and maintained around egalitarian institutions without explicit, official adherence to a norm of substantive economic reciprocity."[39]

Arguments such as this seem to be premised on the idea that we will cultivate feelings of and ethos of solidarity by making the poor jump through hoops, fulfilling some obligation, before they get access to the means of existence. I suspect that that effort will cultivate nearly the opposite of the intended ethos, because to the extent that a policy can cultivate an ethos at all, it will cultivate the values it *displays* not the values it attempts to enforce. A policy that gives only conditional benefits to the poor might be designed to make the poor act like good solidaristic contributors, but it displays the social value that *we give to no one until they give us something first*. It communicates, "We, the group in power, take all the resources for our social project; you get no resources to further your project until we can use your labor as a resource for our project." The rules display selfishness and invites individuals to return selfishness. Each individual should pay the group in power back by refusing to give them anything that isn't paid for, by driving the hardest and most selfish bargain they can. If you want to cultivate an ethos of selfless giving, give selflessly. If you want to cultivate an ethos of selfishness, give with self-serving conditions attached. The poor have good reason to be skeptical of any authority that claims to be generous to them while it gives them less than everyone else and makes them do jobs with poorer working conditions than everyone else to prove their worthiness for this supposed generosity.

Conditional polities not only encourage resentment on the part of recipients but they also encourage selfishness on the part of better-off people in two important ways. First, better-off people are encouraged to look at the weak and the vulnerable as potential cheats who all must continually prove their worth. Second, they are encouraged to think that there is something laudable about their relatively large income in the sense that it is assumed to be disproportionately small in relation to their contribution while low-income people receive salaries that are disproportionately large in relation to their contribution. If this characterization were accurate, people with better working conditions and high wages would be continually giving gifts to the people with lower wages and less desirable working conditions. I'm sure this is not the way liberal-egalitarians want people to look at a work obligation, but I don't think it's controversial to say that if one class of people continually gives and another continually receives, humans tend to think there is something laudable about the giving class and something disrespectful about the receiving class. Humans would tend to think that an obligation develops, and if the difference-principle description is accurate, the poor could never pay it back. So, people with relatively large incomes might feel that the disadvantaged should at least be grateful, respectful, and humble. The poor can reject this characterization and feel bad about the project, or they can accept it and feel bad about themselves. Neither of these is the ethos of mutual respect that White and other egalitarians hope to cultivate.

JPA does not rely on any ethic of contribution to justify taxation. People pay taxes to justify their ownership of a larger share of resources than other people. In an ideally functioning society, the highest incomes are neither praiseworthy nor blameworthy. It is one side of an exchange in an imperfect market. If you took a job that pays a dollar more than the basic income, people should assume that you did it for the dollar. You contributed your labor, and you were fully paid with greater access to resources. Your taxes are not a gift. Once you have accepted more than anyone else gets, you have moved into the realm of the trade model, and you have made application of the voluntarism or obligation model inappropriate. You have to choose whether you want praise for what you do or a high after-tax income. It is inappropriate to ask for both. If you want gratitude for your contribution, contribute on a purely voluntary basis.

It might be better for society to create institutions that reflect an indepentarian ethos. The social project will be as fair and mutually beneficial as the ruling majority is capable of making it. But the ruling majority respects that not every individual agrees. It shows respect even for those who do not respect it. The ruling majority asks for their contribution, but it does not demand it or use threats to obtain it. We attempt to build a society where each individual respects the independence of other individuals. We do not tell them what they want. We let them choose. There are jobs if you want them and there are resources available unconditionally if you don't. We stand in solidarity with you even if you do not reciprocate. If we can show those who disagree with us most that we care about their needs, and that we will not take advantage of them, we give them much more reason to come into accord with us than if we force them to work for our goals.

D. *An Exit Option for the Disadvantaged*

If we want to avoid extorting people to join the project, we should find some non-punishing way to leave them outside the project.

This is how I see an exit option sustained by basic income. Many liberal-egalitarians seem to see no such possibility: everyone either contributes to the project or benefits at its expense. But, there must be a happy medium where one neither contributes to nor benefits at the expense of the project. Because of the assumption of "identity of interests" (discussed above), there would seem to be no Rawlsian objection to a basic income set at a level just enough to compensate a person for the fact that resources have been dominated by a social project they don't want to participate in. If we really have any identity of interests in contributing to the project, it would be in our private interest to take a job rather than to live off the basic income at the level that just compensates us for the loss of our next best option.

In ideal theory, the power to say no would seem to be superfluous because everyone agrees that participation is fair and the right thing to do. But two reasons indicate that it would be useful even in ideal theory. First, even a superfluous exit option might be truer than forced participation to the spirit of mutual cooperation that motivates liberal-egalitarianism. Second, even if everyone agreed to the ideal-theory basic structure, taking people as they are, some will be weak and get themselves fired from their jobs, just as under mandatory participation. Instead of being forced back into another job by whatever punishment enforces mandatory participation, they would live at the level that compensates them for being unable to live by their own efforts. If we are in a position that meets all the criteria for Rawlsian ideal theory, they would say to themselves, "All though this life is not thoroughly bad in an absolute sense, and I could continue to live this way, I realize now that that job really was worth the effort, and so I voluntarily choose to get a new job and try harder."

One might respond by arguing that such a basic income is not feasible. I doubt the empirical claim.[40] But even if it were true, one who counters this argument with the feasibility objection concedes voluntary participation as the first-best option. Mandatory participation is second best, coming into play only when a sufficiently large basic income is unavailable. Chapter 9 discusses the possibility that basic income is not feasible.[41]

E. An Exit Option for Everyone

Rawlsians might worry that advantaged people would use the power to refuse to their advantage in violation of the spirit of the difference principle, but there are several reasons that we might ignore this worry. The greater worry about the more talented is that they will get easy jobs that don't use their full talent, as in the example of Roy the professor/inventor above. I'm not sure how much additional leverage such a person would get from the opportunity to live at the very social minimum. The lower a person's potential income is (i.e., the more disadvantaged she is) the more attractive the basic income becomes. Moving up the scale of advantage the basic income becomes relatively less attractive. High potential-income earners might still take advantage of it in some cases, but if they really are willing to live so far below their potential income, perhaps there is something very unattractive about their job that we are unaware of.

If we allow the least advantaged to choose basic income over their offer—because they are the least advantaged—but we don't let someone else choose that same option, we run the risk of making that person even less advantaged than the formerly least advantaged. Perhaps respect for their day-to-day exercise of a meaningful form of self-ownership, and the use of the identity-of-interests argument requires that we let them do so. At the very least, it provides a check to ensure that the identity of interests is there if we have not quite reached an overlapping consensus.

F. The Inegalitarian Use of Force against the Disadvantaged

One final reason egalitarians should respect independence is that it is distinctly inegalitarian to force the powerless to participate in a project with rules, goals, and methods chosen by more powerful people. Any egalitarian who supports a mandatory-participation economy needs to recognize that even if such an economy is capable of virtually eliminating poverty *ex post* via conditional benefits, it *cannot* eliminate poverty, destitution, and propertylessness *ex ante.* In fact a mandatory-participation economy relies on poverty; it *creates* and *uses* poverty and destitution as a threat to ensure participation. It has to do so because participation is not mandatory unless there is a significant punishment for the refusal to participate. If participation is going to be both mandatory and real (meaning jobs are productive and workers must put forth good effort to remain employed), there has to be some realistic expectation of punishment if they don't participate. Thus, no matter now generous a liberal-egalitarian system might be, as long as it is committed to mandatory participation, it relies on the constant threat of destitution and homelessness to keep workers disciplined. Just as in Nozick's system, propertyless individuals start out in a state of destitution with no legal access to resources other than by agreeing to serve the project designated by the group that controls property. Presumably some people will test the limits. Some people will do a poor job. They will be fired and they will become propertyless. Help will always be waiting, but until these bad people shape up, they will be destitute.

Under mandatory participation, the fear of destitution hangs over the heads of all our most disadvantaged workers, not in the sense that they fear being downsized without unemployment insurance. As long as an individual continues to perform sufficiently, they are protected and insured against unemployment, but the ruling majority want them always to fear being labeled undeserving by refusing to follow orders or by not following those orders well enough to continue to qualify as a worker. It's a simple dichotomy: either workers really do fear being punished for not following orders or jobs aren't really mandatory. All the psychological advantages that Erich Fromm argued will appear when workers no longer fear poverty is not something we want to give to the poor.[42] We could provide freedom from the fear of poverty, but doing so would be too much to give our disadvantaged workers. It might be a good thing in itself, but it wouldn't be worth the loss in discipline among our disadvantaged workers. Even in a first-best ideal society with laws as good as they can be, we cannot have freedom from the fear of poverty because people, being people as they are, wouldn't fulfill their mandatory obligations without it.

Egalitarians who support mandatory participation need to own this argument. They need to admit that, all things considered, the freedom from the fear of poverty is not something they ever want to eliminate, because they choose to use it to discipline the most disadvantaged workers. The ruling coalition should admit, "We deprive individuals of direct access to resources to force dissenters to face destitution not as the consequence for the refusal to *work* but as the consequence for the refusal to work *for us*. We use this strategy to discipline dissenters into accepting our goals, methods, and terms." Something about this position seems to be distinctly inegalitarian.

5. Conclusion

Many modern egalitarians seem to believe that the power to say no is too much freedom for the disadvantaged to have. What is it about the poor that egalitarians are so afraid of? They believe that a government can offer people good jobs at good wages and people will be so lazy that they will still turn them down to live at the bare minimum, and that these jobs can be so good and so fair that government is morally authorized to force individuals to take them. Egalitarians should not be so sure that disputes about the worthiness of a job offer occur because the poor are lazy and not because everyone else made them an offer that is unworthy of acceptance. If egalitarianism is worth pursuing, it is because the weak and the disadvantaged need greater concern, and if so, an egalitarian's first concern should be that the powerful do not take advantage of the poor rather than the reverse. An egalitarian worthy of the name should give benefit of the doubt to the poor.

Is there really any way in which society can ethically divide unowned natural resources such that one person has no access to resources at all? Anyone who advocates conditional access to all resources must believe the answer to that question is yes. The failure to satisfy the obligation to serve the ruling coalition's joint project is sufficient grounds to make them destitute. If egalitarianism is the ideology most favorable to the least advantaged, I do not see how a system that threatens anyone with destitution can claim to be truly egalitarian. It is surprising that people who consider themselves defenders of either equality or liberty would support using this life-threatening power to get less powerful individuals to do what the powerful group decides they should do.

Liberal-egalitarians and right-libertarians are unlikely allies on the issues discussed in the last two chapters. Both supposedly believe that agreement is central to just interaction, but neither of them create an institutional structure in which propertyless individuals have any real opportunity to say no to agreements. They justify their systems of social cooperation on the grounds that the system makes everyone better-off (in terms of their own preferences) than they would be producing by their own efforts, but neither system allows individuals to choose between social cooperation and living by their own efforts or living at the equivalent level. Nozick believes that a right-libertarian capitalist economy with extreme inequality simply turns out to be better for everyone than a state of nature. Many liberal-egalitarians believe that a regulated, market economy can be made to turn out better for everyone. I believe we should let each individual decide whether the economic system is worthy of their participation. Without respect for independence libertarianism displays insufficient concern with liberty, and egalitarianism displays insufficient concern with equality.

CHAPTER 9

On Duty

State what, in your opinion, is the best way to enlist colored men for soldiers.

—*General Sherman (through his agent)*

I think, sir, that all compulsory operations should be put a stop to. The ministers would talk to them, and the young men would enlist.

—*Garrison Frazier*[1]

This chapter considers the question of duty and how it relates to the arguments for freedom from forced interaction presented above. Beginning with the assumption that there are some situations in which individuals have an enforceable obligation to contribute to a joint project, this book considers what limits JPA theory implies for the enforcement of duties. This discussion is largely a response to the objection to basic income on grounds variously described as "exploitation," "reciprocity," or "parasitism." Many political theorists have argued against policies are allowing people to receive an *unconditional* basic income. It takes labor to generate the social product from which basic income is drawn. Therefore, basic income recipients, supposedly, act as parasites, exploiting workers who contribute to the social product without making a reciprocal contribution to it.[2]

I have voiced skepticism about this sort of argument above and elsewhere. However, I don't think my arguments are decisive against any and all potential arguments for a duty to contribute to some joint project in any and all circumstances. I do not think any such argument can be decisive without relying on some premise like there is no such thing as an active duty. But I would like to approach the issue from the opposite direction: assuming active duties exist, what are the limits on a ruling majority coalition's power to enforce them?

Recall from earlier chapters that I do not rely on active duty to justify taxation. People pay taxes to obtain resources and the things we make out of them. If they don't want more than the minimum amount of resourses, they don't have to pay taxes. Thus, taxpayers cannot assert that they have fulfilled a duty by paying a tax. For duty to be fulfilled by work, it must be by the act of work.

This chapter discusses the reasonable limits that a duty of active contribution should have. In the context of the theory outlined above, this chapter argues that maximal substantive and equal freedom for all implies substantial limits on the power of any one person or group (even a majority group) to force unwilling individuals to perform active duties. The chapter argues that there are (relatively) few situations in which an active duty is justified, that there are substantial limits on how a duty can be imposed, and that the group imposing a duty must take on substantial responsibilities in return for forcing people to do things.

Specifically, this chapter argues for four limits on the imposition of an active duty by force. First, the group imposing duties has the responsibility to make decisions democratically. This limit follows directly from the requirement to seek accord, and so I will not argue for it further. However, consistently with what I have argued above, I do not assume that democratic imposition means that the group imposes the duty on itself. Democracy ensures only that people have the *opportunity* to affect the decision. It does not assure that everyone succeeds in having a significant impact on the decision or that everyone agrees that the majority should have the power to enforce its opinion on this issue. The majority imposes the duty by force onto everyone, including those who oppose the idea.

Second, duties must be equally onerous for everyone. One group cannot force others to perform more burdensome duties than they force on themselves. This requirement does not mean that everyone performs the exact same duties. The relative difficulty of one duty could be compensated by reducing the amount of time one is required to perform it relative to one who performs an easier duty.

Third, the imposition of a duty by force can only be justified by necessity. Maximal freedom requires the avoidance of force whenever possible. Therefore, a group must limit its enforcement to necessity. There must be compelling cases both that the duties exist and that enforcement is necessary. Essentially then, enforceable duties are limited to cases of emergency: unavoidable situations requiring action. It is not enough to say, we're all better-off if we all perform this duty. If there is a way to put people outside the circle of obligation, those imposing the duty have a responsibility to do so.

Fourth, by appealing to the urgency of the situation to justify a duty, the ruling coalition takes on the responsibility to get out of the emergency as soon as possible. It cannot simply choose to maintain a situation in which the enforcement of duties is necessary when it could bring about a situation when no enforcement would be necessary.

If the argument (below) for these limits holds, the enforcement of active duties is justifiable in fewer situations and under more restrictive conditions than might otherwise be supposed. That is, the conditions are more restrictive for the group imposing the duty. This chapter argues for those limits, and shows that under those limits, the appeal to duty cannot do what basic income opponents would like it to do: it cannot justify a lifetime commitment to labor market participation. Even if active duties exist, duty can at most justify a minimal service obligation imposed equally on all citizens (rich and poor alike).

Section 1 discusses what can and cannot ground an active duty of participation. It shows that there are cases in which an active duty can be justified but that when one considers the possibility of passive contribution, the case for an active duty is much weaker and much more limited. Section 2 then discusses the limits on the possible imposition of a duty, and connects those limits with the question of whether basic income recipients have a duty to participate in the labor market.

1. What Can and Cannot Justify a Duty

This section discusses what can and cannot justify a duty. It first shows that there are situations in which duties are justified, but it then shows that they are fewer such situations than supposed by those who believe that basic income recipients have a lifetime obligation to contribute to the labor market.

In several places above, this book refers to one type of situation capable of grounding an enforceable active duty: Singer's example of a drowning child or infant:

> **Example 1, the drowning child**: An infant is drowning in a shallow pond. One passerby is capable of saving the infant with minimal effort. The child will die, if the passerby does not make the effort.

Although the passerby's freedom is important, the child's life outweighs it in this extreme situation. In this example, a moral duty to preserve life grounds a duty.

The following example shows a different kind of situation capable of grounding an active duty.

> **Example 2, lifeboat above the falls**: A rowboat is caught in a swift current above a high falls. Unless everyone on board rows with sufficient strength to pull their own weight, the boat will go over the falls and everyone on board will surely die.

This example shows that interdependence is capable of grounding an active duty to contribute to a joint project in at least some cases. The people in this example are urgently and physically interdependent. Everyone's life depends on the success of the joint project. People cannot meet their own needs alone; all are dependent on joint cooperation for survival and thriving. It is difficult to argue against the contention that everyone has an enforceable duty to contribute to the cooperative project under these conditions. It doesn't matter if one person owns the boat or even if one person is physically incapable of rowing. If it is true that everyone on board must pull their weight or all will die, very harsh conclusions follow. We could soften the example. If rowing required only x percent of the able-bodied,[3] there would still be a good case for an enforceable active duty, and there would be ways to enforce it without throwing nonparticipants over the falls. Call this softened version example 2b.

There are two different possibilities about the level of free riding. In the original version of example 2: the likely level of free riding (or, in this case, *any* level of free riding) is larger than the group can sustain without the entire group going over the falls. If so, everyone's life depends on the enforceability of the duty. But assume that in example 2b, the likely level of free riding is easily sustained without any danger of the boat going over the falls. In this case, people's physical survival does not depend on the enforceability of the duty; what depends on enforceability is fairness in the distribution of a burden that is essential to the preservation of life. In example 2b, the argument for enforcement relies on an additional premise of fairness or reciprocity, which is not required in example 2, which requires only the belief that death for all is worse than a temporary loss of freedom. The level of force necessary to maintain everyone's life might be much less than the level of force necessary to maintain both life and this premise of fairness, but I concede that both are allowable grounds for a duty.

Examples 1 and 2 establish two groundings for an active duty: moral responsibility and interdependence. It is possible to draw a connection between them by saying that there are two kinds of interdependence: moral and physical. One could argue that everyone is equally under a moral duty to care for an orphan child. Everyone's life as a moral human being depends on that project. There is a closer connection between physical and moral interdependence than might first appear. All of us are physically dependent on others during part of our lives—at least during childhood and most probably also in cases such as illness, injury, accident, old age, and so on. Therefore, one could argue that we are interdependent on average throughout our lives: each of us depends on others to take care of us during the times in which we are unable to take care of ourselves.

I will not dwell on the difference or the connection between moral and physical interdependence. Most of what I want to say about one applies equally to the other. It is not necessary for me to establish that there are active duties. I am conceding that they exist and examining the extent to which they limit my arguments for independence. My goal is to show that there are strong limits on the group enforcing duties, even if we presume that interdependence exists.

Although this discussion shows that other moral principles can override concern with status freedom and scalar freedom in some circumstances, maximal equal and substantive freedom is still important. If some other principle prevents us from respecting people's independence throughout their lives, we can and should respect their independence for as much of their lives as possible. As earlier chapters argue, freedom cannot be rendered worthless, even if it can be overridden by other principles. Many principles prevent us from giving everyone complete scalar freedom, but we can and should give them maximal equal freedom. These concerns will place important limits on the enforcement of duty.

I now turn to arguments that cannot justify an active duty. One is simply that active cooperation makes us better-off. Saying that we would all be better-off is not a legitimate reason to force somebody to participate.

> **Example 3, legitimate nonparticipant**: Initially everyone lives minimally but adequately as subsistence farmers or hunter-gatherers. Someone figures out that we could all earn pay that will give us a higher standard of living if we all contributed our land and our labor to a joint project called the modern post-industrial economy. The majority of citizens want this project, but Gilligan asks to be left out.

This example shows to the extent that what we get from working together is reflected in our pay, there is no need for nor legitimacy in forcing people to seek that pay. If Gilligan doesn't like the pay relative to what he was doing before, it's very hard to say that he has a duty to contribute to a project designed to get everyone higher private rewards than they were able to generate outside the project. Also, it would be legitimate of Gilligan to say, you can have my land but not my labor. I don't like the pay but I'll take basic income for accepting less access to land than other people.[4] This response seems especially appropriate if the decision to devote most of the world's land to the project is imposed on Gilligan without his consent.

The grounds for a duty has to be something more than mutual benefit, something like interdependence. But even interdependence on labor is not enough. I want to demonstrate that the following argument does not always work: The social product requires labor. Therefore, everyone who would consume something from the social product is under a duty to contribute their labor to social production. I believe this argument is at the heart of most reciprocity- and exploitation-based objections to basic income.[5] The central problem with this argument is that work is not *all* that is required to create the social product.

I have responded to this argument in several articles, arguing that at least some level of basic income must be ***unconditional*** to be ***consistent*** with reciprocity and to protect individuals from exploitation. A property right is the legal right to interfere with people who might want to use some external asset. Typically governments enforce private and public property rights in natural resources without the consent of the people they force to obey those duties. Therefore, unequally held property rights can only be reciprocal if the people who benefit from the imposition of those duties compensate the people on whom those property rights authorize interference. Otherwise, property rights are enforced as a one-way obligation from the have-nots to the haves. Earlier chapters of this book extend that argument, claiming that such compensation must be sufficient to maintain personal independence. I have also argued that the claim of exploitation is misplaced. Basic income is to be paid by the group that dominates resources to potential workers to free them from forced labor and potential exploitation by the group that dominates resources.[6]

I want to extend those arguments further here to show that the poor and the propertyless already contribute to the social project, although they contribute passively. Reciprocity arguments against basic income must be based on some duty to contribute *actively*. But if such arguments take the existence of passive contribution seriously and consider the question of when passive contribution can and cannot be enough, the case for a duty to participate in the labor market is weaker. Consider the following example:[7]

> **Example 4, the well**: Everyone will die of thirst unless one of the seven stranded castaways on Gilligan's Island digs a well. Mr. Howell is glad to do so in exchange for a relatively larger share of land, natural resources, and external assets left by previous generations.

Individuals in this example are interdependent. Everyone needs the well and the well requires human effort. Only Mr. Howell actively contributes to digging the well, but everyone else passively contributes to the well by assigning him ownership of more resources than they receive. Everyone consumes part of the social product, which embodies both labor and resources. Only one person contributes labor to that product, but yet, the simple version of the reciprocity argument doesn't work. Everyone else passively contributes to the digging of the well by being assigned access to a smaller amount of resources than Mr. Howell. The other castaways are not under a duty to contribute their labor simply because the social product embodies labor. Basic income opponents need an argument to explain why *passive contribution*, which seems adequate in this example, is insufficient in the situations in which they wish to impose an active duty.

This example readily translates into the receipt of an unconditional basic income in JPA theory. All wealth is a claim on resources and on the things that we make out of them. The government enforces property rights in resources, giving people incentives to make them into more valuable forms, increasing individual and national wealth. All individuals pay taxes to justify their ownership of resources they hold, and all individuals receive basic income in compensation for the resources they do not hold. If the system works perfectly, those who contribute a lot, get a lot of resources, but of course, there is a great deal of luck and unfairness in the political and economic system. Those who contribute less get less than anyone else, but they get something to compensate for all the resources that have been assigned to others. They get to consume products that embody the labor of others. If they got no compensation, there would be no justification for the assignment of resources to others, for the unfairness of the system, and for the many controversial rules that they are forced to live under against their will.

Basic income opponents need to show either why it is always wrong for the castaways to consume water without contributing labor in the well example or why the well example is not representative of basic income recipients in a modern economy. If the outcome in the well example is morally acceptable, then the mere existence of interdependence is not enough to justify a duty.

The justification for an active duty must be based on interdependence *and* something else, such as the inability to internalize rewards. In the example of the boat on the falls, there is presumably no way to internalize the reward. If a sufficient number volunteer to row, all survive whether they row or not. Those who row have a claim of unfairness against those who literally ride for free. But in the well example, no one rides for free. No one rides without sacrifice. The castaways pay Mr. Howell for what they consume by consuming less than he does. Most of the things people plausibly have duties to do are things that people are paid to do: firefighters, doctors, paramedics, paid care workers, and so forth. As long as the rewards are adequate, the mere existence of labor on which all people depend does not itself justify forcing everyone to labor.

Hopefully, this discussion shows that basic income has the potential to be a legitimate starting point for individuals entering potential cooperation. Recipients are being compensated for not being able to have all the access to resources they might be able to use (alone or in a group of their choosing), for living under rules not entirely of their choice, and for rules that give greater advantages to others. And they contribute passively to the fulfillment of duties by consuming fewer resources than those who are paid for fulfilling active duties of doing anything else.

Perhaps reluctance to accept the potential legitimacy of basic income comes from a contractarian desire to substitute imagined agreement for what I believe should be literal agreement. Return to the four steps I considered in chapter 4. The difference between a voluntary- and a mandatory-participation economy is in step 3. I put the two sets of steps together. Step 3a represents the mandatory-participation move. Step 3b represents the voluntary-participation move.

Step 1: Population begins low and resources are not dominated.
Step 2: Some group comes to dominate resources.
Step 3a: Without compensation for lost access to resources, destitution forces the propertyless into the labor market.
Step 3b: The propertyless receive compensation sufficient to preserve independence. They enter the labor market if jobs are sufficiently attractive.
Step 4: The propertyless (might) take jobs that (hopefully) make them better-off than they were in step 1.

Contractarians seem to want to frame this situation in such a way that the only legitimate choice is between step 1 and step 4. If people were living as subsistence farmers and or hunter-gatherers, it would be legitimate of some coalition to make an offer to create a joint project called post-industrial capitalism and to say that only people who devote *both* their land and their labor to it can share in its benefits,[8] and people might have said yes. But a long and complex history brought us from step 1 to step 4. It's not practical for us to offer that choice. Step 2 has passed and we are unlikely to reverse it. We have to deal with where we are now.

The contractarian solution is to use our imagination to pretend that we actually offered a choice between step 1 and 4. If we take the Hobbesian strategy, we imagine that step 1 was a horrible "state of nature," and so, we conclude step 4 is always better than the alternative. Most contractarians no longer rely on the alternative being utterly horrible, and I've argued that we should include, not limit, the alternative to the "state of nature" but to all other possible social arrangements. If so, the possibility of legitimate nonparticipation grows. However a contractarian might claim, individuals only have a legitimate objection (and therefore a legitimate claim to compensation) if they are real dissenters who actually prefer step 1 to step 4. Everyone else is free riding or gaming the system.

This argument doesn't work because the ruling coalition can't claim credit for making the offer it wishes it could make. Two can play at that game. When the coalition offered to create modern (welfare) capitalism or any other system, individuals could have responded, you can have my land, but you cannot have my labor. Give me unconditional basic income in exchange for land, and then I'll decide whether I want to contribute my labor. The ruling coalition might have said yes to this offer, just as the individual might have said yes to the bundled offer.

But what actually happened was that some group (a complex mix of private owners and government) came to dominate resources. Propertyless individuals have not been given the choice of whether to do things differently. We find ourselves at step 3, and we have to decide whether people are entitled to unconditional compensation for resource domination or not. The indepentarian solution is that we have to obtain literal, individual agreement from wherever we start (unless some compelling duty overrides it). The subjunctive question of what people would have done were we to make them such and such an offer at some early point is irrelevant. What is relevant is that some group has come to dominate resources without the consent of the propertyless. The direction of obligation runs from all those who have to all those who have not, and this compensation must be unconditional both to preserve independence and to function as reciprocal compensation for the liberties that were taken away without consent.

What if this compensation makes some people far better-off than they were in step 1? That's fine. That's how trade works, and that's how compensation for forced trade works. Whether we sell labor, goods, or services, we all give up one thing to get another thing in hopes of becoming as much better-off as possible. I might like my job better than my coworker, but I get the same pay as long as I do the job just as well. If we were all restricted to making trades that would make us no better off than at the start, no one would bother to trade anything. There is something suspicious about a system that applies the trade model to so much of our interaction, but would not allow the propertyless to apply it to the passive contribution that more advantaged people have forced them to make. If we see basic income in this way, it is a legitimate starting point for all people regardless of their preferences.

If basic income is a legitimate starting point, gaming the system or free riding does not exist. To game the system, one must take more than is legitimate. With a legitimate, unconditional starting point, there is no system to game. To free ride, one needs to benefit without sacrifice. Basic income recipients benefit without working, but certainly not without sacrifice. When you think of the enormity of social rules that put people with little property at a disadvantage relative to people with property, it is clear that a propertyless person without a basic income has sacrificed a great deal to make the economy work.

If basic income is a *potentially* legitimate starting point, are there any conditions that would make it illegitimate? Are there some ways that the modern society is more like the lifeboat example than the well example? To make the case that it is more like the lifeboat example, I think one would have to claim that there is a population emergency: there just aren't enough resources available for everyone to create sufficient internalized rewards for people who perform duties relative to receiving a livable basic income. Insufficiently internalized rewards could mean one of two things: it could mean that the basic income is unsustainable because too few people will take the jobs doing the duties (as in example 2), or it could mean that basic income is sustainable only because some people make the sacrifice by taking the under-rewarded jobs, when they would really rather live on basic income (as in example 2b). Although it is difficult to accept a higher reward than someone else *and* claim that one does so purely for selfless reasons, either of these situations creates potential moral problems that might justify a duty to contribute. The next section looks at limits on the imposition of a duty in the presence of these possibilities.

2. Limits on the Imposition of a Duty

The introduction mentioned four limits on the enforcement of active duties: (1) Duties must be enacted democratically; (2) Duties must be equally onerous for all; (3) Duties must be justified by necessity or emergency; and (4) Those imposing the duty have a responsibility to try to get out of the situation in which force is necessary; that is, they have to try to get out of the emergency. I'm not going to argue for democracy any more in this chapter. So, I'll begin with equally onerous duties.

Force involves a sacrifice of freedom. If maximal and equally substantive freedom is a goal, any duties we force on people have to be equally onerous for everyone. If not, we make some less free than others. As earlier chapters argue, differential work and differential reward must be justified by choice.

> **Example 5, lifeboat with rowers and a navigator**: Several castaways find themselves on a lifeboat in the ocean. They need people to row and at least one person to navigate to survive. Everyone agrees that rowing is ten times more difficult and time-consuming than navigation. Not all members are able to navigate.

If the group holds one individual to the duty to navigate while it holds others to the duty to row, the rowers have a legitimate complaint that they are not equally as free as the navigator. Even though both contributions are necessary, a rower behaves reasonably if she refuses to row unless the navigator does enough rowing to equalize the burden. The analogy between this example and a modern, industrial economy is, I hope, obvious. If others can fulfill their duties as highly paid, pleasant jobs, such as corporate executive, fashion model, or university professor, those who are held to a duty to take poorly paid, unpleased jobs, such as dishwasher or nursing home attendant, have a legitimate claim that the duty to contribute is not equally onerous for everyone.

Section 1 argued that force must be justified by necessity to be consistent with equal freedom for all. This limit has many implications.

For one thing, we can't give people credit toward fulfilling duties for doing things that aren't duties.

> **Example 6, lifeboat with rowers and a bookie**: As in example 5, rowers are in a lifeboat on the ocean, but instead of the navigator, the rowers like to gamble, make use of the services of a bookie. Although gambling is not essential to the lifeboat's mission, a majority of the rowers allow the bookie to get out of the duty to row to concentrate fulltime on bookmaking.

In this example, it seems reasonable for any of the rowers to say, "If the bookie doesn't have to row, I don't have to row." The reasonableness of this argument doesn't seem to depend on whether that rower makes use of the bookie's services or not. It is reasonable even for a better to believe that bookmaking is something that should be done only after any duties are fulfilled. Furthermore, if bookmaking is a contribution to rowing, it is indirect and passive, and it undercuts the argument that people have an active duty to participate in rowing. Hopefully, the analogy to basic income is again clear. Much if not most of modern economic activity is dedicated to things that are unnecessary and that people clearly have no duty to do. If duties were limited to those things and applied equally to all people, whatever duty people would have would be much less than a fulltime work obligation, leaving people with a lot of time to pursue either leisure or optional economic activities.

The requirement that force be minimized to necessity also implies that we can't force people to do more than is strictly necessary to do.

> **Example 7, work ethic utopia**: Everyone works 16 hours a day, seven days a week doing difficult physical labor producing pure public goods (i.e., all share equally in the benefits of those goods whether or not they contribute to production). Most members of society agree that this arrangement is the good life. One member objects to this work pace.

The majority has at least one claim based on exploitation and one claim based on equal freedom to hold the dissenter to an enforceable duty. Because all production is devoted to public goods, the dissenter will benefit from the others' labor even if she does not contribute. In the example, everyone does the same work for the same reward, and everyone is in that sense equally free, or more accurately, equally unfree. No one has much freedom at all. Although in the majority opinion, holding everyone to this obligation makes everyone better-off, it is not necessary to force someone with differing preferences to participate. To reach the *maximal* equal freedom they have to pare down the duty to the minimum that is genuinely necessary, even if those who refuse to do more than the minimum will benefit from public goods produced by others. The case for a general work obligation is even weaker if the economy produces private goods for private rewards, because if the rewards for work are internalized, the exploitation charge goes away. Even if it is necessary to hold people to some contributory obligation in a modern economy, it cannot be necessary to hold them to a fulltime work obligation for 40 or 50 years.

Finally, if the ruling coalition appeals to necessity to justify duty, the coalition takes on the responsibility to get out of that emergency as soon as possible to free people from force.

> **Example 8, lifeboat past the point of safety**: Return to the lifeboat above the falls. The lifeboat reaches the point at which it is safely beyond the dangerous current. Although they could row immediately to shore, the majority decides to row farther upstream because they believe they will have a more enjoyable time at that location.

It seems as soon as the boat passes the point of safety, the argument for forcing everyone to row is lost. The same would hold true for a lifeboat on the ocean, if the majority decided not to row in the direction of the nearest island but to row to a much more distant island that they preferred for some reason. It seems that as soon as this decision is made, the argument for the necessity of forcing people to row is lost. If a modern society insists on imposing obligation on the grounds that there is a shortage of resources relative to the size of the population, it takes on the responsibility to get out of the population emergency as soon as possible. It can either commit itself to reduce the population to the point at which a work obligation is no longer necessary, or it can give up on imposing the work obligation.

I will illustrate the connection between these limits to the possibility of a duty of contribution to the modern economy by considering one final example, which puts most of these issues together.

> **Example 9, the floating casino**: The castaways are aboard a giant ship powered like a Roman galleon with rows of oars below decks and a casino above. The floating casino has a complex economy including, not only many different gambling tables, but also fine restaurants, downscale restaurants, massage parlors, electronics stores, sports, and so on. Only a small fraction of the floating casino's economy is devoted to the one essential task of rowing. The rewards for most

> jobs are internalized with differentiated pay. Significant unfairness and inequality exists in the economic system, but the majority decides that the system is as fair and mutually beneficial as possible, and it enforces a fulltime obligation to contribute to the economy in general. The floating casino is not rowing toward the nearest island, or to any island. It rows for the purpose of trade. It is expected that citizens enter the floating casino only by birth and exit only by death.

Except democracy, the floating casino violates every limit on forced obligations. People are forced to do things that aren't necessary. All people are forced to do more hours of work per day than can be justified by necessity. The ruling coalition is making no effort to get out of the situation in which the enforcement of duties is necessary. And the enforced duties are more onerous for some than others, violating equal freedom. Some people are forced into difficult, unpleasant, poorly paid, or low status jobs, while others satisfy their work obligation with easier, pleasant, well paid, or high status jobs. Even if the difference principle (maximizing the advantages of the least advantaged individuals) is applied to wages and working conditions, as long as society forces the least advantaged to participate, the relative burden of their jobs makes them significantly less free than those who are able to get the better jobs.

To rectify this situation while preserving the mandatory obligation, the ruling coalition would have to separate duties from non-duties, limit the use of force to genuine duties, and enforce them equally. In this simplified example, the only necessary duty is rowing.[9] Everyone—rich and poor—would make an equal contribution to rowing. Their basic needs would be satisfied, and the rest of the economy would be based on voluntary participation. But the ruling coalition would still have the responsibility to get out of the emergency that justifies force as soon as possible. If they wanted to get out of that responsibility, they could stop forcing individuals to participate. They can internalize the rewards for rowing, paying people enough to make them want to do it when they can do otherwise, and base the entire economy on voluntary participation.

Applying the same principles I applied in these simplified examples to the modern economy shows that it is extremely difficult, if not impossible, to make a generalized work obligation (i.e. a duty to participate in the labor market) consistent with equal freedom for all. It would force duties on the poor that are far more onerous than the duties forced on people with more advantages in the labor market. It would force people to do many things that clearly aren't duties. It would force people to work many more hours than is necessary to complete the tasks that people might actually have a duty to do. As argued in earlier chapters, differential rewards must be justified by force.

For an enforced contributive duty to be consistent with maximal equal freedom, it would have to be very different from a generalized obligation. The government would have to figure out exactly which economic activities are things that we have a duty to do and which aren't. It would then have to figure out how to share those duties in a way that is as equally burdensome for all, rich and poor alike. It would have to figure out what the minimum amount is that we all have to do, force us all to do that and no more. We would then be free to resume our normal economic activities in a voluntary-participation economy once our duties were completed. Setting this up would be a major undertaking, and in the end it would be more like a national service than a duty to work as currently envisioned. Perhaps citizens would work a few hours a month throughout their lives, or perhaps they would perform one, two, or several years of fulltime service at the beginning of their working lives. Once the duty is completed people would be free to choose whether to participate in optional economic activities for private rewards.

This strategy of dealing with duty changes the four-step process discussed above into a five-step process:

Step 1: Population begins low and resources are not dominated.
Step 2: Some group comes to dominate resources.
Step 3: Everyone performs their active duties, which are equally onerous for all. (Benefits and burdens of these jobs must be equalized as much as possible.)
Step 4: The propertyless receive compensation sufficient to maintain independence for the remainder of their lives. They enter the labor market if jobs are sufficiently attractive.
Step 5: The propertyless (might) take jobs that (hopefully) make them better-off than they were in step 1. (Benefits and burdens of these jobs need not be equalized as long as the differences are chosen.)

Even if the government equalized the burden of the active duties by introducing national service, it would have to appeal to the population-emergency argument to justify forced service.[10] Therefore, the government would have to take on the responsibility of getting out of the population emergency as soon as possible. They would have to find a freedom-respecting method to reduce the birth rate until we reach a point at which sufficient resources are available so that it would not be necessary to force anyone to work for anyone else.

People *do not* have a necessary obligation to reduce the size of the population as long as the current level is sustainable. But if we *choose* to maintain the current population, we can no longer claim the size of the population as a justification for force. If we realize that maintaining the current population is a choice, we cannot say that an unavoidable shortage of resources forces everyone to contribute to a joint project.

The ruling coalition can get out of all of these responsibilities if it simply refrains from directly or indirectly forcing people to work for others. If it introduces a basic income sufficient to maintain everyone's independence and to compensate them for all the rules that disadvantage them relative to others, it makes the economy voluntary, and it doesn't take on all the special responsibilities that come with the enforcement of an active duty.

If we want to force the poor, the disadvantaged, and dissenters to do things for society, we should force ourselves to spend as much time doing things that are just as onerous for the same rewards. If we won't force ourselves to do the same things we force others to do for us, we privilege ourselves at the expense of the freedom of others.

CHAPTER 10

Conclusion

[A] certain small income, sufficient for necessaries, should be secured to all, whether they work or not, and... a larger income, as much larger as might be warranted by the total amount of commodities produced, should be given to those who are willing to engage in some work which the community recognizes as useful. On this basis we may build further.

—*Bertrand Russell*[1]

This book has begun a tentative exploration of justice as the pursuit of accord (JPA) or indepentarianism. JPA involves three central ideas: (1) People's first duty is try to stay out of each other's way. This duty entails the respect for each other's need to maintain core well-being, and their equal entitlement to the most important liberties—that is, to status freedom. (2) When it is not possible to stay out of each other's way, people's duty is to seek accord; to seek an agreement in which each party literally accepts the sacrifices they make in exchange for the sacrifices others make on their behalf. (3) When universal accord is not possible—and it is usually not possible—people's duty is to seek both the widest possible agreement and the minimum negative impact on dissenters (i.e., those who cannot be brought into agreement).

This book has provided an in-depth discussion of only one aspect of indepentarianism: the effort to identify the most important liberties or to provide a theory of status freedom. Chapter 2 argued that status freedom is best understood as effective control self-ownership (ECSO freedom): the effective power to make and to refuse active cooperation with other willing people. To have this power a person must have independence, freedom from directly and indirectly forced service to others. Independent people require civil and political rights, control of their persons, and access to a sufficient amount of resources so that they can meet their basic needs without serving anyone else's interests. Any person or group that interferes with others' ability to meet their needs on their own or with the people of their choice forces them (indirectly but effectively) to serve the interests of at least one person who controls resources. I observed that most political theories and modern democracies usually avoid directly forced service but do not sufficiently avoid indirectly forced service. Therefore, freedom from indirectly forced service takes up much of the discussion of this book.

Chapter 3 discussed the implications of prioritizing the protection of personal independence, arguing that different institutions might be appropriate ways to secure the effective component of personal independence in different societies, but that the best way to do so in a modern industrial society is with an unconditional basic income guarantee.

Chapters 4, 5, and 6 argued for the importance of personal independence from an ethical and a practical perspective. They argue that we need to respect each other's independence to respect each other as truly free and equal citizens and that the protection of independence can be an important mechanism to protect the weak and the vulnerable from poverty, exploitation, and injustice.

Chapters 7 and 8 considered the relationship between the theory of ECSO freedom and other theories of freedom and social justice, arguing that few of the theories discussed fundamentally conflict with respect for personal independence and that most would be stronger and more consistent in their support for substantive freedom and equality if they incorporated respect for independence.

Chapter 9 addressed the question of duty, specifically considering whether people have enforceable obligations to each other that might reduce the concern for independence or reverse the support for basic income argued for in earlier chapters. The chapter showed that JPA doesn't rule out the possibility of enforceable duties, but JPA's support for the most substantive equal freedom for all puts significant limits on the majority's power to force individuals to actively serve others, such that all people would have to perform equally onerous duties for equal pay and that the ruling government would have to commit itself to a good faith effort to get out of the situation in which it is necessary to enforce duties. If circumstances prevent us from respecting everyone's independence throughout their lives, we should hold everyone (rich or poor) to an equally onerous duty of active service for a limited number of years, and then let everyone enjoy their status as free individuals for as many years of their lives as possible.

I do not believe that the recognition of personal independence is all there is to social justice. It is merely a basis on which to build further. I hope to flesh out JPA more in future works, but I do believe the arguments here are significant, and I would like to use this last chapter to underline that significance.

The indepentarian perspective is *not* about speaking for the poor, the propertyless, the disadvantaged, or dissenters. It is about giving them (and everyone else) the power to make their own choices. Perhaps what disadvantaged people want most is better jobs. Nothing in the theory presented here indicates that people who want better jobs should be denied them. What indepentarian theory demands is that people who do not think the jobs on offer are good enough should not be forced to accept them anyway. The jobs society offers to individuals are not good enough unless the individuals we ask to take those jobs say so. Only a society that guarantees unconditional access to the resources people need to live a decent life gives every individual the power to decide when, whether, and under what conditions he or she will participate in social projects with others. A voluntary-participation economy can give every individual an important power to choose that all mandatory-participation economies lack.

I have tried to portray respect for independence as the minimum level of decency that all individuals deserve—no matter how different their perspective might be from ours. It might not be all that we can and should do for everyone, but we are, so far, very short of doing even this much. Most societies attempt to help the poor in one way or another, but even the most generous social support systems tend to attach their aid to paternalistic and sometimes punitive conditions. Disadvantaged people live in many different circumstances. They have many different perspectives. None of us understands all of everyone else's circumstances and perspectives. Therefore, we are wrong to ask the disadvantaged to prove that they are worthy of access to the resources they need to reach a basic level of functioning. We should put the burden of proof on ourselves if we want to convict someone of being unworthy of basic need. Self-restraint on the part of the people making the rules is especially warranted when the type of proof we ask for tends to be extremely self-serving—like asking them to serve our project or prove they cannot. If we want people to cooperate, we should negotiate the terms of cooperation under conditions in which all are free. We have no moral basis to force anyone into the position in which more powerful people are able to dictate the terms of cooperation.

If we care about others, we need to care about them unconditionally. I do not accept that a society somehow fosters greater caring for each other if it forces disadvantaged people to participate in the social project before it allows them to meet their own basic needs. A society that sets up its basic structure so that everyone is able to meet their basic needs unconditionally displays more caring than a society that forces anyone who refuses to participate into a position in which they are unable to meet their most basic needs.

When I read history I see one injustice, being committed over and over again from the rise of the first chiefdoms to the present day. People take some form of advantage over others and force the disadvantaged to serve them. Advantage might be based on race, class, gender, or anything else, but the general form of the advantaged forcing the disadvantaged to serve recurs again and again. Thinking of all the unjust states in history, you take away the elite's power to force the disadvantaged to serve (or to deny them their ability to meet their needs on their own),[2] and you take away their ability to commit almost all of their injustices.

Given this long history of injustice against the propertyless and the disadvantaged by the people who dominate resources, it is surprising to me how many political theorists, Left and Right, believe that the power to say no is too much power for disadvantaged individuals to have. Certainly we can agree that the workers who built the pyramids should have had the power to say no to serving the Pharaoh. Alexander's conscripts, Roman slaves, medieval serfs, Aztec peasants, ancient Chinese harem members, early American slaves, native peoples displaced by colonialism, Victorian proletarians, and Soviet citizens should have had the power to refuse the things the privileged people of their societies force them to do. Yet rather than freeing the people from force, many political philosophers today are focused on perfecting the conditions under which a forced, lifetime work obligation supposedly becomes allowable. We need to realize that advantaged people have spent too much time throughout history forcing disadvantaged people to serve them, and we need to deny that power to anyone. We need to build a community based on solidarity, and the first step for the advantaged to show solidarity toward the less advantaged is to stop forcing them to do things. Without this kind of restraint on the powers of advantaged people, "libertarians" show insufficient concern with freedom and "egalitarians" show insufficient concern for equality.

I have argued that the basic income guarantee is a good institution to secure the effective component of independence in a modern economy, but what ultimately protects each individual's independence is each other individual's support for independence. If people recognize that they and all of their brothers and sisters must be independent to be free, they will find some institution to protect independence.

NOTES

PROLOGUE: THE BIG CASINO

1. D. Brown, *The Da Vinci Code* (London: Bantam, 2003).

1 INTRODUCTION

1. Milton Friedman and Rose Friedman, *Free to Choose: A Personal Statement* (New York: Harcourt Brace Jovanovich, 1980), pp. 137–39. He also argues that efforts to eliminate market inequality will reduce the incentives for people to produce value that is good for everyone. I do not address this issue here, assuming that the importance of incentives is agreed by all parties to this debate.
2. Robert Nozick, *Anarchy, State, and Utopia* (New York: Basic Books, 1974), p. 163. Although Nozick poses this question in an example in which a just distribution exists, he uses it as part of an argument for capitalism with strong property rights.
3. To name just a few: Jeremy Waldron, "Homelessness and the Issue of Freedom," in *Liberal Rights*, ed. Jeremy Waldron (Cambridge: Cambridge University Press, 1993); Herbert Spencer, *Social Statics*, 1st ed.(New York: D. Appleton and Company, 1872); Hillel Steiner, *An Essay on Rights* (Oxford: Blackwell, 1994). See also further discussion of the history of his observation in chapter 7.
4. Although still tentative, these ideas are laid out in a little more detail in Karl Widerquist, *Property and the Power to Say No: A Freedom-Based Argument for Basic Income* (Oxford University: Department of Politics and International Relations, 2006).
5. Anthony Atkinson, *Public Economics in Action: The Basic Income/Flat Tax Proposal* (Oxford: Clarendon Press, 1995); John Cunliffe, Guido Erreygers, and Walter Van Trier, "Basic Income: Pedigree and Problems," in *Real Libertarianism Assessed*, ed. Andrew Reeve and Andrew Williams (New York: Palgrave Macmillan, 2003); Irwin Garfinkel, Chien-Chung Huang, and W. Naidich, "The Effects of a Basic Income Guarantee on Poverty and Income Distribution," in *Redesigning Distribution: Basic Income and Stakeholder Grants as Cornerstones of a More Egalitarian Capitalism*, ed. Bruce Ackerman, Anne Alstott, and Philippe Van Parijs (New York: Verso, 2005); Karl

Widerquist and Michael A. Lewis, "An Efficiency Argument for the Basic Income Guarantee," *International Journal of Environment, Workplace and Employment* 2, no. 1 (2006): 21–43; Guy Standing, *Beyond the New Paternalism: Basic Security as a Right* (New York: Verso, 2002); J. Elster, "Comment on Van der Veen and Van Parijs," *Theory and Society* 15, no. 5 (1986): 709–22; Philippe Van Parijs, *Arguing for Basic Income: Ethical Foundations for a Radical Reform* (New York: Verso, 1992); Philippe Van Parijs, *Real Freedom for All: What (If Anything) Can Justify Capitalism?* (Oxford: Oxford University Press, 1995); Philippe Van Parijs, *What's Wrong with a Free Lunch?* (Boston: Beacon Press, 2001); Philippe Van Parijs, "Basic Income: A Simple and Powerful Idea for the 21st Century" (Paper Presented at the Real Utopias Conference, "Rethinking Redistribution: Designs for a More Egalitarian Capitalism," Madison, WI, 2002); Karl Widerquist, S. Pressman, and Michael A. Lewis, *The Ethics and Economics of the Basic Income Guarantee* (Aldershot, UK: Ashgate, 2005); Allan Sheahen, *Basic Income Guarantee: Your Right to Economic Security* (New York: Palgrave Macmillan, 2012).

6. Thomas Hobbes, *Leviathan* (Glasgow: Collins, 1962).
7. David Hume, "Of the Original Contract," in *Social Contract: Essays by Locke, Hume and Rousseau*, ed. Ernest Barker (Oxford: Oxford University Press, 1960).
8. John Rawls, *A Theory of Justice* (Oxford: Oxford University Press, 1971).
9. Nozick, *Anarchy, State, and Utopia*, p. 160.
10. Peter Vallentyne, "Left-Libertarianism—A Primer," in *Left-Libertarianism and Its Critics: The Contemporary Debate*, ed. P. Vallentyne and H. Steiner (New York: Palgrave, 2000), p. 1.
11. Even a state with a majoritarian government.
12. Van Parijs, *Real Freedom for All*, pp. 30–57.
13. Philip Pettit, *Republicanism: A Theory of Freedom and Government* (Oxford: Clarendon Press, 1997).

2 Status Freedom as Effective Control Self-Ownership

1. J. Heller, *Catch-22* (New York: Simon & Schuster, 1996).
2. E. Foner and J. Brown, *Forever Free: The Story of Emancipation and Reconstruction* (New York: Knopf, 2005).
3. E. D. Townsend, "Minutes of an Interview Between the Colored Ministers and Church Officers at Savannah with the Secretary of War and Major-Gen. Sherman," in *Freedom: A Documentary History of Emancipation, 1861–1867*, ed. Steven F Miller (College Park, MD: Department of History, University of Maryland, 2007), (emphasis original).

4. Foner and Brown, *Forever Free.*
5. *The American Heritage Dictionary.*
6. *The American Heritage Dictionary.*
7. Freedom and liberty can be used synonymously in most circumstances. I use freedom for the overall concept and liberty for specific instance just because it is convenient to do so.
8. This book does not deal directly with the allegation that status freedom is incoherent. It presents a theory of status freedom as an attempt to identify the most important liberties.
9. Status freedom of some sort has been a concern of Elizabeth S. Anderson, "What is the Point of Equality?," *Ethics* 109, no. 2 (January 1999): 287–337; Philip Pettit, *Republicanism: A Theory of Freedom and Government* (Oxford: Clarendon Press, 1997); Joseph Raz, *The Morality of Freedom* (Oxford: Clarendon Press, 1986); Quentin Skinner, *Liberty Before Liberalism* (Cambridge: Cambridge University Press, 1998), but it has been largely absent from works as diverse as Isaiah Berlin, *Four Essays on Liberty* (Oxford: Oxford University Press, 1969); Robert Nozick, *Anarchy, State, and Utopia* (New York: Basic Books, 1974); John Rawls, *A Theory of Justice* (Oxford: Oxford University Press, 1971); John Rawls, *Justice as Fairness: A Restatement* (Cambridge, MA: Harvard University Press, 2001); John Rawls, *Political Liberalism* (New York: Columbia University Press, 2005); Philippe Van Parijs, *Real Freedom for All: What (If Anything) Can Justify Capitalism?* (Oxford: Oxford University Press, 1995).
10. Isaiah Berlin, "Two Concepts of Liberty," in *Four Essays on Liberty*, ed. Isaiah Berlin (Oxford: Oxford University Press, 1969), p. 122.
11. Thomas Pogge, *World Poverty and Human Rights: Cosmopolitan Responsibilities and Reforms* (Oxford: Blackwell, 2002).
12. J. Locke, "Draft of a Representation Containing a Scheme of Methods for the Employment of the Poor," in *John Locke: Political Writings* (Harmondsworth: Penguin Books, 1993); Karl Widerquist, "Lockean Theories of Property: Justifications for Unilateral Appropriation," *Public Reason* 2, no. 3 (2010): 3–26.
13. G. A. Cohen, *Self-Ownership, Freedom, and Equality* (Cambridge: Cambridge University Press, 1995), p. 67.
14. Van Parijs, *Real Freedom for All.*
15. Nozick, *Anarchy, State, and Utopia*; S. Wheeler, "Natural Property Rights as Body Rights," in *Left-Libertarianism and Its Critics: The Contemporary Debate*, ed. P. Vallentyne and H. Steiner (New York: Palgrave, 2000).
16. John Christman, *The Myth of Property: Toward an Egalitarian Theory of Ownership* (New York: Oxford University Press, 1994); Tony Honoré, *Making Law Bind* (Oxford: Oxford University Press, 1987), pp. 166–75.

17. John Christman, "Self-Ownership, Equality, and the Structure of Property Rights," *Political Theory* 19, no. 1 (February 1991): 29.
18. Ibid., p. 39.
19. Ibid., p. 40.
20. Cohen, *Self-Ownership, Freedom, and Equality*, pp. 14–15; Michael Otsuka, *Libertarianism without Inequality* (Oxford: Oxford University Press, 2003), pp. 30–32.
21. A few examples include: Cohen, *Self-Ownership, Freedom, and Equality*; John Cunliffe and Guido Erreygers, "The Enigmatic Legacy of Fourier: Joseph Charlier and Basic Income," *History of Political Economy* 33, no. 3 (2001): 459–84; John Cunliffe and Guido Erreygers, "'Basic Income? Basic Capital!' Origins and Issues of a Debate," *Journal of Political Philosophy* 11, no. 1 (2003): 89–110; John Cunliffe, Guido Erreygers, and Walter Van Trier, "Basic Income: Pedigree and Problems," in *Real Libertarianism Assessed*, ed. Andrew Reeve and Andrew Williams (New York: Palgrave MacMillan, 2003); Magnus Jedenheim-Edling, "The Compatibility of Effective Self-Ownership and Joint World Ownership," *Journal of Political Philosophy* 13, no. 3 (September 2005): 284–304; T. Paine, "Agrarian Justice," in *The Origins of Left-Libertarianism: An Anthology of Historical Writings*, ed. P. Vallentyne and H. Steiner (Basingstoke: Palgrave, 2000);. Robert L. Hale, "Coercion and Distribution in Supposedly Non-Coercive State," *Political Science Quarterly* 38(1923): 470–94; Pierre-Joseph Proudhon, *What Is Property?* (Cambridge: Cambridge University Press, 1994); Otsuka, *Libertarianism without Inequality*; Senera Olsaretti, "Freedom, Force and Choice: Against the Rights-Based Definition of Voluntariness," *Journal of Political Philosophy* 6, no. 1 (1998): 53–78; Senera Olsaretti, *Liberty, Desert and the Market* (Cambridge: Cambridge University Press, 2004); Herbert Spencer, *Social Statics*, 1st ed. (New York: D. Appleton and Company, 1872); Peter Vallentyne and Hillel Steiner, *The Origins of Left-Libertarianism: An Anthology of Historical Writings* (Basingstoke: Palgrave, 2000); Peter Vallentyne and Hillel Steiner, *Left-Libertarianism and Its Critics: The Contemporary Debate* (New York: Palgrave, 2000); Van Parijs, *Real Freedom for All*; Jeremy Waldron, *The Right to Private Property* (Oxford: Clarendon Press, 1988); Jeremy Waldron, *Liberal Rights* (Cambridge: Cambridge University Press, 1993).
22. Olsaretti, "Freedom, Force and Choice," defines force slightly differently, "To say that A is forced to do x means that A does x because A has no acceptable alternative to doing x." Her definition is appropriate to her work because she is concerned whether a person does something *because* she is forced by external factors. I am concerned whether external factors exert force.
23. G. A. Cohen, *History, Labour, and Freedom: Themes from Marx* (Oxford: Clarendon Press, 1988), p. 245, emphasis original.

24. Stuart White, *The Civic Minimum* (Oxford: Oxford University Press, 2003), p. 46.
25. Otsuka, *Libertarianism without Inequality*, p. 32.
26. Ibid.; Kadri Vihvelin and Terrance Tomkow, "The Dif," *Journal of Philosophy* 102, no. 4 (2005): 183–205.
27. See White, *The Civic Minimum* and Cohen. *Self-Ownership, Freedom, and Equality.*
28. Notice that Art's assault on Bob's person is only instrumental to his real aim to get Art to stop breathing in the atmosphere he claims to own. It's interesting that most legal systems recognize blocking access to the atmosphere through strangulation as a terrible crime, while blocking access to the land by establishing "property" is a legally protect right, even though access to land is just as necessary for human survival as access to the atmosphere.
29. Otsuka, *Libertarianism without Inequality*, pp. 18–22 makes this argument very clearly.
30. The coherence of the concept of negative liberty has been challenged on the grounds that although negative duties *directly* imply only negative duties on the part of others, they indirectly require positive duties. The negative right not to be murdered is not very valuable without the positive right to police protection from murder.
31. Jeremy Waldron, "Homelessness and the Issue of Freedom," in *Liberal Rights*, ed. Jeremy Waldron (Cambridge: Cambridge University Press, 1993).
32. Cohen, *Self-Ownership, Freedom, and Equality.*
33. G. A. Cohen, "Once More into the Breach of Self-Ownership: Reply to Narveson and Brenkert," *The Journal of Ethics* 2, no. 1 (1998): 74.
34. Pogge, *World Poverty and Human Rights.*
35. Gerald C. Jr. McCallum, "Negative and Positive Freedom," in *Liberty*, ed. David Leslie Miller (New York: Oxford University Press, 1991).
36. Karl Widerquist, "What Does Prehistoric Anthropology Have to Do with Modern Political Philosophy? Evidence of Five False Claims," in USBIG Discussion Paper Series (USBIG Network, 2010).
37. T. Severin, *In Search of Robinson Crusoe* (New York: Perseus Publishing, 2003).
38. Nurit Bird-David, "Sociality and Immediacy: Or, Past and Present Conversations on Bands," *Man* 29, no. 3 (1994): 583–603.; Tim Ingold, David Riches, and James Woodburn, eds., *Hunters and Gatherers 1: History, Evolution and Social Change* (Oxford: Berg Publishing, 1988); Tim Ingold, David Riches, and James Woodburn, eds., *Hunters and Gatherers 2: Property, Power and Ideology* (Oxford: Berg Publishing, 1988); Allen Johnson and Timothy Earle, *The Evolution of Human Societies: From Foraging Group to Agrarian State*, 2nd ed. (Stanford: Stanford University Press, 2000); James Woodburn, "Stability and Flexibility in Hadza Residential

Groupings," in *Man the Hunter*, ed. Richard Borshay Lee and Irven DeVore (New York: Aline, 1968); James Woodburn, "Egalitarian Societies," *Man* 17, no. 3 (1982): 431–51.

39. Karl Widerquist and Grant McCall, *Prehistoric Myths in Modern Political Philosophy* (Edinburgh: Edinburgh University Press, forthcoming); Ingold, Riches, and Woodburn, *Hunters and Gatherers 1*; Ingold, Riches, and Woodburn, *Hunters and Gatherers 2*; Johnson and Earle, *The Evolution of Human Societies*; Robert L. Kelly, *The Foraging Spectrum: Diversity in Hunter-Gatherer Lifeways* (Washington DC: Smithsonian Institution Press, 1995).
40. H. D. Thoreau, *Walden* (Princeton: Princeton University Press, 1971).
41. Chapter 3 discusses the connection to basic income in further detail.
42. See the discussions of Rawls, Anderson, and White, in chapter 8.

3 Forty Acres and a Mule? Implications of the Duty to Respect Personal Independence

1. J. Heller, *Catch-22* (New York: Simon & Schuster, 1996).
2. Nurit Bird-David, "Sociality and Immediacy: Or, Past and Present Conversations on Bands," *Man* 29, no. 3 (1994): 583–603; Tim Ingold, David Riches, and James Woodburn, eds., *Hunters and Gatherers 1: History, Evolution and Social Change* (Oxford: Berg Publishing, 1988); Tim Ingold, David Riches, and James Woodburn, eds., *Hunters and Gatherers 2: Property, Power and Ideology* (Oxford: Berg Publishing, 1988); Allen Johnson and Timothy Earle, *The Evolution of Human Societies: From Foraging Group to Agrarian State*, 2nd ed. (Stanford: Stanford University Press, 2000).
3. Karl Widerquist, "What Does Prehistoric Anthropology Have to Do with Modern Political Philosophy? Evidence of Five False Claims," in USBIG Discussion Paper Series (USBIG Network, 2010).
4. Or any kind of forced labor, work, employment, or service, whether in a market or not.
5. I will not address the enormous issue of the distinction between a criminal and a dissenter.
6. Magnus Jedenheim-Edling, "The Compatibility of Effective Self-Ownership and Joint World Ownership," *Journal of Political Philosophy* 13, no. 3 (September 2005): 284–304, especially p. 287.
7. It is difficult to determine what is and is not trivial under such circumstances.
8. Assume for the sake of argument that everyone including Mary Ann agrees that they are frivolous luxuries.
9. I am putting off detailed discussion of the JPA theory of property in external assets to a later book.
10. A. Kuflik, "The Inalienability of Autonomy," *Philosophy and Public Affairs* 13(1984): 271–98.

11. John Stuart Mill, *The Essential Works of John Stuart Mill* (New York: Bantam Books, 1965), p. 348; J. Gray, *Mill on Liberty: A Defense* (London: Routledge & Kegan Paul, 1983), p. 93.
12. Robert Nozick, *Anarchy, State, and Utopia* (New York: Basic Books, 1974), p. 331.
13. Hillel Steiner, *An Essay on Rights* (Oxford: Blackwell, 1994), pp. 64–65, 71–72, 232–33.
14. Peter Singer, "Famine, Affluence, and Morality," *Philosophy & Public Affairs* 1, no. 3 (Spring 1972): 229–43.
15. S. Kagan, "The Argument from Liberty," in *In Harm's Way: Essays in Honor of Joel Feinberg*, ed. J. L. Coleman and A. Buchanan (Cambridge: Cambridge University Press, 1994).
16. M. C. Nussbaum, "Human Capabilities, Female Human Beings," in *Women, Culture and Development: A Study in Human Capabilities*, ed. M. C. Nussbaum and J. Glover (Oxford: Clarendon Press, 1995) 33–59; M. C. Nussbaum, *Sex and Social Justice* (Oxford: Oxford University Press, 1999); M. C. Nussbaum, *Women and Human Development: The Capabilities Approach* (Cambridge: Cambridge University Press, 2000); M. C. Nussbaum, "Capabilities as Fundamental Entitlements: Sen and Social Justice," *Feminist Economics* 9 (2003): 33–59; L. Doyal and I. Gough, *A Theory of Human Need* (London: MacMillan Education, 1991); Ingrid Robeyns, "Sen's Capability Approach and Gender Inequality: Selecting Relevant Capabilities," *Feminist Economics* 9, nos. 2–3 (2003): 61–92. Robeyns compares her theory to Doyal and Gough, Nussbaum, and several others and remarks on the extensive overlap.
17. I. Gough, "Lists and Thresholds: Comparing the Doyal-Gough Theory of Human Need with Nussbaum's Capabilities Approach" (Bath, UK: WeD Working Paper 01, 2003).
18. Karl Widerquist, "The Physical Basis of Voluntary Trade," *Human Rights Review* 11, no. 1 (2010): 83–103.
19. Amartya Sen, "Capability and Well-Being," in *The Quality of Life*, ed. A. Sen (Oxford: Clarendon Press, 1993), pp. 41–42.
20. Nussbaum, "Human Capabilities," pp. 83–86; Nussbaum, "Capabilities as Fundamental Entitlements," pp. 41–42.
21. For a more detailed comparison, see Widerquist "Physical Basis."
22. Sen, "Capability and Well-Being."
23. M. Sharif, *Work Behavior of the World's Poor: Theory, Evidence and Policy* (Aldershot, UK: Ashgate, 2003), p. 76.
24. For a description of how basic income guarantee might work and how much it might cost see Irwin Garfinkel, Chien-Chung Huang, and W. Naidich, "The Effects of a Basic Income Guarantee on Poverty and Income Distribution," in *Redesigning Distribution: Basic Income and Stakeholder Grants as Cornerstones of a More Egalitarian Capitalism*, ed. Bruce Ackerman, Anne Alstott, and Philippe Van Parijs (New York: Verso, 2005) 143–174; Anthony Atkinson, *Public Economics in*

Action: The Basic Income/Flat Tax Proposal (Oxford: Clarendon Press, 1995). For a history of the idea see John Cunliffe, Guido Erreygers, and Walter Van Trier, "Basic Income: Pedigree and Problems," in *Real Libertarianism Assessed*, ed. Andrew Reeve and Andrew Williams (New York: Palgrave MacMillan, 2003) 15–28. For a debate of issues surrounding basic income guarantee see Guy Standing, *Beyond the New Paternalism: Basic Security as a Right* (New York: Verso, 2002); Robert J. Van der Veen and Philippe Van Parijs, "A Capitalist Road to Communism," *Theory and Society* 15, no. 5 (1986): 635–55; Philippe Van Parijs, *Arguing for Basic Income: Ethical Foundations for a Radical Reform* (New York: Verso, 1992); Philippe Van Parijs, *Real Freedom for All: What (If Anything) Can Justify Capitalism?* (Oxford: Oxford University Press, 1995); Philippe Van Parijs, *What's Wrong With a Free Lunch?* (Boston: Beacon Press, 2001); Philippe Van Parijs, "Basic Income: A Simple and Powerful Idea for the 21st Century" (Paper presented at the Real Utopias Conference, "Rethinking Redistribution: Designs for a More Egalitarian Capitalism," Madison, WI, 2002); Eva Harman, "Can It Start Small, but End BIG? Expanding Social Assistance in South Africa," *Human Rights Review* 7, no. 4 (2006): 81–99; Karl Widerquist, "A Failure to Communicate: What (If Anything) Can We Learn from the Negative Income Tax Experiments?". *The Journal of Socio-Economics* 34, no. 1 (2005): 49–81; and Karl Widerquist and M. A. Lewis. "An Efficiency Argument for the Basic Income Guarantee." *International Journal of Environment, Workplace and Employment* 2, no. 1 (2006): 21–43.

25. L. C. Thurow, "Cash versus in-Kind Transfers," *The American Economic Review* 64, no. 2 (1974): 190–95.
26. There is evidence of market failure in the health care industry, M. V. Pauly, "Taxation, Health Insurance, and Market Failure in the Medical Economy," *Journal of Economic Literature* 24, no. 2 (1986): 629–75; J. Hurley, "An Overview of the Normative Economics of the Health Sector," in *Handbook of Health Economics*, ed. A. J. Culyer and J. P. Newhouse (Oxford: Elsevier, 2000) 55–118, but there is also a widespread belief that medical care should be provided outside the market because of their importance, B. R. Bergmann, "A Swedish-Style Welfare State or Basic Income: Which Should Have Priority?," *Politics and Society* 32, no. 1 (2004): 107–18; L. C. Thurow, "Government Expenditures: Cash or in-Kind Aid?," *Philosophy and Public Affairs* 5, no. 4 (1976): 361–81.
27. D. Hardy and C. Ward, *Arcadia for All: The Legacy of a Makeshift Landscape* (London: Mansell, 1984); D. Crouch and C. Ward, *The Allotment: Its Landscape and Culture* (Nottingham: Mushroom, 1994); C. Ward, *Anarchy in action* (London: Allen and Unwin, 1973); Stuart White, "A Relevant Anarchism? The Social Philosophy of Colin Ward" (Unpublished Manuscript, Jesus College, Oxford, 2006); J. Robertson, *Future Work* (Aldershot, UK: Gower, 1985).

4 The Importance of Independence I: Framing the Issue

1. M. McCaughan, L. Ballance, and C. Garrison, "Slack Motherfucker," in *Superchunk* (Matador, 1990).
2. Amartya Sen, *Development as Freedom* (New York: Knopf, 1999); Amartya Sen, *Identity and Violence: The Illusion of Destiny* (New York: W. W. Norton & Company, 2006).
3. Sen, *Development as Freedom*, p. 8.
4. L. Doyal and I. Gough, *A Theory of Human Need* (London: MacMillan Education, 1991); J. Drèze and A. K. Sen, *Hunger and Public Action* (Oxford: Clarendon Press, 1989); M. C. Nussbaum, *Women and Human Development: The Capabilities Approach* (Cambridge: Cambridge University Press, 2000); M. C. Nussbaum and J. Glover, *Women, Culture and Development: A Study of Human Capabilities* (Oxford: Clarendon Press, 1995); Amartya Sen, *Poverty and Famines: An Essay on Entitlement and Deprivation* (Oxford: Clarendon Press, 1981); Sen, *Development as Freedom*; M. Sharif, *Work Behavior of the World's Poor: Theory, Evidence and Policy* (Aldershot, UK: Ashgate, 2003).
5. To cite only a few: Stuart White, *The Civic Minimum* (Oxford: Oxford University Press, 2003), p. 17; Elizabeth S. Anderson, "What is the Point of Equality?" *Ethics* 109, no. 2 (January 1999): 287–337; John Rawls, "The Priority of Right and Ideas of the Good," *Philosophy and Public Affairs* 17, no. 4 (1988): 251–76; John Rawls, *Justice as Fairness: A Restatement* (Cambridge, MA: Harvard University Press, 2001), p. 257.
6. For efficiency-based criticism of the traditional welfare system, see Karl Widerquist and Michael A. Lewis, "An Efficiency Argument for the Basic Income Guarantee," *International Journal of Environment, Workplace and Employment* 2, no. 1 (2006): 21–43.
7. Anderson, "What is the Point of Equality?" 287–337; J. Elster, "Comment on Van der Veen and Van Parijs," *Theory and Society* 15, no. 5 (1986): 709–22; John Rawls, "Reply to Alexander Musgrave," *Quarterly Journal of Economics* 88, no. 4 (1974): 633–55; Rawls, *Justice as Fairness* p. 179; Stuart White, "Liberal Equality, Exploitation, and the Case for an Unconditional Basic Income," *Political Studies* 45, no. 2 (1997): 312–26; White, *The Civic Minimum*; Stuart White, "Fair Reciprocity and Basic Income," in *Real Libertarianism Assessed*, ed. Andrew Reeve and Andrew Williams (New York: Palgrave MacMillan, 2003) pp. 136–160; Gijs Van Donselaar, *The Benefit of Another's Pains: Parasitism, Scarcity, Basic Income* (Amsterdam: University of Amsterdam Department of Philosophy, 1997); Gijs Van Donselaar, "The Stake and Exploitation," in *The Ethics of Stakeholding*, ed. K Dowding, Jurgen De Wispelaere, and S. White (New York: Palgrave Macmillan, 2003). pp. 94–113.

8. For example, A. Levine, "Fairness to Idleness: Is There a Right Not to Work," *Economics and Philosophy* 11, no. 2 (1995): 255–74.
9. Philippe Van Parijs, *Real Freedom for All: What (If Anything) Can Justify Capitalism?* (Oxford: Oxford University Press, 1995), p. 108.
10. Van Donselaar, *The Benefit of Another's Pains*; Van Donselaar, "The Stake and Exploitation"; Gijs Van Donselaar, *The Right to Exploit: Parasitism, Scarcity, and Basic Income* (Oxford: Oxford University Press, 2009); White, "Liberal Equality, Exploitation"; White, *The Civic Minimum*; White, "Fair Reciprocity and Basic Income".
11. H. Arendt, "Work, Labor, Action," in *The Portable Hannah Arendt*, ed. P. Baehr (London: Penguin, 2000) pp. 167–81. Arendt draws a distinction between work and labor, demonstrating that labor is more connected with necessity, the cycle of life, and transience. But there is a great deal of overlap in the way we use the two terms, and both are used for many different things.
12. Independent traders might provide a service in the sense that they do something that others value, but unlike a self-employed contractor they are not in service in the sense of taking direction from someone else.
13. White (2003), *The Civic Minimum*, p. 91.
14. Ibid., pp. 113–18. Although White argues that caregiving can count as part of a social contribution, he does not believe that it reduces the paid work expectation to zero in most cases.
15. The apparent view of the US welfare system since the "reform" of 1996 is an example of the first definition. The apparent view before 1996 was an example of the second definition, although time spent caregiving was apparently considered to be much less of a contribution than making money. Anthony Atkinson's "participation income" is essentially an example of the third definition, although he does not count all the time spent making money as a social contribution. Anthony Atkinson, "The Case for a Participation Income," *Political Quarterly* 67 (1996): 67–70.
16. Even gaming the system could be justified if the system was unfair.
17. White (2003) *The Civic Minimum*, pp. 161–62.
18. Earlier chapters have discussed the distinction between active and passive cooperation.
19. That is, those without a competing obligation.
20. Karl Marx, *Selected Writings* (Indianapolis: Hackett Publishing Company, 1994).
21. Karl Widerquist, "What Does Prehistoric Anthropology Have to Do with Modern Political Philosophy? Evidence of Five False Claims," in USBIG Discussion Paper Series (USBIG Network, 2010); Karl Widerquist and Grant McCall, *Prehistoric Myths in Modern Political Philosophy* (Edinburgh: Edinburgh University Press, forthcoming).

22. Anderson, "What is the Point of Equality?", pp. 287–337; Elster, "Comment on Van der Veen and Van Parijs" pp. 709–721; Rawls, "Reply to Alexander Musgrave", pp. 633–655; Rawls, *Justice as Fairness*, p. 179; White, "Liberal Equality, Exploitation" pp. 312–26; White, *The Civic Minimum*, p. 17; White, "Fair Reciprocity and Basic Income", p. 136–60; Van Donselaar, *The Benefit of Another's Pains*, pp. 166–90; Van Donselaar, "The Stake and Exploitation.", pp. 94–113.
23. The lack of compensation is usually justified by claiming either that it would violate the rights of property holders or that it would violate the principle of reciprocity, giving the propertyless something for nothing. I have argued elsewhere that the direction of obligation runs in the opposite way. Only unconditional payments from property owners to the propertyless fulfill the principle of reciprocity, compensating them for the liberties lost in step 2. Karl Widerquist, "Reciprocity and the Guaranteed Income," *Politics and Society* 33 (1999): 386–401.
24. See chapter 9.

5 The Importance of Independence II: Freedom and Integrity

1. StoneE-Producktions, "Quotes from Our Native Past," StoneE Producktions, http://www.ilhawaii.net/~stony/quotes.html.
2. See chapter 9.
3. John Rawls, *A Theory of Justice* (Oxford: Oxford University Press, 1971), p. 4.
4. As in Robert Nozick, *Anarchy, State, and Utopia* (New York: Basic Books, 1974), p. 184.
5. Agreement is present in some way in nearly every theory of justice, but chapter 8 argues that literal agreement is underemphasized in Elizabeth S. Anderson, "What Is the Point of Equality?," *Ethics* 109, no. 2 (January 1999): 287–337; Nozick, *Anarchy, State, and Utopia*; Rawls, *A Theory of Justice*; John Rawls, *Justice as Fairness: A Restatement* (Cambridge, MA: Harvard University Press, 2001); John Rawls, *Political Liberalism* (New York: Columbia University Press, 2005); Stuart White, *The Civic Minimum* (Oxford: Oxford University Press, 2003). Agreement is more important in Brian Barry, *A Treatise on Social Justice, Volume 2: Justice as Impartiality* (Oxford: Clarendon Press, 1989); A. Gibbard, "Natural Property Rights," in *Left-Libertarianism and Its Critics*, ed. P. Vallentyne and H. Steiner (Basingstoke: Palgrave, 2000) pp. 23–30; G. A. Cohen, *Self-Ownership, Freedom, and Equality* (Cambridge: Cambridge University Press, 1995); John Christman, *The Myth of Property: Toward an Egalitarian Theory of Ownership* (New York: Oxford University Press, 1994); Michael Otsuka, *Libertarianism without Inequality* (Oxford: Oxford University Press, 2003); Philip Pettit,

Republicanism: A Theory of Freedom and Government (Oxford: Clarendon Press, 1997); Joseph Raz, *The Morality of Freedom* (Oxford: Clarendon Press, 1986). Van Parijs argues for maximizing the least advantaged individuals' freedom to do whatever they might want to do, but the agreement of the least advantaged individuals to the projects they end up participating in has little or nothing to do with the motivation for the theory, Philippe Van Parijs, *Real Freedom for All: What (If Anything) Can Justify Capitalism?* (Oxford: Oxford University Press, 1995).

6. Peter Singer, "Famine, Affluence, and Morality," *Philosophy & Public Affairs* 1, no. 3 (Spring 1972): 229–43.
7. C. Pateman, *The Sexual Contract* (Cambridge: Polity, 1988); G. D. H. Cole, *Self-Government in Industry* (London: G. Bell and Sons, 1919), p. 34.
8. Ronald Dworkin, *Sovereign Virtue: The Theory and Practice of Equality* (Cambridge, MA: Harvard University Press, 2000), pp. 266–70.
9. Ronald Dworkin, *Life's Dominion: An Argument about Abortion, Euthanasia, and Individual Freedom.* (New York: Vintage Books, 1993), pp. 201–02.
10. Ibid., p. 223.
11. Dworkin, *Sovereign Virtue*, p. 270.
12. Ibid., pp. 270–72.
13. Rawls, *Political Liberalism*, pp. 54–58.
14. Rawls, *A Theory of Justice*; Rawls, *Justice as Fairness*, p. 257.
15. Nozick, *Anarchy, State, and Utopia.*
16. R. Plant, *Politics, Theology and History* (Cambridge: Cambridge University Press, 2001); S. Caney, "Liberal Legitimacy, Reasonable Disagreement and Justice," in *Pluralism and Liberal Neutrality*, ed. R. Bellamy and M. Hollis (Illford: Frank Cass, 1999), pp. 19–36.
17. Fabienne Peter. "Choice, Consent, and the Legitimacy of Market Transactions," *Economics and Philosophy* 20, no. 1 (2004): 1–18.
18. G. A. Cohen, *History, Labour, and Freedom: Themes from Marx* (Oxford: Clarendon Press, 1988), pp. 239–54.

6 The Importance of Independence III: Market Vulnerability

1. Johann Wolfgang von Goethe, *The Maxims and Reflections of Goethe* (New York: Macmillan, 1906), p. 91.
2. Karl Widerquist and M. A. Lewis, "An Efficiency Argument for the Basic Income Guarantee," *International Journal of Environment, Workplace and Employment* 2, no. 1 (2006): 21–43.
3. Adam Smith, *The Wealth of Nations* (Oxford: Oxford University Press, 1976 [1776]).
4. A. M. D. Whinston Mas-Colell and J. R. Green, *Microeconomic Theory* (Oxford: Oxford University Press, 1995).

5. Smith, *The Wealth of Nations.*
6. Mas-Colell and Green, *Microeconomic Theory.*
7. Smith, *The Wealth of Nations*, book I, chapter 8, paragraph 12.
8. R. E. Goodin, *Protecting the Vulnerable* (Chicago: University of Chicago Press, 1985), pp. 198, 189–204; R. E. Goodin, *Reasons for Welfare* (Princeton, NJ: Princeton University Press, 1988), pp. 332–59; R. E. Goodin, "Self-Reliance Versus the Welfare State," *Journal of Social Policy* 14 (1985): 25–47.
9. Stuart White, *The Civic Minimum* (Oxford: Oxford University Press, 2003), p. 17.
10. P. J. Hammond, "Some Assumptions of Neoclassical Economic Theology," in *Joan Robinson and Modern Economic Theory*, ed. G. R. Feiwel (London: Macmillan, 1989), pp. 210–12; J. L. Coles and P. J. Hammond, "Walrasian Equilibrium without Survival: Existence, Efficiency and Remedial Policy," in *Choice, Welfare and Development: A Festschrift in Honour of Amartya K. Sen*, ed. K. Baru, P. Pattanaik, and K. Suzumura (Oxford: Clarendon Press, 1995).
11. J. A. Mirrlees, "Optimal Tax Theory: A Synthesis," *Journal of Public Economics* 6 (1976): 327–58.
12. Karl Widerquist, "A Failure to Communicate: What (If Anything) Can We Learn from the Negative Income Tax Experiments?," *The Journal of Socio-Economics* 34, no. 1 (2005): 49–81.
13. S. Bouquin, "Social Minima in Europe: The Risks of Cumulating Income-Sources," in *The Ethics and Economics of the Basic Income Guarantee*, ed. Karl Widerquist, M. A. Lewis, and S. Pressman (Aldershot, UK: Ashgate, 2005), pp. 212–31.
14. T. Funiciello, *The Tyranny of Kindness* (New York: Grove/Atlantic, 1994).
15. How well it works is a matter of debate in political theory. Jeremy Waldron, *Law and Disagreement* (Oxford: Oxford University Press, 1999).
16. They also have the power to use their property to influence the political process, but I'm looking only at powers in the market right now.
17. I'm ignoring the option of surviving by foraging through other people's garbage, because it fails to provide a minimum standard of decency.
18. Steven J. Brams and Alan D. Taylor, "An Envy-Free Cake Division Protocol," *The American Mathematical Monthly* 102, no. 1 (January 1995): 9–18.
19. John Rawls. *A Theory of Justice* (Oxford: Oxford University Press, 1971).
20. Townsend, "Minutes of an Interview between the Colored Ministers and Church Officers at Savannah with the Secretary of War and Major-Gen. Sherman," in *Freedom: A Documentary History of Emancipation, 1861–1867*, ed. Steven F Miller (College Park, MD: Department of History, University of Maryland, 2007).

21. This statement does not imply that voluntary participation encourages selfishness any more than mandatory participation. It is just as selfish to avoid punishment as it is to seek reward.
22. C. Pateman, *The Problem of Political Obligation* (New York: Wiley, 1979); C. Pateman, *The Sexual Contract* (Cambridge: Polity, 1988); C. Pateman, *The Disorder of Woman* (Cambridge: Polity, 1989).
23. Susan Moller Okin, *Justice, Gender, and the Family* (New York: Basic Books, 1989), pp. 135–70.
24. For a discussion of the reasons see ibid.
25. Ibid.
26. Funiciello, *The Tyranny of Kindness.*
27. Goodin (1985) *Protecting the Vulnerable*, p. 197.
28. Okin, *Justice, Gender, and the Family.*
29. For a discussion of unequal legal rights within the family see Pateman, *The Disorder of Woman*, especially chapter 4, pp. 71–89.

7 What Good Is a Theory of Freedom That Allows Forced Labor? Independence and Modern Theories of Freedom

1. D. A. Coe, "Take This Job and Shove It" (Family Album: Bear Family, 1978).
2. Theorists who have focused almost entirely on freedom in the scalar sense include, Isaiah Berlin, *Four Essays on Liberty* (Oxford: Oxford University Press, 1969); Robert Nozick, *Anarchy, State, and Utopia* (New York: Basic Books, 1974); John Rawls, *A Theory of Justice* (Oxford: Oxford University Press, 1971); John Rawls, *Justice as Fairness: A Restatement* (Cambridge, MA: Harvard University Press, 2001); John Rawls, *Political Liberalism* (New York: Columbia University Press, 2005); Philippe Van Parijs, *Real Freedom for All: What (If Anything) Can Justify Capitalism?* (Oxford: Oxford University Press, 1995). Notable exceptions include Joseph Raz, *The Morality of Freedom* (Oxford: Clarendon Press, 1986); Philip Pettit, *Republicanism: A Theory of Freedom and Government* (Oxford: Clarendon Press, 1997); Elizabeth S. Anderson, "What is the Point of Equality?," *Ethics* 109, no. 2 (January 1999): 287–337.
3. Cicero compared wage work to slavery in the first century BCE, Marcus Tullius Cicero, *De Officiis*, trans. Walter Miller, Loeb ed. (Cambridge, MA: Harvard University Press, 1913), Richard J. Arneson, "Should Surfers Be Fed?," in *Real Libertarianism Assessed*, ed. Andrew Reeve and Andrew Williams (New York: Palgrave Macmillan, 2003), p. XLII.
4. Alan Barnard, *Hunter-Gatherers: In History, Archeology, and Anthropology* (New York: Berg, 2004); Robert L. Bettinger, *Hunter-Gatherers: Archeology and Evolutionary Theory* (New York: Plenum Press, 1991); Lewis R. Binford, *In Pursuit of the Past: Decoding*

the Archeological Record (Berkeley: University of California Press, 1983); Nurit Bird-David, "The Giving Environment: Another Perspective on the Economic System of Gatherer-Hunters," *Current Anthropology* 31, no. 2 (1990): 189–96; Christopher Boehm, *Hierarchy in the Forest: The Evolution of Egalitarian Behavior* (Cambridge, MA: Harvard University Press, 2001); Morton H. Fried, *The Evolution of Political Society: An Essay in Political Anthropology* (New York: Random House, 1967); John Gowdy, ed. *Limited Wants, Unlimited Means: A Reader on Hunter-Gatherer Economics and the Environment* (Washington, DC: Island Press, 1998); Kristen Hawkes, "Is Meat the Hunter's Property? Big Game, Ownership, and Explanations of Hunting and Sharing," in *Meat-Eating and Human Evolution*, ed. Craig B. Stanford and Henry T. Bunn (Oxford: Oxford University Press, 2001), pp. 219–36; Kim Hill and A. Magdalena Hurtado, *Ache Life History: The Ecology and Demography of a Foraging People* (New York: Aldine de Gruyter, 1996); Richard Borshay Lee, "Primitive Communism and the Origin of Social Inequality," in *the Evolution of Political Systems: Sociopolitics in Small-Scale Sedentary Societies*, ed. S. Upham (Cambridge: Cambridge University Press, 1990), pp. 225–46; Richard Borshay Lee, ed. *The Cambridge Encyclopedia of Hunters and Gatherers* (Cambridge: Cambridge University Press, 1999); Richard Borshay Lee and Richard Daly, "Foragers and Others," in *The Cambridge Encyclopedia of Hunters and Gatherers*, ed. Richard Borshay Lee and Richard Daly (Cambridge: Cambridge University Press, 1999), pp. 1–19; Richard Borshay Lee and Irven DeVore, eds., *Man the Hunter* (New York: Aldine, 1968); Paul Roscoe, "The Hunters and Gatherers of New Guinea," *Current Anthropology* 43, no. 1 (2002): 153–62; Karl Widerquist, "What Does Prehistoric Anthropology have to do with Modern Political Philosophy? Evidence of Five False Claims," in USBIG Discussion Paper Series (USBIG Network, 2010); James Woodburn, "Stability and Flexibility in Hadza Residential Groupings," in *Man the Hunter*, ed. Richard Borshay Lee and Irven DeVore (New York: Aline, 1968); James Woodburn, "Egalitarian Societies," *Man* 17, no. 3 (1982): 431–51; James Woodburn, "'Sharing Is Not a Form of Exchange': An Analysis of Property-Sharing in Immediate-Return Hunter-Gatherer Societies," in *Property Relations: Renewing the Anthropological Tradition*, ed. Hann C. M. (Cambridge: Cambridge University Press, 1998), pp. 48–63.

5. Matthew S. Bandy, "Fissioning, Scalar Stress, and Social Evolution in Early Village Societies," *American Anthropologist* 106, no. 2 (2004): 322–33; Allen Johnson, "Horticulturalists: Economic Behavior in Tribes," in *Economic Anthropology*, ed. Stuart Platter (Stanford: Stanford University Press, 1989); Allen Johnson and Timothy Earle, *The Evolution of Human Societies: From Foraging Group to Agrarian State*, 2nd ed. (Stanford: Stanford University Press, 2000); M. D. Sahlins, "Poor Man, Rich Man, Big-Man, Chief: Political Types in Melanesia and

Polynesia," *Comparative Studies in Society and History* 5, no. 3 (1963): 285–303; Richard Walter, Ian Smith, and Chris Jacomb, "Sedentism, Subsistence and Socio-Political Organization in Prehistoric New Zealand," *World Archaeology* 38, no. 2 (2006): 274–90; Widerquist, "What Does Prehistoric Anthropology," pp. 30–35.

6. Robert L. Carneiro, "A Theory of the Origin of the State," *Science* 169, no. 3947 (1970): 733–38.
7. David Graeber, *Debt: The First 5,000 Years* (Brooklyn, NY: Melville House, 2011), pp. 49–52.
8. John Locke, *Two Treatises of Government* (Cambridge: Cambridge University Press, 1960), "Second Treatise, §27.
9. Jean-Jacques Rousseau, *A Discourse: What is the Origin of Inequality among Men, and Is It Authorized by Natural Law?* trans. G. D. H. Cole (Austin, TX: Constitution Society, 1998), The First Part.
10. Adam Smith, *The Wealth of Nations* (Oxford: Oxford University Press, 1976), book I, chapter 8, paragraph 12.
11. T. Paine, "Agrarian Justice," in *The Origins of Left-Libertarianism: An Anthology of Historical Writings*, ed. P. Vallentyne and H. Steiner (Basingstoke: Palgrave, 2000), pp. 81–98.
12. CooperativeIndividualism.org, "Agrarian Justice," http://www.cooperativeindividualism.org/paine_agrarianjustice_01.html.
13. Marcus Cunliffe, *Chattel Slavery and Wage Slavery: The Anglo-American Context, 1830–1860* (Athens, GA: University of Georgia Press, 1979); John Cunliffe, "Left Libertarianism: Historical Origins," in *The Origins of Left Libertarianism: An Anthology of Historical Writings*, ed. P. Vallentyne and H. Steiner (Basingstoke: Palgrave, 2000), pp. 1–8; John Cunliffe and Guido Erreygers, "The Enigmatic Legacy of Fourier: Joseph Charlier and Basic Income," *History of Political Economy* 33, no. 3 (2001): 459–84; John Cunliffe, Guido Erreygers, and Walter Van Trier, "Basic Income: Pedigree and Problems," in *Real Libertarianism Assessed*, ed. Andrew Reeve and Andrew Williams (New York: Palgrave Macmillan, 2003), pp. 15–28; Mikhail Bakunin, *Bakunin On Anarchy: Selected Works by the Activist Father of World Anarchism*, trans. Sam Dolgoff (New York: A. A. Knopf, 1972); Pierre-Joseph Proudhon, *What Is Property?* (Cambridge: Cambridge University Press, 1994); Karl Widerquist, "Libertarianism," in *The International Encyclopedia of Public Policy: Governance in a Global Age, Volume 3*, ed. Phillip O'Hara (Perth: GPERU, 2009).
14. Karl Marx and Frederick Engles, "The Communism Manifesto," in *Selected Writings*, ed. Lawrence H. Simon (Indianapolis: Hackett Publishing Company, 1994), pp. 157–86.
15. Herbert Spencer, *Social Statics*, 1st ed. (New York: D. Appleton and Company, 1872), pp. 131–38.
16. Henry George, *Social Problems* (New York: Henry George & Co., 1886); Henry George, *Progress and Poverty* (New York: Dutton, 1976).

17. Robert L. Hale, "Coercion and Distribution in Supposedly Non-Coercive State," *Political Science Quarterly* 38(1923): 471–73.
18. Jeremy Waldron, *Liberal Rights* (Cambridge: Cambridge University Press, 1993).
19. Amartya Sen, *Identity and Violence: The Illusion of Destiny* (New York: W. W. Norton & Company, 2006); Amartya Sen, *Development as Freedom* (New York: Knopf, 1999); Amartya Sen, *Poverty and Famines: An Essay on Entitlement and Deprivation* (Oxford: Clarendon Press, 1981), pp. 172–73.
20. G. A. Cohen, *Self-Ownership, Freedom, and Equality* (Cambridge: Cambridge University Press, 1995); G. A. Cohen, *History, Labour, and Freedom: Themes from Marx* (Oxford: Clarendon Press, 1988); Michael Otsuka, *Libertarianism without Inequality* (Oxford: Oxford University Press, 2003); Michael Otsuka, "Self-Ownership and Equality: A Lockean Reconciliation," *Philosophy and Public Affairs* 27(1998): 65–92; Brian Barry, "Real Freedom and Basic Income," *The Journal of Political Philosophy* 4, no. 3 (1996): 242–76; Fabienne Peter, "Choice, Consent, and the Legitimacy of Market Transactions," *Economics and Philosophy* 20, no. 1 (2004): 3; Senera Olsaretti, *Liberty, Desert and the Market* (Cambridge: Cambridge University Press, 2004), p. 71; Andrew Levine, "Fairness to Idleness: Is There a Right Not to Work?," *Economics and Philosophy* 11, no. 2 (1995): 261–62; Hillel Steiner, *An Essay on Rights* (Oxford: Blackwell, 1994); Hillel Steiner, "Left Libertarianism and the Ownership of Natural Resources," *Public Reason* 1, no. 1 (2009): 1–8; A. Zelleke, "Distributive Justice and the Argument for an Unconditional Basic Income," *Journal of Socio-Economics* 34, no. 1 (2005): 3–15.
21. Peter, "Choice, Consent"; Levine, "Fairness to Idleness," pp. 255–74.
22. Noam Chomsky, "The Relevance of Anarcho-syndicalism: Noam Chomsky Interviewed by Peter Jay," Chomsky.info, http://www.chomsky.info/interviews/19760725.htm.
23. Peter Vallentyne and Hillel Steiner, *The Origins of Left-Libertarianism: An Anthology of Historical Writings* (Basingstoke: Palgrave, 2000); Peter Vallentyne and Hillel Steiner, *Left-Libertarianism and Its Critics: The Contemporary Debate* (New York: Palgrave, 2000).
24. Tibor R. Machan, *Libertarianism Defended* (Aldershot, UK: Ashgate, 2006), p. 273.
25. Nozick, *Anarchy, State, and Utopia*.
26. Onora, O., "Nozick's Entitlements," in *Reading Nozick: Essays on Anarchy, State, and Utopia*, ed. J. Paul (Oxford: Basil Blackwell, 1981), pp. 305–322.
27. Nozick, *Anarchy, State, and Utopia*, pp. 178–79, footnote, emphasis original.
28. Ibid., p. 177.
29. Ibid., p. 182.

30. Widerquist, "What Does Prehistoric Anthropology," pp. 1–54; Karl Widerquist and Grant McCall, *Prehistoric Myths in Modern Political Philosophy* (Edinburgh: Edinburgh University Press, forth coming).
31. Nozick, *Anarchy, State, and Utopia*, pp. 150–73.
32. Ibid., p. 157.
33. Ibid., p. ix.
34. Cohen, *Self-Ownership, Freedom, and Equality*, p. 36.
35. Nozick's inconsistency on the priority of liberty over Pareto optimality has also been pointed out by Cohen, *Self-Ownership, Freedom, and Equality*, pp. 81–82 and Eric Mack, "Nozick on Unproductitivty: The Unintended Consequences," in *Reading Nozick: Essays on Anarchy, State, and Utopia*, ed. Jeffrey Paul (Oxford: Basil Blackwell, 1983), pp. 169–90.
36. Or to banks, to landlords, to consumer-clients, or even to a prescribed position in a socialist or egalitarian system.
37. See chapter 9.
38. Cohen, *Self-Ownership, Freedom, and Equality*, pp. 19–37.
39. Raz, *The Morality of Freedom*, p. 369, parentheses original.
40. Ibid., pp. 369–71.
41. Ibid., p. 371.
42. Berlin, *Four Essays on Liberty*, p. 168.
43. J. Gray, *Isaiah Berlin* (New York: HarperCollins, 1995), p. 21.
44. Pettit, *Republicanism*; Daniel Raventos and David Casassas, "Republicanism and Basic Income: The Articulation of the Public Sphere from Repolitization of the Private Sphere" (Paper presented at the Ninth International Congress of the Basic Income Guarantee Network, Geneva, 2002); Quentin Skinner, *Liberty before Liberalism* (Cambridge: Cambridge University Press, 1998).
45. Skinner, *Liberty before Liberalism*, p. 43.
46. Pettit, *Republicanism*; Philip Pettit, "Republicanism," *The Stanford Encyclopedia of Philosophy*, http://plato.stanford.edu/archives/spr2003/entries/republicanism/. Accessed November 5, 2012.
47. Frank Lovett, "Republicanism," *The Stanford Encyclopedia of Philosophy*, http://plato.stanford.edu/entries/republicanism/.
48. Ibid.
49. Pettit, *Republicanism*, pp. 78–79.
50. Ibid.
51. Frank Lovett, "Domination and Distributive Justice," *The Journal of Politics* 71, no. 3 (2009): 817–30; Philip Pettit, "A Republican Right to Basic Income?," *Basic Income Studies* 2, no. 2 (2008): 1–8; Raventos and Casassas, "Republicanism and Basic Income," pp. 1–8.
52. Pettit, *Republicanism*, p. 69.
53. Jeremy Waldron, "Homelessness and the Issue of Freedom," in *Liberal Rights*, ed. Jeremy Waldron (Cambridge: Cambridge University Press, 1993), pp. 309–38.

54. Ibid.
55. Karl Marx, *Capital, Volume One* (Moscow: Progress Publishers, 1887); Karl Marx, *Selected Writings* (Indianapolis: Hackett Publishing Company, 1994). Whether the situation Marx describes exists or not is immaterial for the argument here. It can function in this argument purely as an example. According to Peter Singer, "The Right to be Rich or Poor," in *Reading Nozick: Essays on Anarchy, State, and Utopia*, ed. J. Paul (Oxford: Basil Blackwell, 1981), p. 39, "The fundamental Marxist objection to classical liberalism," is that "people may make choices, but they do so under given historical circumstances." The influence of historical circumstances may be important, but I hold that the propertyless are not only influenced but also constrained to the point of force, to be more important.
56. Yitzhak Benbaji, "The Doctrine of Sufficiency: A Defense," *Utilitas* 17, no. 3 (November 2005): 310–32; Paula Casal, "Why Sufficiency Is Not Enough," *Ethics* 117, no. 2 (January 2007): 296–326; Roger Crisp, "Equality, Priority, and Compassion," *Ethics* 113, no. 4 (2003): 745–63; Roger Crisp, "Egalitarianism and Compassion," *Ethics* 114 (2004): 119–26; Harry Frankfurt, "Equality as a Moral Ideal," *Ethics* 98, no. 1 (October 1987): 21–43; Liam Shields, "The Prospects for Sufficientarianism," *Utilitas* 24, no. 1 (2012): 101–17; Karl Widerquist, "How the Sufficiency Minimum Becomes a Social Maximum," *Utilitas* 22, no. 4 (2010): 474–80.
57. Widerquist (2010). "How the Sufficiency Minimum," pp. 474–80.
58. Shields, "The Prospects for Sufficientarianism," pp. 101–17.
59. Axel Gosseries, "Sufficientarianism," in *Routledge Encyclopedia of Philosophy*, ed. E. Craig (London: Routledge, 2011).
60. A. Gibbard, "Natural Property Rights," in *Left-Libertarianism and its Critics*, ed. P. Vallentyne and H. Steiner (Basingstoke: Palgrave, 2000), pp. 23–30; Peter Vallentyne, "Left-Libertarianism—A Primer," in *Left-Libertarianism and Its Critics: The Contemporary Debate*, ed. P. Vallentyne and H. Steiner (New York: Palgrave, 2000), pp. 1–22; Vallentyne and Steiner, *The Origins of Left-Libertarianism*; Vallentyne and Steiner, *Left-Libertarianism and Its Critics*.
61. In simple terms, left-libertarians (and to a great extent real libertarians) look at the problem of securing equal access to resources as a simple problem of the equalization of resource rents taking the size of the population and the amount of resources in public and private hands as given. JPA does not take these three variables as given, and so the problem of securing equal access to resources is more complex. There is no fixed value of revenue to equalize. We must come up with a society-wide bargain to determine how many resources are held privately, under what terms, and at what price.
62. Van Parijs, *Real Freedom for All*, p. 23.

8 If You're an Egalitarian, Why Do You Want to Be the Boss of the Poor? Independence and Liberal-Egalitarian Theories of Justice

1. John Locke, *Two Treatises of Government* (Cambridge: Cambridge University Press, 1960). "Second Treatise," § 22.
2. C. Pateman, *The Disorder of Woman* (Cambridge: Polity, 1989), p. 71.
3. Elizabeth S. Anderson, "What Is the Point of Equality?," *Ethics* 109, no. 2 (January 1999): 287–337; John Rawls, *A Theory of Justice* (Oxford: Oxford University Press, 1971); John Rawls, "Reply to Alexander Musgrave," *Quarterly Journal of Economics* 88 (1974): 633–55; John Rawls, "The Priority of Right and Ideas of the Good," *Philosophy and Public Affairs* 17, no. 4 (1988): 251–76; John Rawls, *Political Liberalism* (New York: Columbia University Press, 1993); John Rawls, *Justice as Fairness: A Restatement* (Cambridge, MA: Harvard University Press, 2001); Stuart White, "Liberal Equality, Exploitation, and the Case for an Unconditional Basic Income," *Political Studies* 45, no. 2 (1997): 312–26; Stuart White, *The Civic Minimum* (Oxford: Oxford University Press, 2003); Stuart White, "Fair Reciprocity and Basic Income," in *Real Libertarianism Assessed*, ed. Andrew Reeve and Andrew Williams (New York: Palgrave Macmillan, 2003).
4. White (2003), *The Civic Minimum* p. 17.
5. John Rawls, *A Theory of Justice, Revised Edition* (Cambridge, MA: Harvard University Press, 1999), pp. xv, 96.
6. Anderson, "What Is the Point of Equality?" p. 318; White (2003) *The Civic Minimum*, pp. 17, 77, 91 Rawls, "The Priority of Right," p. 257.
7. Jail was the solution in Edward Bellamy's utopia. E. Bellamy, *Looking Backward, 2000–1887* (Harmondsworth: Penguin Books, 1982).
8. Anderson, "What Is the Point of Equality?," pp. 288–89.
9. Ibid., pp. 315, 326.
10. Ibid., p. 318.
11. Ibid., p. 327.
12. Ibid., p. 318.
13. Ibid., p. 327.
14. White (2003) *The Civic Minimum*, p. 17.
15. In detail, elimination of the proletarian condition is five conditions, non-immiseration, market security, work as challenge, minimized class differences, and nondiscrimination. Ibid., pp. 87–90.
16. Ibid., chapter 4.
17. Karl Marx, *Capital, Volume One* (Moscow: Progress Publishers, 1887), chapter 26.
18. Rawls, *A Theory of Justice*, p. 4.
19. Ibid.; Rawls, *Political Liberalism*; Rawls, *Justice as Fairness*; L. Wenar 2008, "John Rawls," *Stanford Encyclopedia of Philosophy*, http://plato.stanford.edu/entries/rawls/. Accessed July 31, 2012

20. Jean-Jacques Rousseau, *Discourse on Political Economy and the Social Contract*, trans. Christopher Betts (Oxford: Oxford University Press, 1994).
21. Rawls, *Political Liberalism*, pp. 54–58.
22. Philippe Van Parijs, *Real Freedom for All: What (If Anything) Can Justify Capitalism?* (Oxford: Oxford University Press, 1995); Simon Birnbaum, *Basic Income Reconsidered: Social Justice, Liberalism, and the Demands of Equality* (New York: Palgrave Macmillan, 2012).
23. Rawls, *A Theory of Justice*, p. 275; Rawls, *A Theory of Justice, Revised Edition*, p. 243.
24. L. Wenar 2008, "John Rawls," *Stanford Encyclopedia of Philosophy*, http://plato.stanford.edu/entries/rawls/. Accessed July 31, 2012
25. John Rawls, *Political Liberalism*, p. 7.
26. Ronald Dworkin, "What is Equality? Part 2: Equality of Resources," *Philosophy and Public Affairs* 10, no. 4 (1981): 312.
27. Alexander Brown, "The Slavery of the Not So Talented," *Ethical Theory and Moral Practice* 14, no. 2 (2011): 185–96. I apply the idea differently here.
28. It could be that society would not always exercise that power because incentive might be more effective in many cases than restricted options, but it would be morally permissible for society to exercise that power whenever it increased the output of the social project.
29. Rawls, *A Theory of Justice, Revised Edition*, p. 96.
30. Rawls, *Justice as Fairness*, p. 179.
31. Rawls, *Political Liberalism*, pp. 54–58.
32. Perhaps they could get higher wages by making someone else even more disadvantaged.
33. Rawls, "The Priority of Right," p. 257. He makes a similar argument in Rawls, *Justice as Fairness*, p. 179.
34. White (2003) *The Civic Minimum*, p. 17; Rawls, *A Theory of Justice*, p. 3.
35. Along with the minimum interference with those who do not want to participate.
36. Rawls, *A Theory of Justice*, p. 343.
37. Stuart White, "What do Egalitarians Want?," in *Equality*, ed. Jane Franklin (London: Institute for Public Policy Research, 1997), pp. 59–82; White (2003) *The Civic Minimum*.
38. Rawls, *A Theory of Justice*, pp. 60–64.
39. White, *The Civic Minimum*, pp. 215, 218.
40. A great deal of research on basic income and similar policies indicates that a reasonably generous guaranteed income is feasible: Karl Widerquist, "A Failure to Communicate: What (If Anything) Can We Learn from the Negative Income Tax Experiments?," *The Journal of Socio-Economics* 34, no. 1 (2005): 49–81; Karl Widerquist and M. A. Lewis, "An Efficiency Argument for the Basic Income

Guarantee," *International Journal of Environment, Workplace and Employment* 2, no. 1 (2006): 21–43; Karl Widerquist, S. Pressman, and Michael A. Lewis, *The Ethics and Economics of the Basic Income Guarantee* (Aldershot, UK: Ashgate, 2005); Robert Levine et al., "A Retrospective on the Negative Income Tax Experiments: Looking Back at the Most Innovative Field Studies in Social Policy," in *The Ethics and Economics of the Basic Income Guarantee*, ed. Karl Widerquist, Michael A. Lewis, and Steven Pressman (Aldershot, UK: Ashgate, 2005); Karl Widerquist and Michael W. Howard, eds., *Alaska's Permanent Fund Dividend: Examining its Suitability as a Model* (New York: Palgrave Macmillan, 2012).

41. One might also respond that the alternative to social participation *is* thoroughly bad in an absolute sense. Chapter 2 argues against this position as a reason against providing an exit option.
42. Erich Fromm, "The Psychological Aspects of the Guaranteed Income," in *The Guaranteed Income*, ed. Robert Theobald (New York: Doubleday, 1966).

9 On Duty

1. E. D. Townsend, "Minutes of an Interview between the Colored Ministers and Church Officers at Savannah with the Secretary of War and Major-Gen. Sherman," in *Freedom: A Documentary History of Emancipation, 1861–1867*, ed. Steven F. Miller (College Park, MD: Department of History, University of Maryland, 2007).
2. Elizabeth S. Anderson, "What Is the Point of Equality?," *Ethics* 109, no. 2 (January 1999): 287–337; B. R. Bergmann, "A Swedish-Style Welfare State or Basic Income: Which Should Have Priority?," *Politics and Society* 32, no. 1 (2004): 107–18; J. Elster, "Comment on Van der Veen and Van Parijs," *Theory and Society* 15, no. 5 (1986): 709–22; Gijs Van Donselaar, *The Benefit of Another's Pains: Parasitism, Scarcity, Basic Income* (Amsterdam: University of Amsterdam Department of Philosophy, 1997); Gijs Van Donselaar, "The Stake and Exploitation," in *The Ethics of Stakeholding*, ed. K Dowding, Jurgen De Wispelaere, and S. White (New York: Palgrave Macmillan, 2003), pp. 94–113; Gijs Van Donselaar, *The Right to Exploit: Parasitism, Scarcity, and Basic Income* (Oxford: Oxford University Press, 2009). Stuart White, "Liberal Equality, Exploitation, and the Case for an Unconditional Basic Income," *Political Studies* 45, no. 2 (1997): 312–26; Stuart White, "Fair Reciprocity and Basic Income," in *Real Libertarianism Assessed*, ed. Andrew Reeve and Andrew Williams (New York: Palgrave Macmillan, 2003), pp. 136–60; Stuart White, *The Civic Minimum* (Oxford: Oxford University Press, 2003).
3. As in the flood example from chapter 4.
4. This example is essentially the same as Van Parijs's Crazy-Lazy challenge. Philippe Van Parijs, *Real Freedom for All: What (If Anything) Can Justify Capitalism?* (Oxford: Oxford University Press, 1995).

5. Anderson, "What is the Point of Equality?" pp. 287–337; Bergmann, "A Swedish-Style Welfare State" pp. 107–18; Elster, "Comment on Van der Veen and Van Parijs" pp, 709–22; Van Donselaar, "The Stake and Exploitation", pp. 94–113; Van Donselaar, *The Right to Exploit* pp. 101–162. White, "Liberal Equality, Exploitation", pp. 312–26; White, "Fair Reciprocity and Basic Income" pp. 136–60; White, *The Civic Minimum*, pp. 59–69.
6. Karl Widerquist, "Reciprocity and the Guaranteed Income," *Politics and Society* 33 (1999): 386–401; Karl Widerquist, "Does She Exploit or Doesn't She?," in *The Ethics and Economics of the Basic Income Guarantee*, ed. Karl Widerquist, Michael A. Lewis, and Steven Pressman (Aldershot, UK: Ashgate, 2005), pp. 138–62; Karl Widerquist, "Who Exploits Who?," *Political Studies* 54, no. 3 (October 2006): 444–64; Karl Widerquist, *Property and the Power to Say No: A Freedom-Based Argument for Basic Income* (Oxford University: Department of Politics and International Relations, 2006). The fourth of these references lays out some the property theory eluded to in this work. I hope to lay it out in greater detail in a future work.
7. Originally mentioned in chapter 4.
8. As long as offering this choice doesn't ask them to permanently sacrifice their status as free individuals. See chapter 3 for arguments that people need to retain the power to refuse throughout their lives to remain free.
9. Perhaps we can assume flying fish land on everyone's plate every evening. The complexity of need is not the point of the example.
10. There might be some other kind of emergency that could justify some permanent obligations, such as jury duty. I don't discuss these issues here. I assume any such duties would not be terribly time-consuming compared to emergency justification such as natural disaster, overpopulation, or invasion.

10 Conclusion

1. Bertrand Russell, *Proposed Roads to Freedom* (New York: Blue Ribbon Books, 1918), p. 110.
2. Murder, which also occurs over and over throughout history, is simply an extreme case of denying another person the effective freedom to meet her own needs—a very immediate and extremely denial of independence.

Bibliography

Anderson, Elizabeth S. "What Is the Point of Equality?" *Ethics* 109, no. 2 (January 1999): 287–337.

Arendt, H. "Work, Labor, Action." In *The Portable Hannah Arendt*, edited by P. Baehr, pp. 167–81. London: Penguin, 2000.

Arneson, Richard J. "Should Surfers Be Fed?" In *Real Libertarianism Assessed*, edited by Andrew Reeve and Andrew Williams, pp. 95–110. New York: Palgrave Macmillan, 2003.

Atkinson, Anthony. "The Case for a Participation Income." *Political Quarterly* 67 (1996): 67–70.

———. *Public Economics in Action: The Basic Income/Flat Tax Proposal.* Oxford: Clarendon Press, 1995.

Bakunin, Mikhail. *Bakunin on Anarchy: Selected Works by the Activist Father of World Anarchism.* Translated by Sam Dolgoff. New York: A. A. Knopf, 1972.

Bandy, Matthew S. "Fissioning, Scalar Stress, and Social Evolution in Early Village Societies." *American Anthropologist* 106, no. 2 (2004): 322–33.

Barnard, Alan. *Hunter-Gatherers: In History, Archeology, and Anthropology.* New York: Berg, 2004.

Barry, Brian. "Real Freedom and Basic Income." *The Journal of Political Philosophy* 4, no. 3 (1996): 242–76.

———. *A Treatise on Social Justice, Volume 2: Justice as Impartiality.* Oxford: Clarendon Press, 1989.

Bellamy, E. *Looking Backward, 2000–1887.* Harmondsworth: Penguin Books, 1982.

Benbaji, Yitzhak. "The Doctrine of Sufficiency: A Defense." *Utilitas* 17, no. 3 (November 2005): 310–32.

Bergmann, B. R. "A Swedish-Style Welfare State or Basic Income: Which Should Have Priority?" *Politics and Society* 32, no. 1 (2004): 107–18.

Berlin, Isaiah. *Four Essays on Liberty.* Oxford: Oxford University Press, 1969.

———. "Two Concepts of Liberty." In *Four Essays on Liberty*, edited by Isaiah Berlin, pp. 118–172. Oxford: Oxford University Press, 1969.

Bettinger, Robert L. *Hunter-Gatherers: Archeology and Evolutionary Theory.* New York: Plenum Press, 1991.

Binford, Lewis R. *In Pursuit of the Past: Decoding the Archeological Record.* Berkeley: University of California Press, 1983.

Bird-David, Nurit. "The Giving Environment: Another Perspective on the Economic System of Gatherer-Hunters." *Current Anthropology* 31, no. 2 (1990): 189–96.

———. "Sociality and Immediacy: Or, Past and Present Conversations on Bands." *Man* 29, no. 3 (1994): 583–603.

Birnbaum, Simon. *Basic Income Reconsidered: Social Justice, Liberalism, and the Demands of Equality*. New York: Palgrave Macmillan, 2012.

Boehm, Christopher. *Hierarchy in the Forest: The Evolution of Egalitarian Behavior*. Cambridge, MA: Harvard University Press, 2001.

Bouquin, S. "Social Minima in Europe: The Risks of Cumulating Income-Sources." In *The Ethics and Economics of the Basic Income Guarantee*, edited by Karl Widerquist, M. A. Lewis, and S. Pressman, pp. 212–31. Aldershot, UK: Ashgate, 2005.

Brams, Steven J. and Alan D. Taylor. "An Envy-Free Cake Division Protocol." *The American Mathematical Monthly* 102, no. 1 (January 1995): 9–18.

Brown, Alexander. "The Slavery of the Not So Talented." *Ethical Theory and Moral Practice* 14, no. 2 (2011): 185–96.

Brown, D. *The Da Vinci Code*. London: Bantam, 2003.

Caney, S. "Liberal Legitimacy, Reasonable Disagreement and Justice." In *Pluralism and Liberal Neutrality*, edited by R. Bellamy and M. Hollis, pp. 19–36. Illford: Frank Cass, 1999.

Carneiro, Robert L. "A Theory of the Origin of the State." *Science* 169, no. 3947 (1970): 733–38.

Casal, Paula. "Why Sufficiency Is Not Enough." *Ethics* 117, no. 2 (January 2007): 296–326.

Chomsky, Noam. "The Relevance of Anarcho-Syndicalism: Noam Chomsky Interviewed by Peter Jay." Chomsky.info, http://www.chomsky.info/interviews/19760725.htm.

Christman, John. *The Myth of Property: Toward an Egalitarian Theory of Ownership*. New York: Oxford University Press, 1994.

———. "Self-Ownership, Equality, and the Structure of Property Rights." *Political Theory* 19, no. 1 (February 1991): 28–46.

Cicero, Marcus Tullius. *De Officiis*. Translated by Walter Miller. Loeb edn. Cambridge, MA: Harvard University Press, 1913. http://www.constitution.org/rom/de_officiis.htm. Accessed November 11, 2012.

Coe, D. A. "Take This Job and Shove It." Family Album: Bear Family, 1978.

Cohen, G. A. *History, Labour, and Freedom: Themes from Marx*. Oxford: Clarendon Press, 1988.

———. "Once More into the Breach of Self-Ownership: Reply to Narveson and Brenkert." *The Journal of Ethics* 2, no. 1 (1998): 57–96.

———. *Self-Ownership, Freedom, and Equality*. Cambridge: Cambridge University Press, 1995.

Cole, G. D. H. *Self-Government in Industry*. London: G. Bell and Sons, 1919.

Coles, J. L. and P. J. Hammond. "Walrasian Equilibrium without Survival: Existence, Efficiency and Remedial Policy." In *Choice, Welfare and Development: A Festschrift in Honour of Amartya K. Sen*, edited by K. Baru, P. Pattanaik, and K. Suzumura. Oxford: Clarendon Press, 1995, pp. 32–64.

CooperativeIndividualism.org. "Agrarian Justice." http://www.cooperativeindividualism.org/paine_agrarianjustice_01.html.

Crisp, Roger. "Egalitarianism and Compassion." *Ethics* 114 (2004): 119–26.

———. "Equality, Priority, and Compassion." *Ethics* 113, no. 4 (2003): 745–63.

Crouch, D. and C. Ward. *The Allotment: Its Landscape and Culture*. Nottingham: Mushroom, 1994.

Cunliffe, John. "Left Libertarianism: Historical Origins." In *The Origins of Left Libertarianism: An Anthology of Historical Writings*, edited by P. Vallentyne and H. Steiner, pp. 1–8. Basingstoke: Palgrave, 2000.

Cunliffe, John and Guido Erreygers. "'Basic Income? Basic Capital!' Origins and Issues of a Debate." *Journal of Political Philosophy* 11, no. 1 (2003): 89–110.

———. "The Enigmatic Legacy of Fourier: Joseph Charlier and Basic Income." *History of Political Economy* 33, no. 3 (2001): 459–84.

Cunliffe, John, Guido Erreygers, and Walter Van Trier. "Basic Income: Pedigree and Problems." In *Real Libertarianism Assessed*, edited by Andrew Reeve and Andrew Williams, pp. 15–28. New York: Palgrave Macmillan, 2003.

Cunliffe, Marcus. *Chattel Slavery and Wage Slavery: The Anglo-American Context, 1830–1860*. Athens, GA: University of Georgia Press, 1979.

Doyal, L. and I. Gough. *A Theory of Human Need*. London: Macmillan Education, 1991.

Drèze, J. and A. K. Sen. *Hunger and Public Action*. Oxford: Clarendon Press, 1989.

Dworkin, Ronald. *Life's Dominion: An Argument About Abortion, Euthanasia, and Individual Freedom*. New York: Vintage Books, 1993.

———. *Sovereign Virtue: The Theory and Practice of Equality*. Cambridge, MA: Harvard University Press, 2000.

———. "What Is Equality? Part 2: Equality of Resources." *Philosophy and Public Affairs* 10, no. 4 (1981): 283–345.

Elster, J. "Comment on Van Der Veen and Van Parijs." *Theory and Society* 15, no. 5 (1986): 709–22.

Foner, E. and J. Brown. *Forever Free: The Story of Emancipation and Reconstruction*. New York: A. A. Knopf, 2005.

Frankfurt, Harry. "Equality as a Moral Ideal." *Ethics* 98, no. 1 (October 1987): 21–43.

Fried, Morton H. *The Evolution of Political Society: An Essay in Political Anthropology*. New York: Random House, 1967.

Friedman, Milton and Rose Friedman. *Free to Choose: A Personal Statement.* New York: Harcourt Brace Jovanovich, 1980.

Fromm, Erich. "The Psychological Aspects of the Guaranteed Income." In *The Guaranteed Income: Next Step in Socioeconomic Evolution?*, edited by Robert Theobald. New York: Doubleday, 1966, pp. 183–93.

Funiciello, T. *The Tyranny of Kindness.* New York: Grove/Atlantic, 1994.

Garfinkel, Irwin, Chien-Chung Huang, and W. Naidich. "The Effects of a Basic Income Guarantee on Poverty and Income Distribution." In *Redesigning Distribution: Basic Income and Stakeholder Grants as Cornerstones of a More Egalitarian Capitalism*, edited by Bruce Ackerman, Anne Alstott, and Philippe Van Parijs, pp. 143–74. New York: Verso, 2005.

George, Henry. *Progress and Poverty.* New York: Dutton, 1976.

———. *Social Problems.* New York: Henry George & Co., 1886.

Gibbard, A. "Natural Property Rights." In *Left-Libertarianism and Its Critics*, edited by P. Vallentyne and H. Steiner, pp. 23–30. Basingstoke: Palgrave, 2000.

Goethe, Johann Wolfgang von. *The Maxims and Reflections of Goethe.* New York: Macmillan, 1906.

Goodin, R. E. *Protecting the Vulnerable.* Chicago: University of Chicago Press, 1985.

———. *Reasons for Welfare.* Princeton, NJ: Princeton University Press, 1988.

———. "Self-Reliance versus the Welfare State." *Journal of Social Policy* 14 (1985): 25–47.

Gosseries, Axel. "Sufficientarianism." In *Routledge Encyclopedia of Philosophy*, edited by E. Craig. London: Routledge, 2011. http://www.rep.routledge.com/article/S112. Accessed July 18, 2012.

Gough, I. "Lists and Thresholds: Comparing the Doyal-Gough Theory of Human Need with Nussbaum's Capabilities Approach." WeD Working Paper 01, Bath, UK, 2003.

Gowdy, John, ed. *Limited Wants, Unlimited Means: A Reader on Hunter-Gatherer Economics and the Environment.* Washington, DC: Island Press, 1998.

Graeber, David. *Debt: The First 5,000 Years.* Brooklyn, NY: Melville House, 2011.

Gray, J. *Isaiah Berlin.* New York: HarperCollins, 1995.

———. *Mill on Liberty: A Defense.* London: Routledge & Kegan Paul, 1983.

Hale, Robert L. "Coercion and Distribution in Supposedly Non-Coercive State." *Political Science Quarterly* 38 (1923): 470–94.

Hammond, P. J. "Some Assumptions of Neoclassical Economic Theology." In *Joan Robinson and Modern Economic Theory*, edited by G. R. Feiwel. London: Macmillan, 1989, pp. 186–257.

Hardy, D. and C. Ward. *Arcadia for All: The Legacy of a Makeshift Landscape.* London: Mansell, 1984.

Harman, Eva. "Can It Start Small, but End Big? Expanding Social Assistance in South Africa." *Human Rights Review* 7, no. 4 (2006): 81–99.

Hawkes, Kristen. "Is Meat the Hunter's Property? Big Game, Ownership, and Explanations of Hunting and Sharing." In *Meat-Eating and Human Evolution*, edited by Craig B. Stanford and Henry T. Bunn, pp. 219–36. Oxford: Oxford University Press, 2001.

Heller, J. *Catch-22*. New York: Simon & Schuster, 1996.

Hill, Kim and A. Magdalena Hurtado. *Ache Life History: The Ecology and Demography of a Foraging People*. New York: Aldine de Gruyter, 1996.

Hobbes, Thomas. *Leviathan*. Glasgow: Collins, 1962.

Honoré, Tony. *Making Law Bind*. Oxford: Oxford University Press, 1987.

Hume, David. "Of the Original Contract." In *Social Contract: Essays by Locke, Hume and Rousseau*, edited by Ernest Barker. Oxford: Oxford University Press, 1960, pp. 207–236.

Hurley, J. "An Overview of the Normative Economics of the Health Sector." In *Handbook of Health Economics*, edited by A. J. Culyer and J. P. Newhouse, pp. 55–118. Oxford: Elsevier, 2000.

Ingold, Tim, David Riches, and James Woodburn, eds. *Hunters and Gatherers 1: History, Evolution and Social Change*. Oxford: Berg Publishing, 1988.

———, eds. *Hunters and Gatherers 2: Property, Power and Ideology*. Oxford: Berg Publishing, 1988.

Jedenheim-Edling, Magnus. "The Compatibility of Effective Self-Ownership and Joint World Ownership." *Journal of Political Philosophy* 13, no. 3 (September 2005): 284–304.

Johnson, Allen. "Horticulturalists: Economic Behavior in Tribes." In *Economic Anthropology*, edited by Stuart Platter, pp. 49–77. Stanford: Stanford University Press, 1989.

Johnson, Allen and Timothy Earle. *The Evolution of Human Societies: From Foraging Group to Agrarian State*. 2nd ed. Stanford: Stanford University Press, 2000.

Kagan, S. "The Argument from Liberty." In *In Harm's Way: Essays in Honor of Joel Feinberg*, edited by J. L. Coleman and A. Buchanan, pp. 16–41. Cambridge: Cambridge University Press, 1994.

Kelly, Robert L. *The Foraging Spectrum: Diversity in Hunter-Gatherer Lifeways*. Washington DC: Smithsonian Institution Press, 1995.

Kuflik, A. "The Inalienability of Autonomy." *Philosophy and Public Affairs* 13 (1984): 271–98.

Lee, Richard Borshay, ed. *The Cambridge Encyclopedia of Hunters and Gatherers*. Cambridge: Cambridge University Press, 1999.

———. "Primitive Communism and the Origin of Social Inequality." In *The Evolution of Political Systems: Sociopolitics in Small-Scale Sedentary Societies*, edited by S. Upham, pp. 225–46. Cambridge: Cambridge University Press, 1990.

Lee, Richard Borshay and Richard Daly. "Foragers and Others." In *The Cambridge Encyclopedia of Hunters and Gatherers*, edited by Richard

Borshay Lee and Richard Daly, pp. 1–19. Cambridge: Cambridge University Press, 1999.

Lee, Richard Borshay and Irven DeVore, eds. *Man the Hunter.* New York: Aldine, 1968.

Levine, Andrew. "Fairness to Idleness: Is There a Right Not to Work?" *Economics and Philosophy* 11, no. 2 (1995): 255–74.

Levine, Robert, Harold Watts, Robinson Hollister, Walter Williams, Alice O' Connor, and Karl Widerquist. "A Retrospective on the Negative Income Tax Experiments: Looking Back at the Most Innovative Field Studies in Social Policy." In *The Ethics and Economics of the Basic Income Guarantee*, edited by Karl Widerquist, Michael A. Lewis, and Steven Pressman. Aldershot, UK: Ashgate, 2005, pp. 95–106.

Locke, John. "Draft of a Representation Containing a Scheme of Methods for the Employment of the Poor." In *John Locke: Political Writings*, pp. 446–61. Harmondsworth: Penguin Books, 1993.

———. *Two Treatises of Government*, Second Treatise, §27. Cambridge: Cambridge University Press, 1960.

Lovett, Frank. "Domination and Distributive Justice." *The Journal of Politics* 71, no. 3 (2009): 817–30.

———. "Republicanism." *The Stanford Encyclopedia of Philosophy*, http://plato.stanford.edu/entries/republicanism/.

Machan, Tibor R. *Libertarianism Defended.* Aldershot, UK: Ashgate, 2006.

Mack, Eric. "Nozick on Unproductitivty: The Unintended Consequences." In *Reading Nozick: Essays on Anarchy, State, and Utopia*, edited by Jeffrey Paul, pp. 169–90. Oxford: Basil Blackwell, 1983.

Marx, Karl. *Capital, Volume One.* Moscow: Progress Publishers, 1887.

———. *Selected Writings.* Indianapolis: Hackett Publishing Company, 1994.

Marx, Karl and Frederick Engles. "The Communism Manifesto." In *Selected Writings*, edited by Lawrence H. Simon, pp. 157–86. Indianapolis: Hackett Publishing Company, 1994.

Mas-Colell, A. M. D. Whinston, and J. R. Green. *Microeconomic Theory.* Oxford: Oxford University Press, 1995.

McCallum, Gerald C. Jr. "Negative and Positive Freedom." In *Liberty*, edited by David Leslie Miller, pp. 100–22. New York: Oxford University Press, 1991.

McCaughan, M., L. Ballance, and C. Garrison. "Slack Motherfucker." In *Superchunk*. Matador, 1990.

Mill, John Stuart. *The Essential Works of John Stuart Mill.* New York: Bantam Books, 1965.

Mirrlees, J. A. "Optimal Tax Theory: A Synthesis." *Journal of Public Economics* 6 (1976): 327–58.

Nozick, Robert. *Anarchy, State, and Utopia.* New York: Basic Books, 1974.

Nussbaum, M. C. "Capabilities as Fundamental Entitlements: Sen and Social Justice." *Feminist Economics* 9 (2003): 33–59.

———. "Human Capabilities, Female Human Beings." In *Women, Culture and Development: A Study in Human Capabilities*, edited by M. C. Nussbaum and J. Glover, pp. 61–104. Oxford: Clarendon Press, 1995.

———. *Sex and Social Justice*. Oxford: Oxford University Press, 1999.

———. *Women and Human Development: The Capabilities Approach*. Cambridge: Cambridge University Press, 2000.

Nussbaum, M. C. and J. Glover. *Women, Culture and Development: A Study of Human Capabilities*. Oxford: Clarendon Press, 1995.

O' Neill, O. "Nozick's Entitlements." In *Reading Nozick: Essays on Anarchy, State, and Utopia*, edited by Jeffrey Paul, pp. 305–22. Oxford: Basil Blackwell, 1981.

Okin, Susan Moller. *Justice, Gender, and the Family*. New York: Basic Books, 1989.

Olsaretti, Senera. "Freedom, Force and Choice: Against the Rights-Based Definition of Voluntariness." *Journal of Political Philosophy* 6, no. 1 (1998): 53–78.

———. *Liberty, Desert and the Market*. Cambridge: Cambridge University Press, 2004.

Otsuka, Michael. *Libertarianism without Inequality*. Oxford: Oxford University Press, 2003.

———. "Self-Ownership and Equality: A Lockean Reconciliation." *Philosophy and Public Affairs* 27 (1998): 65–92.

Paine, T. "Agrarian Justice." In *The Origins of Left-Libertarianism: An Anthology of Historical Writings*, edited by P. Vallentyne and H. Steiner. pp. 81–98. Basingstoke: Palgrave, 2000.

Pateman, C. *The Disorder of Woman*. Cambridge: Polity, 1989.

———. *The Problem of Political Obligation*. New York: Wiley, 1979.

———. *The Sexual Contract*. Cambridge: Polity, 1988.

Pauly, M. V. "Taxation, Health Insurance, and Market Failure in the Medical Economy." *Journal of Economic Literature* 24, no. 2 (1986): 629–75.

Peter, Fabienne. "Choice, Consent, and the Legitimacy of Market Transactions." *Economics and Philosophy* 20, no. 1 (2004): 1–18.

Pettit, Philip. "A Republican Right to Basic Income?" *Basic Income Studies* 2, no. 2 (2008): 1–8.

———. "Republicanism." *The Stanford Encyclopedia of Philosophy*, http://plato.stanford.edu/archives/spr2003/entries/republicanism/.

———. *Republicanism: A Theory of Freedom and Government*. Oxford: Clarendon Press, 1997.

Plant, R. *Politics, Theology and History*. Cambridge: Cambridge University Press, 2001.

Pogge, Thomas. *World Poverty and Human Rights: Cosmopolitan Responsibilities and Reforms*. Oxford: Blackwell, 2002.

Proudhon, Pierre-Joseph. *What Is Property?* Cambridge: Cambridge University Press, 1994.

Raventos, Daniel and David Casassas. "Republicanism and Basic Income: The Articulation of the Public Sphere from Repolitization of the Private

Sphere." Paper presented at the Ninth International Congress of the Basic Income Guarantee Network. Geneva, 2002.

Rawls, John. *Justice as Fairness: A Restatement.* Cambridge, MA: Harvard University Press, 2001.

———. *Political Liberalism.* New York: Columbia University Press, 1993.

———. "The Priority of Right and Ideas of the Good." *Philosophy and Public Affairs* 17, no. 4 (1988): 251–76.

———. "Reply to Alexander Musgrave." *Quarterly Journal of Economics* 88 (1974): 633–55.

———. *A Theory of Justice.* Oxford: Oxford University Press, 1971.

———. *A Theory of Justice, Revised Edition.* Cambridge, MA: Harvard University Press, 1999.

Raz, Joseph. *The Morality of Freedom.* Oxford: Clarendon Press, 1986.

Robertson, J. *Future Work.* Aldershot, UK: Gower, 1985.

Robeyns, Ingrid. "Sen's Capability Approach and Gender Inequality: Selecting Relevant Capabilities." *Feminist Economics* 9, nos. 2–3 (2003): 61–92.

Roscoe, Paul. "The Hunters and Gatherers of New Guinea." *Current Anthropology* 43, no. 1 (2002): 153–62.

Rousseau, Jean-Jacques. *Discourse on Political Economy and the Social Contract.* Translated by Christopher Betts. Oxford: Oxford University Press, 1994.

———. *A Discourse: What Is the Origin of Inequality among Men, and Is It Authorized by Natural Law?* The First Part. Translated by G. D. H. Cole. Austin, TX: Constitution Society, 1998. [1754].

Russell, Bertrand. *Proposed Roads to Freedom.* New York: Blue Ribbon Books, 1918.

Sahlins, M. D. "Poor Man, Rich Man, Big-Man, Chief: Political Types in Melanesia and Polynesia." *Comparative Studies in Society and History* 5, no. 3 (1963): 285–303.

Sen, Amartya. "Capability and Well-Being." In *The Quality of Life*, edited by A. Sen, pp. 30–53. Oxford: Clarendon Press, 1993.

———. *Development as Freedom.* New York: A. A. Knopf, 1999.

———. *Identity and Violence: The Illusion of Destiny.* New York: W.W. Norton & Company, 2006.

———. *Inequality Reexamined.* Cambridge, MA: Harvard University Press, 1992.

———. *Poverty and Famines: An Essay on Entitlement and Deprivation.* Oxford: Clarendon Press, 1981.

Severin, T. *In Search of Robinson Crusoe.* New York: Perseus Publishing, 2003.

Sharif, M. *Work Behavior of the World's Poor: Theory, Evidence and Policy.* Aldershot, UK: Ashgate, 2003.

Sheahen, Allan. *Basic Income Guarantee: Your Right to Economic Security* New York: Palgrave Macmillan, 2012.

Shields, Liam. "The Prospects for Sufficientarianism." *Utilitas* 24, no. 1 (2012): 101–17.

Singer, Peter. "Famine, Affluence, and Morality." *Philosophy & Public Affairs* 1, no. 3 (Spring 1972): 229–43.

———. "The Right to Be Rich or Poor." In *Reading Nozick: Essays on Anarchy, State, and Utopia*, edited by Jeffrey Paul, pp. 37–53. Oxford: Basil Blackwell, 1981.

Skinner, Quentin. *Liberty before Liberalism*. Cambridge: Cambridge University Press, 1998.

Smith, Adam. *The Wealth of Nations*. Oxford: Oxford University Press, 1976. [1776].

Spencer, Herbert. *Social Statics*. 1st ed. New York: D. Appleton and Company, 1872.

Standing, Guy. *Beyond the New Paternalism: Basic Security as a Right*. New York: Verso, 2002.

Steiner, Hillel. *An Essay on Rights*. Oxford: Blackwell, 1994.

———. "Left Libertarianism and the Ownership of Natural Resources." *Public Reason* 1, no. 1 (2009): 1–8.

StoneE-Producktions. "Quotes from Our Native Past." StoneE Producktions, http://www.ilhawaii.net/~stony/quotes.html.

Thoreau, H. D. *Walden*. Princeton: Princeton University Press, 1971.

Thurow, L. C. "Cash versus in-Kind Transfers." *The American Economic Review* 64, no. 2 (1974): 190–95.

———. "Government Expenditures: Cash or in-Kind Aid?". *Philosophy and Public Affairs* 5, no. 4 (1976): 361–81.

Townsend, E. D. "Minutes of an Interview between the Colored Ministers and Church Officers at Savannah with the Secretary of War and Major-Gen. Sherman." In *Freedom: A Documentary History of Emancipation, 1861–1867*, edited by Steven F. Miller. College Park, MD: Department of History, University of Maryland, 2007. http://www.history.umd.edu/Freedmen/savmtg.htm. Accessed September 20, 2011.

Vallentyne, Peter. "Left-Libertarianism—a Primer." In *Left-Libertarianism and Its Critics: The Contemporary Debate*, edited by P. Vallentyne and H. Steiner. pp. 1–22. New York: Palgrave, 2000.

Vallentyne, Peter and Hillel Steiner. *Left-Libertarianism and Its Critics: The Contemporary Debate*. New York: Palgrave, 2000.

———. *The Origins of Left-Libertarianism: An Anthology of Historical Writings*. Basingstoke: Palgrave, 2000.

Van der Veen, Robert J. and Philippe Van Parijs. "A Capitalist Road to Communism." *Theory and Society* 15, no. 5 (1986): 635–55.

Van Donselaar, Gijs. *The Benefit of Another's Pains: Parasitism, Scarcity, Basic Income*. Amsterdam: University of Amsterdam Department of Philosophy, 1997.

———. *The Right to Exploit: Parasitism, Scarcity, and Basic Income*. Oxford: Oxford University Press, 2009.

Van Donselaar, Gijs. "The Stake and Exploitation." In *The Ethics of Stakeholding*, edited by K Dowding, Jurgen De Wispelaere, and S. White, pp. 94–113. New York: Palgrave Macmillan, 2003.

Van Parijs, Philippe. *Arguing for Basic Income: Ethical Foundations for a Radical Reform*. New York: Verso, 1992.

———. "Basic Income: A Simple and Powerful Idea for the 21st Century." Paper presented at the Real Utopias Conference, "Rethinking Redistribution: Designs for a More Egalitarian Capitalism". Madison, WI, 2002.

———. *Real Freedom for All: What (If Anything) Can Justify Capitalism?* Oxford: Oxford University Press, 1995.

———. *What's Wrong with a Free Lunch?* Boston: Beacon Press, 2001.

Vihvelin, Kadri and Terrance Tomkow. "The Dif." *Journal of Philosophy* 102, no. 4 (2005): 183–205.

Waldron, Jeremy. "Homelessness and the Issue of Freedom." In *Liberal Rights*, edited by Jeremy Waldron, pp. 309–38. Cambridge: Cambridge University Press, 1993.

———. *Law and Disagreement*. Oxford: Oxford University Press, 1999.

———. *Liberal Rights*. Cambridge: Cambridge University Press, 1993.

———. *The Right to Private Property*. Oxford: Clarendon Press, 1988.

Walter, Richard, Ian Smith, and Chris Jacomb. "Sedentism, Subsistence and Socio-Political Organization in Prehistoric New Zealand." *World Archaeology* 38, no. 2 (2006): 274–90.

Ward, C. *Anarchy in Action*. London: Allen and Unwin, 1973.

Wenar, L. "John Rawls." *Stanford Encyclopedia of Philosophy*, http://plato.stanford.edu/entries/rawls/.

Wheeler, S. "Natural Property Rights as Body Rights." In *Left-Libertarianism and Its Critics: The Contemporary Debate*, edited by P. Vallentyne and H. Steiner. New York: Palgrave, 2000, pp. 171–193.

White, Stuart. *The Civic Minimum*. Oxford: Oxford University Press, 2003.

———. "Fair Reciprocity and Basic Income." In *Real Libertarianism Assessed*, edited by Andrew Reeve and Andrew Williams, pp. 136–60. New York: Palgrave Macmillan, 2003.

———. "Liberal Equality, Exploitation, and the Case for an Unconditional Basic Income." *Political Studies* 45, no. 2 (1997): 312–26.

———. "A Relevant Anarchism? The Social Philosophy of Colin Ward." Unpublished Manuscript. Jesus College, Oxford, 2006.

———. "What Do Egalitarians Want?" In *Equality*, edited by Jane Franklin, pp. 59–82. London: Institute for Public Policy Research, 1997.

Widerquist, Karl. "Does She Exploit or Doesn't She?" In *The Ethics and Economics of the Basic Income Guarantee*, edited by Karl Widerquist, Michael A. Lewis, and Steven Pressman, pp. 138–62. Aldershot, UK: Ashgate, 2005.

———. "A Failure to Communicate: What (If Anything) Can We Learn from the Negative Income Tax Experiments?" *The Journal of Socio-Economics* 34, no. 1 (2005): 49–81.

———. "How the Sufficiency Minimum Becomes a Social Maximum." *Utilitas* 22, no. 4 (2010): 474–80.

———. "Libertarianism." In *The International Encyclopedia of Public Policy: Governance in a Global Age, Volume 3*, edited by Phillip O'Hara. Perth: GPERU, 2009. http://works.bepress.com/widerquist/8/. Accessed October 1, 2011.

———. "Lockean Theories of Property: Justifications for Unilateral Appropriation." *Public Reason* 2, no. 3 (2010): 3–26.

———. "The Physical Basis of Voluntary Trade." *Human Rights Review* 11, no. 1 (2010): 83–103.

———. *Property and the Power to Say No: A Freedom-Based Argument for Basic Income.* Oxford, UK: Department of Politics and International Relations, Oxford University, 2006.

———. "Reciprocity and the Guaranteed Income." *Politics and Society* 33 (1999): 386–401.

———. "What Does Prehistoric Anthropology Have to Do with Modern Political Philosophy? Evidence of Five False Claims." In USBIG Discussion Paper Series. USBIG Network, 2010.

———. "Who Exploits Who?" *Political Studies* 54, no. 3 (October 2006): 444–64.

Widerquist, Karl and Michael W. Howard, eds. *Alaska's Permanent Fund Dividend: Examining Its Suitability as a Model.* New York: Palgrave Macmillan, 2012.

Widerquist, Karl and Michael A. Lewis. "An Efficiency Argument for the Basic Income Guarantee." *International Journal of Environment, Workplace and Employment* 2, no. 1 (2006): 21–43.

Widerquist, Karl and Grant McCall. *Prehistoric Myths in Modern Political Philosophy.* Edinburgh: Edinburgh University Press, forthcoming.

Widerquist, Karl, S. Pressman, and Michael A. Lewis. *The Ethics and Economics of the Basic Income Guarantee.* Aldershot, UK: Ashgate, 2005.

Woodburn, James. "Egalitarian Societies." *Man* 17, no. 3 (1982): 431–51.

———. "'Sharing Is Not a Form of Exchange': An Analysis of Property-Sharing in Immediate-Return Hunter-Gatherer Societies." In *Property Relations: Renewing the Anthropological Tradition*, edited by Hann C. M., pp. 48–63. Cambridge: Cambridge University Press, 1998.

———. "Stability and Flexibility in Hadza Residential Groupings." In *Man the Hunter*, edited by Richard Borshay Lee and Irven DeVore, pp. 103–10. New York: Aline, 1968.

Zelleke, A. "Distributive Justice and the Argument for an Unconditional Basic Income." *Journal of Socio-Economics* 34, no. 1 (2005): 3–15.

About the Author

Karl Widerquist is an associate professor of Philosophy at SFS-Qatar, Georgetown University. He holds two doctorates—one in Political Theory from Oxford University (2006) and one in Economics from the City University of New York (1996). Before coming to Georgetown he was a lecturer in Political Theory at the University of Reading (UK) and a Murphy Fellow at Tulane University in New Orleans (LA). His primary research interest is in distributive justice—the ethics of who has what. He writes on issues of freedom, property rights, political decision-making, and the methodology of philosophical philosophy.

He is coauthor of *Economics for Social Workers* (2002) and of the forthcoming book, tentatively titled, *Prehistoric Myths in Modern Political Philosophy: Challenging Stone Age Stories* (forthcoming). He is coeditor of four books, including *The Ethics and Economics of the Basic Income Guarantee* (2005), *Alaska's Permanent Fund Dividend: Assessing Its Suitability as a Model* (2012), *Exporting the Alaska Model: Adapting the Permanent Fund Dividend for Reform around the World* (2012), and *Basic Income: An Anthology of Contemporary Research* (forthcoming). He is the editor of *Basic Income News* (binews.org) and a former editor of the academic journal *Basic Income Studies*. He has published more than 20 scholarly articles and book chapters, including publications in *Political Studies*, *Utilitas*, *Eastern Economic Journal*, *Politics and Society*, and *Politics, Philosophy, and Economics*. He writes the *Alaska Dividend Blog* and the *Basic Income Guarantee Blog* for USBIG.net and binews.org. He has published more than a dozen opinion and editorial pieces.

Index

The manufacturer's authorised representative in the EU is Springer Nature Customer Service Centre GmbH, Europaplatz 3, 69115 Heidelberg, Germany. If you have any concerns regarding our products, please contact ProductSafety@springernature.com

Printed and bound by CPI Group (UK) Ltd, Croydon, CR0 4YY
23/09/2026
02221520-0017